Fugal Composition

Used by permission of The British Library.

Fugal Composition

A Guide to the Study of Bach's '48'

Joseph Groocock

Edited by Yo Tomita

Contributions to the Study of Music and Dance, Number 65

GREENWOOD PRESS
Westport, Connecticut • London

Library of Congress Cataloging-in-Publication Data

Groocock, Joseph, 1913–1997.
  Fugal composition : a guide to the study of Bach's '48' / Joseph Groocock ; edited by Yo Tomita.
    p. cm.—-(Contributions to the study of music and dance, ISSN 0193–9041 ; no. 65)
  Includes bibliographical references (p.) and index.
  ISBN 0–313–32323–2 (alk. paper)
    1. Fugue.   2. Bach, Johann Sebastian, 1685–1750. Fugues. I. Tomita, Yo.   II. Title.
MT59.G84 2002
  786′.1872′092—dc21   2002069600

British Library Cataloguing in Publication Data is available.

Library of Congress Catalog Card Number: 2002069600
ISBN: 0–313–32323–2
ISSN: 0193–9041

First published in 2003

Greenwood Press, 88 Post Road West, Westport, CT 06881
An imprint of Greenwood Publishing Group, Inc.
www.greenwood.com

Printed in the United States of America

∞™

The paper used in this book complies with the
Permanent Paper Standard issued by the National
Information Standards Organization (Z39.48–1984).

10 9 8 7 6 5 4 3 2 1

Contents

Contents

Editorial Preface and Acknowledgments

This is in essence a concise textbook on fugue, drawing examples exclusively from J. S. Bach's *Well-Tempered Clavier*, Books I and II, familiarly known in the English-speaking world as "The 48." For undergraduate students, the first four chapters are an appropriate introduction to the basic concept of fugue. The subsequent chapters deal with the analysis of individual fugues; here the author classifies them into eight groups according to the complexities of their construction (see Chapter 5), from which the reader may gain further insight into Bach's compositional strategies and his masterly handling of contrapuntal devices. To many readers, the book will also serve as a convenient and reliable analytical guide to all the fugal movements—not only the forty-eight fugues but also the four preludes that are written in fugal style—in this celebrated work. In whichever way it is used, what emerges is Bach's ingenious craftsmanship, as the author demonstrates powerfully the extraordinary diversity of his fugal technique and style in all its richness and beauty.

The accuracy of information and scholarly integrity of the author's final text are the editor's responsibility. Readers may take it that my editorial intervention to the author's text is mostly confined to these areas. There are places where I have altered the text if, in the editor's view, it needs revision; in such cases I have given my reasons in a note. Also in the notes is further information from more recent scholarship (in particular from manuscript studies) that sheds important light on interpreting the particular point under discussion and other scholars' conflicting views on the specific point. The last point may prove particularly useful for those readers who are critically seeking various ways in which one can interpret a specific point. In addition, I have supplied in square brackets additional information if it is considered to be of assistance. An annotated bibliography will help those readers who may wish to consult further references. Finally and most importantly, I have paid a great deal of attention to improving the layout and precision of the analytical diagrams that accompany the discussion of all the fugues, where a bird's-eye view of the various elements of fugal structure is given.

It may be quite unusual to disclose so frankly what I did with this book as the editor; it is nevertheless an important matter to distinguish our tasks and responsibilities, because this is a posthumous publication, and I did not have the opportunity to meet and discuss this book with its remarkable author, Dr. Joseph Groocock (1913–97), who was one of the most prominent figures in the musical life of Dublin for many decades, teaching until he died at the age of 83. His son-in-law, one of his former students, tells me of his uncompromising yet generous nature:

His method was to lead by example; he would pose a contrapuntal problem and ask his pupils to come up with as many solutions as we could, while he on the blackboard swiftly outnumbered us. The Bachelor of Music degree in Trinity College for a number of years was taught almost solely by him, and all hinged on the writing of chorale, canon, invention and fugue. His bible was Bach; his harshest criticism was "would Bach have done that?" (softened frequently by "he *could* have.") He would test our solutions, making chords in the air with his hands; then he would praise our efforts, gently pointing out our gaffes by pretending to admire our daring. He is remembered with deep gratitude by many people, not only his students, for his painstaking kindness and thoughtfulness in times of personal difficulty. He "abominated fuss" but was approachable and charming in any company; to the last he was full of humour, impossibly energetic, endlessly interested in the people he met, and warmly appreciative of kindness in others.

It took little time for me to realize the depth of knowledge and originality of Dr. Groocock's analytical approach to Bach's fugues when I was asked to look at his neat typescript.

What appeared to me at first to be a quite formidable task was reduced considerably by the most generous support that I received from his widow Mrs. Dorene Groocock and his son-in-law Andrew Robinson. I cannot imagine how I could have reached this stage without their help; I appreciate all their detailed and constructive criticism at various stages of my work, as it was so important for striking the right balance between retaining its original quality and my broadening of its scholarly appeal.

Having clarified my editorial role and its background, it now seems appropriate to comment, however briefly, on the key features of this book that can be perceived as strengths or weaknesses in the light of all the published books and articles listed in the bibliography. I hope this puts the significance of this book into perspective.

The author approaches Bach's fugal writing from a compositional perspective; he seldom takes a detour expounding on such matters as the emotional substance of the fugue subjects, which one can draw out forever (as seen in the books by Fuller-Maitland, Gray, Dickinson, and Keller), or the stylistic traits that one can identify in the other works by Bach and his contemporaries (the approach becoming increasingly common in recent literature, for instance, by Schulenberg). He assumes that his readers are already familiar with the music itself, thus avoiding the usual commentary business and moving straight into the analysis of Bach's craft. This may suggest to readers that the author's approach resembles that of Iliffe and Sampson, in which case they are mistaken. The differences are evident in the depth of his thought and the sharpness of his observations. In this regard, it may be worth pointing out that a more recent monograph by Dürr agrees with the author on numerous accounts, both disagreeing frequently with Czaczkes, whose study is considered the classic work by many. However, the author differs from Dürr in the manner in which the construction of the fugue is viewed; while the author sees all the fugues as ternary in design (see Chapter 6), the tradition of German scholarship perceives them in a freer, multisectional design. Readers who seek more straightforward, practical advice on issues relating to performance should refer to Tovey, Bruhn, and Schulenberg, as well as a forthcoming monograph, *The Well-tempered Clavier of J.S. Bach: A Context* (Yale University Press) by David Ledbetter, who is incidentally one of the author's former pupils.

The single most outstanding feature of Dr. Groocock's analytical method is the way that he refers to the keys by roman numerals (i.e., handling the key information relative to the tonic), rather than simply stating the key name as an absolute reference. To many readers, it will be an unfamiliar way to analyze the key structure of a fugue, even though the method itself would be familiar in harmonic analysis. There are advantages and disadvantages. While I made certain editorial amendments (by adding the keys in square brackets) to reduce the burden on the reader, it is important that the reader accepts its merit, for the author's system makes perfect sense when the key structure of several fugues is compared (see pages 30, 60, 81, and 107), revealing interesting aspects of Bach's compositional procedures.

ACKNOWLEDGMENTS

The editor wishes to thank the Trinity Trust for its financial assistance in preparing this manuscript, Dr. Martin Adams of Trinity College Dublin for his help in the most friendly way imaginable at various points of this project, Mr. Hugh Cobbe for supplying the frontispiece for this book and the British Library, London, for their permission to reproduce it, Mr. Eric Levy and Ms. Nina Duprey of Greenwood Publishing for their most courteous and professional assistance in preparing this book, and finally and most importantly, Mrs. Dorene Groocock and Mr. Andrew Robinson for their editorial assistance and encouragement throughout.

Yo Tomita
Belfast, June 2002

Introduction

This book is addressed primarily to those who are beginning the study of fugue, though it may also be of interest to those who are safely past their examinations and who wish to delve more deeply into this fascinating study.

Fugue usually appears on the syllabus during the latter part of a university music course, the assumption being that a student by this time has gained a reasonable level of skill in harmony and counterpoint, in ear-training and general musicianship. Fugues test all these aspects of musical technique.

The ability to write a good fugue depends on the ability to think fugally, and this can certainly not be learned overnight. Progress may seem slow, but with the mastery of each stage there is increasing satisfaction. Unfortunately, this is often overshadowed by one besetting worry, namely, being able to write a good fugue under examination conditions at the end of the course.

Whether the examination is one year or two years away, it is inevitable and hangs like the sword of Damocles over all. The teacher, well aware of this, is sometimes tempted to opt for safety and to adopt the method of training advocated by most textbooks, that is, to instruct the class in the "rules" of fugue and to encourage students to write many fugues of one stereotyped pattern. Whatever does not seem to have a direct bearing on the main objective (the examination) must be completely ignored. He may even pass on the advice given by one writer who says that none of the fugues of Bach should be studied, because Bach did not have to write a fugue in three hours under examination conditions.

This advice is manifestly absurd. It is as if one were to attempt to teach sonata form while scrupulously avoiding the study of any actual sonatas by Haydn, Mozart, or Beethoven. Furthermore, it is likely that most members of the class already play Bach on the piano. Are they then to be told to stop doing this until after the examination? Or at least to shut their ears and their minds to what their fingers enjoy playing?

That type of training that teaches fugue without reference to Bach may be interesting as a kind of mental gymnastic. It may be successful up to a point in the mere preparation for an examination, but it is certainly not concerned with musical values, least of all with the sounds of music. In aiming solely at the requirements of an examination, it must surely fail utterly in the truer object of fugal study. In short, it must miss the unique opportunity afforded at this time for becoming more deeply acquainted with the work of the composer for whom fugue was not only a technique but a sensitive medium for the expression of some of his finest thoughts and feelings.

It is surely preferable to start from the premise that Bach was the supreme writer of fugues. It is then only sensible to base a course of study on Bach's examples rather than on any set of rules and regulations invented after his lifetime. One of the more enlightened textbooks, *The Technique and Spirit of Fugue* by George Oldroyd (Oxford, 1948), does indeed start from this premise, even though it is written from the realistic viewpoint of examination requirements. Oldroyd refers constantly to Bach throughout his book and in particular to the "48," and he concludes with this remark: "I hope this little book in the cause of Fugue may encourage many a student 'to work his way into the manner and thought' of that deep-minded and truth-loving man John Sebastian Bach. I could wish for no greater reward." (page 191)

Fugue has always been regarded as a severe musical discipline. Its value as a discipline is in no way lessened when it is taught according to the methods of Bach rather than by obedience to an imposed system of rules and regulations. Except for the rare case of a student who dislikes Bach's music, the study of fugue can be associated with lively interest from the start and can give increased pleasure with each stage of progress. Fugues written in the examination room should be able to exhibit technical skill and at the same time be expressive pieces of music, when the training has been based on the best musical examples.

Let us then start with the "48," playing them and listening to them and discovering how they work. They consist of many different types of fugue, short and long, simple and complex. Between them they sum up most of what can be done in the name of fugal composition.

The very richness and diversity of the fugues in the "48" call for the most detailed study. They do not easily yield up all their secrets to anyone who is not prepared to do a great deal of hard work. Indeed, without expert guidance students can easily lose their way in the "48" and end up with frustration rather than enlightenment. What has been written in the following pages is an attempt to provide that guidance. Since this book is based on my own experience of teaching fugue to university students, I hope that other teachers may find it a useful aid to their own work, even though it is addressed mainly to the student. Obviously, my book must be used in conjunction with a complete text of the "48," preferably a plain text with numbered bars, such as the two volumes published by the Associated Board. Since my purpose has been to supplement, rather than necessarily to replace, any worthwhile textbook in use, I have not included any specific problems.

In studying Bach's fugues, we should be concerned with every aspect of his craftsmanship. In order to gain an insight into his "manner and thought," the most thorough analysis is necessary, but analysis should always be followed by playing and listening to a complete fugue. This is especially true when we come to the great stretto fugues, when it is possible to become so absorbed in points of technique that we can easily forget to apply the only true criterion of their value, namely, their effectiveness in performance.

I wish to acknowledge my indebtedness to my teacher, Sir Thomas Armstrong, to the writers George Oldroyd and Ebenezer Prout, and to Donald Francis Tovey, whose commentaries in the Associated Board edition of the "48" are a model of concise and scholarly information. My own deep interest in the "48" was stimulated by the sensitive playing of Claud Biggs, who during his years in Dublin contributed so much to our enjoyment and understanding of this music. Finally, I must pay tribute to my uncle, the late Thomas Sheppard, who first showed me how to model my own early attempts at fugal composition on examples from the "48." He convinced me during my student days that if ever I became a teacher, this is the method by which I would try to teach.

Joseph Groocock

1

Fugal Style

What is a fugue? There is no short or simple answer to this question. We commonly speak of a fugue in much the same way that we speak of a minuet, but we are using terms that are not in the same category. Two pieces called minuets may be written in different styles, but they have in common a type of form that makes them both minuets. Two pieces of music called fugues may have little or no common form. We call them both fugues in this case because they are both written in a fugal style. We can learn this style only by imbibing it from many examples of good fugal writing. We cannot learn to write a good fugue by applying a set of rules. Arthur Benjamin makes this point clear in *A New Dictionary of Music* when he writes: "The great masters of fugue such as Bach do not confine the fugue to a strict pattern, though time-wasting academic theorists have done so."[1] Vaughan Williams, in *Grove's Dictionary*, had this to say: "A fugue is a musical movement in which a definite number of parts or voices combine in stating and developing a single theme, the interest being cumulative."[2] As far as it goes, this is quite a good definition. It throws light on the main principles that govern a large number of fugues, without adding any time-wasting academic theories. It says something about the general style of a fugue, without stipulating that it must be written in a particular form. By the time that we have examined critically a large number of fugues in the "48," we shall have a clearer idea of the extraordinary freedom of form that they display.

As an introduction to a detailed study of the "48," let us examine the first two fugues from Book 1 (**I.1** and **I.2**), observing their common features and their differences:

1. Each fugue starts with its *subject* in a single voice.
2. Other voices then enter in turn in imitation of the first voice, at dominant or tonic pitch. When all the voices have entered (four in the first fugue, three in the second), the *exposition* is complete.
3. After the exposition the subject reappears several times in one or another voice, at different pitch and at least once in a key other than tonic or dominant.
4. Toward the end of each fugue the subject reappears at least once in the tonic key.
5. Each fugue ends with a *coda* on a *tonic pedal*.

Little more can be said about the features that they have in common. Their differences are very striking:

Fugue in C major (I.1)	Fugue in C minor (I.2)
1. The *answer* (bars 2–4) is an exact replica of the subject at dominant pitch (*real answer*).	The *answer* (bars 3–5) differs in one small detail from the subject (*tonal answer*).
2. The opening voice accompanies the answer with free counterpoint.	The opening voice accompanies the answer with a *countersubject* (a theme that recurs with other entries).
3. The subject is present in almost every bar of the fugue.	Subject entries are separated by *episodes*.
4. After the exposition the subject or answer is nearly always in *stretto* (i.e., with one entry overlapping another).	There is no stretto.

Even a superficial examination of the first two fugues has revealed that they are of two distinct types; the first is a stretto fugue without episodes, and the second is an episodic fugue without stretto. As we explore the "48," we shall find that most fugues tend to be of one or the other type, though the principles of stretto and episodic treatment are not necessarily opposed, since some fugues effectively blend both principles.

Every serious study has its vocabulary of technical terms, and fugue is no exception. Some of these terms are peculiar to fugue, while others are terms already in common use in nonfugal music but are applied with a special meaning. Fortunately, all these terms are easier to define than fugue itself:

• The *subject* is the main theme announced at the outset and recurring throughout the fugue.
• The *answer* is the first entry of the second voice, at the pitch of the dominant.(or in the key of the dominant).
• A *codetta* is a short connecting passage between entries.[3]
• A *countersubject* is a secondary theme with which the first voice may accompany the second voice and that recurs along with other entries of subject or answer.

- The *exposition* is the first section of a fugue, during which all the voices enter once, either with subject or answer.[4]
- A *redundant entry* is an extra entry of subject or answer after the exposition, in the tonic or dominant key (i.e., before modulation to a related key).
- A *counterexposition* is a second set of entries in all voices, usually in the tonic or dominant keys and often in opposite order of subject–answer from that of the exposition.
- An *episode* is a passage between entries, normally using figure-development and often providing a modulation.[5]
- A *subsidiary subject* is a second or third subject introduced during the course of a fugue and capable of being combined with the main subject.
- *Inversion* means turning a melody or a melodic figure upside down, so that all rising intervals are replaced by similar falling intervals, and vice versa.
- *Interchange* means the displacement of two or more melodic lines, so that a lower part becomes an upper part, and vice versa.
- *Augmentation* means the presentation of the subject to notes of double the original length.
- *Diminution* means the presentation of the subject in notes of half the original length.[6]
- *Stretto* means the overlapping of two or more entries of subject or answer.
- A *coda* is a passage rounding off a fugue, often on a tonic pedal.

2

Answering a Fugue Subject

The first two fugues of the "48" show two different types of answer, *real* and *tonal*, the latter differing in one note from a real answer. Since the writing of an answer is normally the first step to be taken in composing a fugue, it is important at the outset to understand why one type of answer is preferable to another. Many a would-be fugalist might well be deterred by the fact that Prout[1] devoted fifty-four pages of his treatise (about a fifth of the whole book) to his rules and examples of how answers are made. The answer also occupies about the same proportion of Oldroyd's book.[2] This seems to suggest that the first step may not always be a simple one. Bach, however, has made the main principles clear.

ANSWERING A NONMODULATING SUBJECT

Real Answers

In **I.1** the subject ends on the third beat of bar 2, and the answer begins as soon as it can, on the second half of the same beat. It is an exact transposition of the subject a *perfect fifth higher*. The answer is made in the same way in the following fugues: **I.1, 5, 14, 20; II.5, 13, 19, 22, 23**.

Instead of entering a perfect fifth higher, the answer may enter a *perfect fourth lower*: **I.6; II.Pr.3** (bars 25–50), **8, 10, 18**. Occasionally, the answer is a twelfth higher (**II.4**) or an eleventh lower (**I.10**).

The answer may enter just before the subject has finished, overlapping it by one or more notes: **I.4, 9, 15; II.6, 9**.

The Codetta

It is not always possible to bring in the answer either immediately after the subject or overlapping its last note or two. The subject is then extended by a short linking passage called a codetta. In **II.10** the subject ends at the seventh note of bar 6; the following codetta not only fills up time but also harmonizes the entry of the answer on the dominant. In **II.23** the subject ends at the first note of bar 4; the following codetta brings the opening voice down to a pitch at which the answer can enter above it.

Tonal Answers

1. When a subject begins on the dominant, the answer generally begins on the tonic. Apart from this one note, the rest of the answer is normally a real one: **I.3, 11, 12, 13, 16, 21, Pr.14; II.2, 12, 14, 15, 16, 17, 20, 24**. In **I.21** the tonal change is made in both the first and the third notes of the answer. This brings us to the second reason for using a tonal answer.
2. When the dominant occurs among the first few notes of a subject, this one note is generally answered by the tonic: **I.2, 8, 17, 22; II.7**.

Under the following circumstances a real answer is used:

- if the dominant occurs among the first few notes of a subject but without emphasis: **I.9, 10; II.18**.
- if the dominant occurs some distance from the beginning of a subject (this is a matter for individual judgment): **I.1, 5, 6, 14, 15, 20; II.4, 5, 6, 8, 10, 19, 22**.
- if it is felt that a tonal answer would completely spoil the shape of a subject (e.g., by destroying a sequential pattern): **II.13, [also 18]**.[3]

Some Special Cases of Tonal Answers

The Use of a Datonic Auxiliary Note

In **II.1** the subject has the dominant for its first and third notes. As in **I.21** both these notes are answered by the tonic. There is also a difference of interval from the first note to the second, the whole tone $g'-f'-g'$ of the subject being answered by the semitone $c''-b'-c''$. Bach evidently regards the second note in each case as a diatonic auxiliary note.

The principle can also work the other way round. In **II.11** the subject has the dominant for its fourth note. This note is answered by the tonic. The semitone $f'-e'-f'$ of the subject is answered by the whole tone $c'-b\flat-c'$. In **II.21** the answer is treated in a similar way.

An Implied Dominant Chord Near the Beginning of the Subject

In **I.23** the fifth note of the subject is the dominant. It is felt to be near enough to the beginning to be answered by the tonic. In addition, Bach has lowered the preceding three notes. Why? He could have thought differently about the dominant note in the subject (which, after all, is not right at the beginning) and given a real answer. But this would have made an abrupt change of key at the second note of the answer, and normally he prefers to keep the tonic key for the first few notes of an answer, whenever this is possible. The lowering of the fifth note alone would not have avoided the sudden change of key, whereas the answer as it stands certainly does. In addition, he seems to have felt that the dominant chord is outlined by the second, fourth, and fifth notes of the subject; he therefore wrote an answer in which the corresponding notes outline the tonic chord.[4]

I.19 is a rather more puzzling case. The dominant does not occur in the subject until the moment when the answer enters; yet Bach has lowered the pitch of the second and third notes of the answer. The explanation may be that he felt the second note of the subject to be the third of the dominant chord rather than the mere leading-note. He therefore answered this note by the third of the tonic chord, rather than by the leading-note in the dominant key.[5] Having made this decision, he lowered the following note as well, in order to preserve the leaping fourths of the subject.[6]

ANSWERING A MODULATING SUBJECT

The answers so far examined, whether real or tonal, have all followed subjects that begin and end in the same key. Occasionally, a subject ends in a related key, and this is almost always the dominant. In such a case either a real answer or an ordinary tonal answer would normally modulate to the key of the supertonic, and further entries will produce modulations to the submediant and the mediant. Tonality is entirely obscured, and there is little hope of ever reestablishing the main key. Obviously, a more drastic change must be made in the answer if the tonality is to be kept within bounds. Before examining how this is done in three fugues of the "48," there are important facts to be learned from the one fugue in which a modulating subject *is* given a real answer, **I.10**.

From the second beat of bar 2 the subject is clearly aiming at some sort of cadence in the dominant key. At the second beat of bar 4 the answer in itself seems equally to be aiming at a cadence in the supertonic. The first bass note of bar 5, melodically speaking, is a *tierce de Picardie* in F♯ minor. But the harmony suggested by the countersubject in bar 4 makes the first beat of bar 5 a dominant chord in B minor, rather than a tonic chord in F♯ minor. The treatment works here, precisely because this is a two-part fugue. If a similar treatment is applied to a three-part fugue, it is bound to lead to confused tonality.

A modulating subject ends in the dominant key; its answer sounds most natural when it ends in the tonic key. In order to achieve this, the answer must be persuaded to end a tone lower than if it were a real or tonal answer. Careful judgment is required in deciding exactly at which point of the answer to lower its pitch by one tone. The answer, as so modified, must, if possible, be not less melodious than the subject. The shape of the subject should not be drastically altered (e.g., by answering a rising semitone in the subject by a falling semitone in the answer). Above all, the answer should be readily harmonizable, avoiding both harmonic tautology and harmonic vagueness. We can now examine Bach's ways of solving the problem.

Case 1: I.7

In the subject the change of key is made by the step of a semitone after the quaver rest. In the answer the semitone is changed into a minor third. The result is smooth and natural-sounding.

Since a modulating subject begins in the tonic key and ends in the dominant key, it would be reasonable to assume that the answer should do the reverse, beginning in the dominant and ending in the tonic. This may sometimes happen but certainly does not happen in **I.7**, where the whole of the answer is in the tonic key.[7] Three factors operate in this particular case: the codetta in the second half of bar 2 has already reestablished the tonic key; the answer is a tonal one (beginning on the tonic); and the countersubject in bar 3 uses the notes of the tonic key.

Case 2: I.18

The subject begins in G♯ minor and ends in D♯ minor. It lacks the convenient rest that punctuated the subject of **I.7**, so that there is no obvious moment at which to make the drop of a tone. Its two keys are linked by the interval of an augmented fourth, which is such a distinctive interval that it demands to be retained in the answer. Therefore, the change must be made at an earlier point. Experiments will show that every possible modification of the answer sounds absurd, except the one that Bach has chosen, where the drop of a tone is made after the very first note.[8] From its second note onward, the answer faithfully imitates every interval of the subject, ending in the main key at the first note of bar 5.

More is involved here than the mere drop of a tone. The second note of the subject, *f♯*, is the leading-note in the tonic key. The second note of the answer, *b♯*, is the leading-note in the *sub*dominant key. The modulation from tonic key to dominant key is thus balanced by a corresponding modulation from subdominant to tonic key.[9] The subdominant key, however, is merely suggested, not established, as the countersubject clearly indicates before the end of bar 3.

Case 3: I.24

The subject, beginning in B minor and ending in F♯ minor, uses all the notes of the chromatic scale. Not only does it have the most distinctive shape of all the subjects in the "48," but also it implies an unusually rich pattern of chord progressions. Bach answers the first note tonally, then repeats the intervals of the subject as far as the fourth note. After the fourth note he makes the drop of a tone. From this point onward, all the intervals in the answer exactly match those of the subject.

While it is easy to relate the bare facts about this answer, some clarification is desirable if it is to be taken as a model for the solution of similar problems. In the first place Bach has applied the tonal convention not only to the first note but also to the fifth note of the subject. Therefore, from the fifth note of the answer onward, the answer is already at the right pitch for it to end in B minor rather than C♯ minor. In the second place Bach has provided in the first five notes of the answer not only a melodic but also a harmonic counterpart to the first five notes of the subject. (*f♯′*, the first note of the subject, implies dominant harmony and is answered by *b*, the tonic; the next two notes of the subject, *d′* and *b*, imply tonic harmony and are answered by *a* and *f♯*, implying the dominant minor chord; the next two notes of the subject, *g′* and *f♯′*, are understood as a decoration of dominant harmony, and are therefore answered by *d′* and *b*, implying the tonic chord.)

From this point onward, a different principle is applied. All harmony is now related to the key in which the subject or answer ends:

subject: *b′–a♯′* implies V of IV major (key: F♯ minor)
          e′–d♯′ implies IV major (key: F♯ minor)
answer: *e′–d♯′* implies V of IV major (key: B minor)
          a–g♯ implies IV major (key: B minor)

Bach is always most scrupulous about matters of implied harmony and tonality in the first answer of a fugue. Later he often changes the shape of the original answer, as in bar 10 of this fugue.

Subdominant Answers

If the subject of **II.3** is reckoned to consist of only four notes (as indeed it does in many entries of this fugue), then the answer is a normal tonal answer. If the subject is reckoned to last until some way into bar 2, then the answer is different from any so far considered. Having made the tonal change at the fourth note, the answer continues at this lowered pitch, thus modulating to the subdominant key.

There are no other cases in the "48" of a subdominant answer to an opening subject, though they are found among the organ fugues. In those fugues of the "48" that introduce one or two subsidiary subjects into the middle section, those subjects are always given a subdominant answer: **II.4, 14, 18, 23.**

The double fugue that ends **I.Pr.7** in itself seems to have a subdominant answer. In the tonal context, however, it is clear that the double fugue begins in the key of the dominant, so that the normal subject–answer relationship is reversed.

Here, for reference, is a list of the various types of answer in the "48":

Fugal Composition

Real answers:

I.1, 4, 5, 6, 9, 14, 15, 20

II.4, 5, 6, 8, 9, 10, 13, 18, 19, 22, 23, Pr.19

Tonal answers:

I.2, 3, 7†, 8, 11, 12, 13, 16, 17, 21, 22, 24†, Pr.14

II.2, 7, 12, 14, 15, 16, 17, 20, 24

Answers to modulating subjects:

I.7‡, 10, 18, 24‡

Special cases of tonal answers:

I.19, 23

II.1, 11, 21

Subdominant answers:

I.Pr.7 (bars 25–70)

II.3, 4 (second subj., bars 35–36),
14 (second subj., bars 20–22;
third subj., bars 36–38),
18 (second subj., bars 61–70),
23 (second subj., bars 28–33)

Notes: † These are answers to modulating subjects.
‡ These are also tonal answers.

3

Countersubjects

The opening voice, having finished the subject, goes on to accompany the
answer in the second voice with some form of counterpoint. When this
counterpoint recurs with other entries, it is regarded as a countersubject.

Most commonly, a countersubject is used to accompany entries of the
subject or answer (but not necessarily all entries) throughout a fugue.
Sometimes, however, it is used only in the exposition. Some fugues have two
or even three countersubjects in the exposition. Some fugues have no
countersubject in the exposition but add a countersubject after the exposition
is finished. A new countersubject can be introduced after the exposition,
either to take the place of the original countersubject or to add itself to the
texture. Some fugues have no countersubject at all. All this diversity of pattern
can be tabulated for reference:

Countersubjects introduced in the exposition and recurring after it:

I.2, 3, 6, 7, 9, 10, 11, 12, 13, 14, 15, 16, 21,   II.4, 6, 8, 9, 10, 13, 16, 17, 18, 20, 22
24 & Pr.14

Countersubjects in the exposition only:

I.18, 20, 23   II.2, 7, 23, 24

Countersubjects introduced after the exposition:

I.13 (in addition to the original C),   II.21 (no C in exp.),
19 (no C in exp.)   24 (replacing original C)

Two countersubjects in the exposition:

I.2, 3, 18, 21, 23 (12 has three Cs)   II.17, 20

Fugues without a countersubject:

I.1, 4, 5, 8, 17, 22   II.1, 3, 5, 11, 12, 14, 15, 19, & Pr.3
(bars 25–50)

A good countersubject fulfills four conditions:

1. It affords both rhythmic and melodic contrast with the answer.
2. It contains rhythmic or melodic figures which can be used for separate development.
3. It provides adequate harmonic support for the answer.
4. It is interchangeable in pitch with the answer.

Here I discuss each with some examples:

1. Rhythmic and melodic contrast are very noticeable in the first countersubject of **I.2**. The countersubject is an effective accompaniment to the answer and is also easily recognizable as a tune in its own right. The same is true of **I.3**, where the sequential pattern of semiquavers contrasts admirably with the leaping figures of the answer. If the subject consists wholly or mainly of long notes, as in **I.12**, then the countersubject uses shorter notes. Conversely, if the subject consists wholly or mainly of short notes, then the countersubject uses longer notes, as in **II.18**. If the subject uses notes of varied length, as in **I.6**, then the countersubject also uses notes of varied length, in opposite phase to those of the subject.
2. Episodes are often made out of material first introduced by a countersubject. The first countersubject of **I.2** starts with a downward scale, and this scale forms the basis of all five episodes, either direct or inverted.
3. The combination of answer and countersubject in **I.2** is satisfactory as two-part harmony. At the same time it allows the possibility of a third part to complete the harmonic sense (as in bars 20–22).
4. In **I.2** the first countersubject in bar 3 acts as a bass to the answer. In bar 7 the subject is in the bass, and the first countersubject is in the soprano.

THE ORDER OF ENTRIES AND INTERCHANGE

In **I.2** the three voices enter in the order of middle, soprano, and bass. The interchange therefore occurs during the exposition:

I.2, exp.   A   C
              S   C   –
                      S

But this order of entry is not found in every fugue. For instance, in **I.3** the order of entry is soprano, middle, and bass. The countersubject is above the answer in bar 3 and again above the subject in bar 5. The themes are not interchanged until the redundant entry of bar 10.

I.3, exp.   S   C   –   bar 10:   A
                  A   C   C
                      S   –

Sometimes the interchange is still further delayed, as in **II.9**, where the countersubject is always below the answer or the subject during the exposition and is not heard above the subject until bar 35:

```
II.9, exp.                    A    bar 35:  C
                         S    C             ―
                    A    C    ―             S
               S    C    ―    ―
```

Two themes are interchangeable at the octave when the upper part can be transposed an octave lower and so become a bass to the other part. The same effect can be obtained by transposing the lower part an octave higher so that it is above the other part. Every harmonic interval is now replaced by its inversion, a second becoming a seventh, a third becoming a sixth, and so on. Since an octave becomes a unison, and vice versa, it is obvious that no interval of the original combination must exceed an octave.

Two themes are interchangeable at the fifteenth when the upper part can be transposed two octaves lower and so become a bass to the other part. The same effect can be had by transposing the lower part two octaves higher, so that it is above the other part. (Or the upper part can be transposed one octave lower, and the lower part one octave higher.) This form of interchange must be used if any interval between the two themes is greater than an octave.

Subject and countersubject interchangeable at the octave:

    I.9, 11, 13, 14, 18   **II.7, 8, 9, 17, 22**

Subject and countersubject interchangeable at the fifteenth:

    I.2, 3, 6, 7, 10, 12, 15, 16, 20, 23, 24, &   **II.2, 4, 6, 10, 13, 16, 18, 20, 23, 24**
    Pr.14

When the fifteenth is the interval of interchange, a countersubject generally moves with more melodic freedom, covering a wider range.

In the complete analysis of the fugues we find that Bach frequently used counterpoint interchangeable at other intervals besides the octave and the fifteenth, but not as a rule for the first countersubject. An exceptional case is that of **II.16**, where the answer and the countersubject are interchangeable at the tenth or twelfth as well as the fifteenth.

TWO COUNTERSUBJECTS IN THE EXPOSITION

When a third voice makes its entry in the exposition, the first voice, having stated in turn the subject and the countersubject, may continue with free counterpoint. This counterpoint, if it recurs with later entries, must be regarded as a second countersubject. It will usually have some distinctive features of melody or rhythm that make it easily distinguishable when it recurs. It will also in most cases be able to contribute figures for development in episodes. It must be written in interchangeable counterpoint with both the subject and the first countersubject so that the combination of three themes is equally effective, with any one of them acting as bass to the others. **I.2** uses a second countersubject in the exposition, entering inconspicuously after the rests in bar 7, where its main function appears to be the completion of the harmony. Its importance as a second countersubject is proved by its later use with almost every entry of the subject or answer (along with the first countersubject), and its figure in the first four notes of bar 8 provides material for the two lower voices for the whole of the episode beginning at bar 13.

I.2	bars	7	11	15	20	(also possible)	
		C^I	S	C^I	S	C^{II}	C^{II}
		C^{II}	C^{II}	A	C^I	C^I	S or A
		S	C^I	C^{II}	C^{II}	S or A	C^I

EXPOSITION WITHOUT A COUNTERSUBJECT

Some of the finest fugues in the "48" have no countersubject in the exposition. They are quite numerous, amounting to almost one-third of the whole collection, thus proving the absurdity of the rule given in some textbooks that every fugue *must* have a countersubject. Experiments, however, will show that the avoidance of a regular countersubject does not make it easier to write a good fugue and may lead to one of two results: if the accompanying counterpoint is distinctive in character, it will seem to demand treatment as thematic material and consequent repetition; otherwise, the fugue is liable to have too much diversity and too little unity. If, on the other hand, the counterpoint is little more than mere harmonization, it can produce dullness and lack of interest. Fugues that are successful without a regular countersubject generally have some special characteristics.

The first of these is *stretto*. When a subject is designed expressly for stretto, so that this is the most important element in the fugue, then a countersubject could be a distracting element in the whole plan. **I.1, 8** and **II.3** are examples of this.

Both **I.22** and **II.5** have masterly stretti, but stretto is not their sole concern. In each of them Bach seems intent to preserve unity at all cost: in **I.22** by using a figure from the subject in almost every bar of the fugue and in **II.5** by developing a figure from the subject into complex passages of canon in every episode.

In certain fugues the main subject is later combined with one or two subsidiary subjects. A countersubject in the exposition again might prove a distracting element in the whole plan. This may be felt with **I.4** and **II.14**.

When each entry in the exposition is accompanied by different counterpoint, there is, strictly speaking, no regular countersubject, but one of these counterpoints may in fact be repeated after the exposition, as a type of countersubject. We find this in **II.1**, where the lower voice in bars 5–9 is repeated in bars 25–29 and again in bars 51–55, always, however, below an entry. In **II.15** the entry of the bass in bars 15–20 is accompanied by a two-part structure (bars 16–19), which is repeated exactly in bars 34–37, with interchange in bars 41–44. In **II.21** there is no countersubject in the exposition, but two countersubjects are introduced at bar 33, and afterward they accompany every entry. **I.19** has no countersubject in the exposition but adds a countersubject of distinctive type after the exposition, to be repeated once more in its original form and yielding figures for development. In three fugues, **II.11, 12,** and **19,** there is no countersubject, but the exposition provides melodic or rhythmic figures for later development. **I.17** is of similar type; the accompaniment to the answer in bar 2 is sometimes referred to as a countersubject.[1] Since, however, it never reappears in the same form but in one of a dozen varied shapes, its purpose is plainly to provide melodic figures for later use. **I.5** is so much dominated by its lively subject, whose first figure is repeated in almost every bar, and is moreover the most purely harmonic of all the fugues; its simple, direct appeal would be lessened by the presence of a countersubject.

THE MODIFICATION OF A COUNTERSUBJECT

Fugues with a Real Answer

A countersubject, at its first appearance, is written to fit the answer. When answer and subject are identical in shape, there is no obvious need to alter the countersubject when it is used along with the entry of the subject in the third voice. The countersubject is unaltered in the following fugues: **I.6, 9, 14; II.6, 13, 22.**

While we might expect this to be the general rule, we find instead that Bach more often chose to modify the countersubject on its second appearance, in greater or lesser degree. The modification usually improves a melodic line or adds an interesting harmonic interval.

- In **II.8** a comparison of bars 3 and 7 shows the commonest type of modification (i.e., at its opening).
- In **II.4** the bass is a free part in bars 5–6; the suspension gives it both harmonic and rhythmic strength but necessitates the octave leap in the countersubject instead of the original sixth.
- In **II.9** the countersubject in the bass of bar 3 continues its melodic figures into bar 4, whereupon it becomes technically a free part. Since the bass at this point already uses the first figure of the countersubject, the tenor reproduces only that part of it that starts with the rising scale.
- In **II.23** a very subtle modification takes place at bar 10. The previous codetta in bar 9 has already used the first figure of the countersubject; the tenor moves into the countersubject with the third note of bar 10, preceding it in the most natural-sounding way with a continuation of the canon of the codetta.

Sometimes the recurrent part of the countersubject does not begin until halfway through the answer. In **II.7** we cannot tell where the countersubject proper begins, and only on its second appearance can we realize that it begins with the tied note of bar 9, which is reproduced in bars 16 and 23. Likewise, in **I.15** it begins with the last four notes of bar 6, reproduced in bar 12.

Because he is writing keyboard fugues, Bach takes occasional liberties with strict part-writing. In **II.10** the countersubject of bars 7–12 is reproduced with the subject entry of bar 13, but its broken chord figures are now spread over two voices. Only at bar 15 does it settle down as a middle voice with the minims of bars 9–10. Its ending also is altered in order to join more neatly into the following episode.

One of the strangest cases of the treatment of a countersubject in the exposition is that of **I.20**. Only the first bar and a half of the countersubject of bars 4–6 are reproduced with the next two entries, and in an unusual manner. The two-part structure of bars 4–5 is written so that it is interchangeable at the fifteenth or the twelfth. It is interchanged at the twelfth for the bass entry of bar 8 and at the fifteenth for the tenor entry of bar 11. This means that three successive entries, in E minor, A minor, and E minor, are all accompanied by a repetition of virtually the same tune, beginning each time on A. Furthermore at bars 8–9 the countersubject is divided between soprano and alto, while at bar 11 it is used in the alto when we would have expected it to be in the bass.

Fugues with a Tonal Answer

When a subject begins with the dominant, and the countersubject begins after the first note of the tonal answer, the following entry of the subject can usually be accompanied by the countersubject without any modification: **I.16; II.17, 20**.

When the tonal change is made after the beginning of the answer, the countersubject may be so written that it requires no modification for the next entry. In **I.2** the downward scale of the first countersubject does not allow modification; it, in fact, produces an interesting new dissonance when it is used with the subject in bar 7. More often the countersubject is modified at the moment of the tonal change, so that it fits the subject as neatly as it fitted the answer: **I.3, 12, 13, 21; II.16**.

For harmonic reasons Bach sometimes modifies the countersubject at a different moment from the tonal change, as in **I.23**. He also freely changes the position of semitones in order to strengthen the sense of tonality, as in **I.11**. Finally, even when the tonal change was at the first note, he sometimes prefers to alter the beginning of the countersubject at its second appearance, as in **II.24**.

Fugues with a Modulating Subject

In **I.18** the change of pitch is made after the first note of the answer; the countersubject is so written that it fits the subject at bar 5 without any alteration.

In **I.7** the change of pitch is made after the rest. When the countersubject is reproduced with the subject entry at bar 6, it is modified during the beat before the rest, producing, in fact, a smoother melodic shape than on its first appearance.

I.24 is a more complex example. The change of pitch has been made at the fifth note of the answer, and the distinctive shape of the countersubject does not seem to invite modification around this point. Instead of making a small modification, either earlier or later, Bach has chosen to reproduce the semiquaver figures of bar 4 in an inverted form at bar 9 in the alto, continuing with the descending crotchets in the tenor. He uses the same device in the tenor and bass of bars 13–14.

The examples given in this chapter will have shown something of the width of Bach's outlook with regard to the use of countersubjects. In the first place he did not regard it as a necessity to have a countersubject at all, and we are free to follow him in our own experiments if we wish, bearing in mind that it is harder to write a good fugue that way! (It is of interest to observe that there are slightly more fugues without a countersubject in Book II than in Book I and that Book II was compiled after twenty further years of composing experience.)

When Bach decided on a countersubject, he did so in order to give increased thematic interest to a fugue. He never regarded his countersubjects as unalterable entities, to be forced into the texture at all cost, but freely altered them as he felt inclined, always for some good musical reason.

4

The Exposition

At the very outset of a fugue there is freedom of choice as to the order in which the voices enter.

TWO-VOICE EXPOSITION

In both examples from the "48" the leading voice is the soprano:

```
S   C
  A
```

I.10, Pr.14

THREE-VOICE EXPOSITION

Of the six possible orders of entry Bach used four, with a distinct preference for two of them[1]:

No Countersubject	One Countersubject	Two Countersubjects

1
```
S   –   –          S   C   –          S   C'   C''
  A   –              A   C              A   C'
    S                  S                  S
```

I.19; **I.6, 7, 13, 15;** **I.3, 21**
II.Pr.3, 11, 12, 15 **II.10, 18**

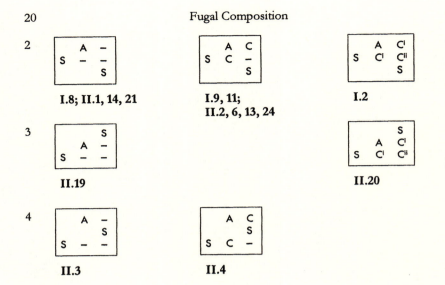

2   I.8; II.1, 14, 21   I.9, 11;   I.2
                              II.2, 6, 13, 24

3   II.19   II.20

4   II.3   II.4

FOUR-VOICE EXPOSITION

Of the twenty-four possible orders, Bach used seven, five of them being
cyclic[2]:

No Countersubject   **One Countersubject**   **Two Countersubjects**

1   II.7, 9   II.23

2   II.16   I.18, 23

3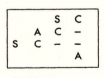

I.16, 20; II.22

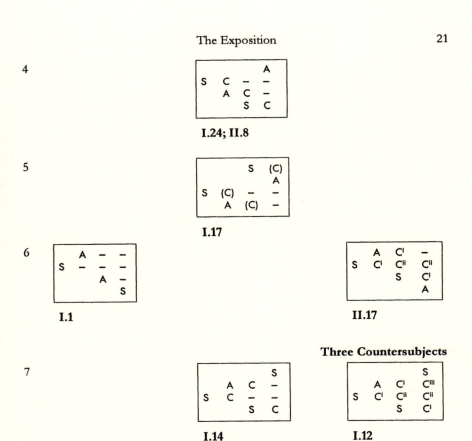

4

I.24; II.8

5

I.17

6

I.1

II.17

Three Countersubjects

7

I.14

I.12

In 6 and 7 the cyclic order is not maintained. In addition, the sequence of subject–answer is irregular, as also in one fugue the sequence of C^i–C^{ii}.

FIVE-VOICE EXPOSITION

Theoretically, a five-part fugue could start in any one of 120 ways. In the two five-part fugues of the "48" Bach chose two orders that are diametrically opposed:

1

I.4

2

I.22

5

A Classification of the "48"

Now that preliminaries have been dealt with, the way is open to study all the fugues in detail. There is no sense in doing this in a haphazard fashion; some plan of orderly study is required. The obvious order might seem to be to go straight through from the beginning of Book I, but this is likely to lead to a great deal of confusion because of the wide differences between one fugue and another. Fortunately, it is possible to classify all the fugues in eight fairly well-defined groups, and it is strongly recommended that a reasonable number of fugues in one group should be studied before going on to the next group.

GROUP 1: FUGUES FOR TWO VOICES

(Minor)   **I.10, Pr.14**

GROUP 2: FUGUES FOR THREE VOICES, WITHOUT STRETTO

With countersubject: Without countersubject:
(Major)   **I.3, 7, 9, 21; II.13**   **II.1, 11, 15, 19**
(Minor)   **I.2; II.10, 20**   **II.12**

GROUP 3: FUGUES FOR THREE VOICES, WITH STRETTO

With countersubject: Without countersubject:
(Major)   **I.11, 15**   **II.3, Pr.3**
(Minor)   **I.6; II.6**   **I.8**

GROUP 4: FUGUES FOR FOUR VOICES, WITHOUT STRETTO

With countersubject: Without countersubject:
(Major)   **I.23; II.17**   **I.5, 17**
(Minor)   **I.12, 14, 18, 24; II.8, 16**

GROUP 5: FUGUES FOR FOUR VOICES, WITH STRETTO

With countersubject: Without countersubject:
(Major)   **II.7, 9**   **I.1; II.5**
(Minor)   **I.16, 20; II.2, 22**

GROUP 6: FUGUES FOR THREE VOICES, WITH (NEW) COUNTERSUBJECT INTRODUCED AFTER THE EXPOSITION

(Major)   **I.13, 19; II.21**
(Minor)   **II.24**

GROUP 7: FUGUES FOR THREE OR FOUR VOICES WITH SUBSIDIARY SUBJECTS

(Major)   **I.Pr.7, Pr.19; II.23**
(Minor)   **II.4, 14, 18**

GROUP 8: FUGUES FOR FIVE VOICES

(Minor)   **I.4, 22**

Group 1: Fugues for Two Voices

I.10: FUGUE IN E MINOR

Bars	1	2	3	4	5	6	7	8	9	10	11	12	13	14	15	16	17	18	19	20	21
S	S————C--------							EP.1			S————C--------				EP.2					C--------	
B	A————										C--------/A————									S————	
	i		v			v–III					III–♭VII	♭VII		♭VII–iv						iv–i	

Bars	22	23	24	25	26	27	28	29	30	31	32	33	34	35	36	37	38	39	40	41	42
S	A————		EP.3						C--------A————				EP.4					S————		Coda	
B	-C--------								S————C--------										S—	S—	
	i		i–♭vii						♭vii–iv	iv		iv–i						i		i	

Note: the sign / denotes a perfect cadence.

The subject ends at the second note of bar 3[1]: the answer, therefore, overlaps the subject. It is a real answer, even though the subject has modulated to the key of the dominant.[2] The sense of early modulation to a third key is, however, avoided by making the answer with a *tierce de Picardie* and treating it as the dominant chord in B minor rather then the tonic chord in F♯ minor. The countersubject begins during the second beat of bar 3 and is used with every entry of the subject or answer until the beginning of the final section (bar 39). Even there it occurs in partial form.

This fugue ranges freely through most of the nearly related keys:

$$i–v–III–♭VII–iv$$

It also uses the more distant key of ♭VII minor [d] (bar 30). Most of these key changes are of transitional type, and a sectional effect is avoided by the relative absence of perfect cadences, of which there are only two: in D major (bars 12–13) and E minor (bars 41–42).

After the exposition the remainder of the fugue consists of alternating episodes and pairs of entries. The episodes are related as follows:

Episode 1 (bars 5–11):   soprano: leaping and scalic figures
                          bass: altered form of countersubject

The two-bar pattern is repeated in falling sequence.

Episode 2 (bars 15–20):   soprano: scalic figure
                          bass: leaping figure

The one-bar pattern is interchanged at every bar, in falling sequence.

Episode 3 (bars 24–30): = interchange of episode 1 (with adjustment in bar 29)
Episode 4 (bars 34–39): = interchange of episode 2

The last complete entry of the subject is that of bars 32–33 in the subdominant key. In the final section (bar 39) the soprano has the first half of the subject in the tonic, followed a bar later by the bass with the first half of the subject (slightly altered).[3] The short coda (bar 41) alludes to the second half of the subject, with *tierce de Picardie* as in the answer at bar 5.

The importance of this two-voice fugue can easily be overlooked. Because everything that happens in it is crystal-clear, its many subtleties may pass unnoticed.

The fugue has a very carefully controlled key structure. Until the final section the entries are always grouped in pairs, each pair echoing at various pitches the original subject–answer relationship:

Subject:	**Answer:**
E minor modulating to B minor	B minor, ending on its dominant chord
G major modulating to D major	D major, ending on its dominant chord
A minor modulating to E minor	E minor, ending on its dominant chord
D minor modulating to A minor	A minor, ending on its dominant chord
½ subject in E minor	
½ subject in E minor	

This precise scheme of key changes will not necessarily be found in any other fugue. But we shall find that it is common practice to modulate first to the relative major key as this fugue does (or if a fugue starts in a major key, then to modulate to the relative minor) and to include a modulation to the subdominant later on.

FORM

A fugue, like any other piece of music, must have a clearly recognizable form. It must achieve a satisfactory balance between the opposing principles of unity and diversity. There are no hard-and-fast rules as to how this can be done, but a study of this fugue will reveal several aspects of formal organization that may serve as a guide to the study of more complex fugues.

Melodic Contrast

This operates in two ways:

a. contrast between subject and countersubject
b. contrast between passages of subject-plus-countersubject, and episodes

Tonality

There are three main key areas:

i.   the exposition (bars 1–5):   keys of tonic and dominant
ii. the middle section (bars 5–38):   various keys
iii. the final section (bars 39–42):   tonic key

Main Divisions of the Fugue

The obvious divisions are the three just mentioned. In addition there is the sense of punctuation caused by perfect cadences. While these are not so apparent and are often hard to determine in a two-voice structure, there would seem to be only two perfect cadences: in D major (bars 12–13) and E minor (bars 41–42). A third factor enters into this particular fugue because of the prevalence of interchange. Bars 20–38 are an exact repetition in an interchanged form of bars 1–19 (apart from the adjustment of pitch in bar 29),[4] so that the overall form may be seen as three divisions, slightly different from those discussed under "Tonality" earlier[5]:

1. bars 1–19:   keys of E minor and B minor
                 Episode 1
                 keys of G major and D major
                 Episode 2
2. bars 20–38: keys of A minor and E minor (= interchange of bars 1–19)
                 Episode 3
                 keys of D minor and A minor
                 Episode 4
3. bars 39–42: key of E minor

Interrelation of the Episodes

An important principle is demonstrated by the episodes of this fugue. Whatever material is used (figures from subject or countersubject, new figures) the episodes are interrelated:

Episode 3 is an interchange of episode 1 (apart from bar 29), at different pitch.
Episode 4 is an interchange of episode 2, at different pitch.

The episodes of this fugue all use a falling sequence, based on a pattern of chord roots that fall by fifths (or fall a fifth and rise a fourth). This we shall find is by far the commonest type of chord progression, being used in almost three-quarters of all 200 or more episodes within the fugues of the "48." There is a change of chord at each bar, with the exception of bars 10 and 29, where each bar implies two chords.

Episode 1: F♯ major, B minor, E major, A minor, D major, G major and D major;
            exactly matched by
Episode 3: B major, E minor, A major, D minor, G major, C major and A major.

Episode 2: A major, D major, G major, C major and E major; exactly matched by
Episode 4: E major, A major, D major, G major and B major.

I.PR.14: PRELUDE IN F♯ MINOR

Bars	1	2	3	4	5	6	7	8	9	10	11	12
S	S————(C)——		EP.1	C————	EP.2	S———C———		EP.3	S———		EP.4	S—
B	(C)————A——			S———		C———A——			C———			/(C)--
	i	i–v		i		III	♭VII		v			v

Bars	13	14	15	16	17	18	19	20	21	22	23	24
S	—C———(C)———S(inv)			EP.5			(C)——S———			S———C———		-Coda
B	——S——S(inv)——(C)-						S———(S)——	ext.		(C)——S———		/
	v	iv	III	III–i			i	i		i	i	

In all but name this prelude is a fugue for two voices, its subject being announced above a tonic pedal at the opening. (This is reproduced as an upper pedal in the dominant key at bars 12–13 and in the main key at bar 22.) For purposes of analysis the "middle voice" in these passages has been treated as if it belonged to either the bass or the soprano.

Though it is very short, this fugue uses nearly as many keys as **I.10**, with entries of the subject or answer in i, v, III, ♭VII, and iv [i.e., f♯, c♯, A, E and b]. Formally, it is in two almost equal sections bounded by the perfect cadences in the dominant (bar 12) and the tonic (bar 24).

Since the subject begins on the dominant, the answer is a tonal one. The effect of the leap at the beginning of the answer is to retain the tonic key for a few notes, before modulating into the dominant key.

In playing or listening to this fugue, we can always be aware that we are in the middle of an entry of subject or answer, but it is not always easy to notice the exact moment when an entry begins. No less than ten of the fourteen entries are slightly different from the subject and answer of bars 1 and 2. The redundant entry of the subject in the bass at bar 4 starts with a semiquaver instead of the original quaver; three other subject entries also start with a shortened first note approached by scale steps (bar 13, bass; bar 22, "middle voice"; bar 23, bass). In other cases Bach has changed the beginning of an entry by inserting one or more notes (bar 9, soprano; bar 20, soprano). He has done something similar in bar 7, where the harmonic context shows that the bass entry is that of the answer. In the soprano of bar 6 he has varied the beginning of the subject entry in the key of A major by leaping up from *c#''* instead of stepping from *e''*.

Bach has also used what at first appears to be a rhythmic displacement of some of the entries (bar 12, "middle voice"; bar 13, bass), but these entries sound perfectly natural, and there is no audible effect of rhythmic change. Bach evidently regarded one bar of common time at a slow or moderate tempo as equivalent to two bars of two time. That the third beat can be as strong as the first is borne out by the placing of the two perfect cadences (bars 12 and 24). Unless one is prepared for this way of writing (and it is extremely common), one could easily miss the beginning of an entry, especially if it happens to be that of the inverted subject (as in the bass of bars 14–15 and the soprano of bars 15–16).

The countersubject appears in three different forms. Its outline is first traced by the "middle voice" of bar 1 (reappearing at bars 12–13 and 22). It can also be felt in the chords of bars 14–16 and 19. This outline is partially filled up by the soprano in bar 2 and in this form is easily recognizable, in spite of some changes of interval in the bass of bar 9. In its complete form the countersubject has the same rhythm as the subject but moves mainly in contrary motion with it (bars 4, 7, 13–14, 23, soprano; bar 6, bass).

As with **I.10** a fairly large proportion of this fugue (ten bars out of twenty four) is not directly concerned with the subject or answer. The single entries or pairs of entries are obviously separated in time by the episodes. But since the episodes (at least in this fugue) are not aimed primarily at contrast but rather at the continuous development of figures from the subject or the countersubject (chiefly the former), their effect is to bind together rather than to separate:

Episode 1 (bars 3–4) uses an upward leap and the subject figure in a two-part canon. The first semiquaver group in the bass is a continuation of the previous falling sequence in the answer.

Episode 2 (bars 5–6) is a variant of episode 1. It has the same rhythmic pattern, but the soprano now uses the inverted subject figure. The bass again starts as a continuation of the previous falling sequence, then goes on with a rising sequence.

Episode 3 (bars 8–9) is a variant of episode 2. It has the same bass, again linked to the falling sequence of the answer, but the soprano introduces fresh material.

Episode 4 (bars 10–12) is a development of previous material. The soprano starts as part of the falling sequence of the previous subject and continues with wider separation of the semiquaver and quaver figures. In bar 11 the semiquaver figures now widen the rising third to a rising sixth (recalling the quaver figures of bar 2). Meanwhile, the bass in bar 10 uses the inverted subject figure, then proceeds in bar 11 to a free inversion of the quaver figure of bar 2.

Episode 5 (bars 16–19) starts at the halfway point of bar 16, with further allusion to the inverted subject and countersubject figures in the bass, while the soprano adds a downward scale that would range over more than two octaves but for the two upward leaps of a seventh.

The imperfect cadence in bar 19 marks the end of development, and the final section is concerned with the restatement of the subject in the main key. In each of the four subject entries that follow there is a different accompaniment. Bar 19 is climactic in effect, with its rising chords (recalling the outline countersubject of bar 1). Perhaps the most effective moment of the fugue is the rest at bar 20 instead of the expected chord. After the rest the subject is in tenths between soprano and bass. Bar 21 can be considered a phrase extension toward the cadence, since it lacks the pattern of previous episodes. The entry in bar 22 reverts to the pattern of bar 1, but now with an upper pedal. The entry in the bass of bar 23 has the full countersubject for the first time since bar 13, its beginning being more clearly marked by the quaver rest. Bar 24 is a miniature **coda**, recalling the cadence of bar 12.

THE KEYSCHEMES OF THE FUGUES IN GROUP 1

	Exposition	Development	Final Section
I.10	i v EP	III, ♭VII EP iv i EP ♭vii iv EP	i i
I.Pr.14	i v EP i EP	III ♭VII EP v EP v, v iv III EP	i i i i

7

Group 2: Fugues for Three Voices, without Stretto

With countersubject:		Without countersubject:
(Major)	**I.3, 7, 9, 21; II.13**	**II.1, 11, 15, 19**
(Minor)	**I.2; II.10, 20**	**II.12**

In this chapter we examine thirteen fugues that follow the same basic plan as the two-voice fugues of Group 1, except that they use three voices. Reduced to its simplest terms, that plan is:

Exposition
Episodes and entries in related keys
Entry (or entries) in the main key

We shall find that this basic plan is treated in various ways.

EXPOSITION

There is no rule as to the order of entry. Theoretically, the three voices can enter in any one of six different ways: this group uses three of the following:

Soprano – middle – bass (8 fugues)
Middle – soprano – bass (3 fugues)
Bass – middle – soprano (2 fugues)

In four fugues the exposition is a simple one, each voice entering without delay: **I.3, 21; II.1, 13**.

In four fugues the entry of the second or third voice is delayed by a codetta, which is often an extension of the last figure of the subject (or answer or countersubject) but which sometimes introduces new ideas: **I.7** (bar 2), **9** (bar 3); **II.10** (bars 6 and 12), **15** (bars 6–8 and 13–15).

In six fugues the entry of the third voice is delayed by a passage longer and/or more involved than a codetta; this will be regarded as an episode, even though it comes within the exposition: **I.2** (bars 5–6), **7** (bars 4–5); **II.11** (bars 9–14), **12** (bars 8–11), **19** (bar 4), **20** (bars 5–6).

Five fugues of this group have their exposition extended by a redundant entry of the answer: **I.3** (bar 10), **7** (bar 10), **21** (bar 13); **II.11** (bar 21), **19** (bar 7).

In two fugues there is a counterexposition, in which each voice enters once more with either subject or answer in the keys of tonic or dominant but usually in a different order from the entries of the exposition: **I.9** (bars 6–10); **II.13** (bars 20–40).

MIDDLE SECTION

At the end of the exposition (or after the redundant entry or the counterexposition) all these fugues have at least one entry of subject or answer in a related key; six fugues use two related keys; four fugues use three related keys.

FINAL SECTION

This varies greatly, from a single entry of the subject in the main key (or two or three entries of the subject), to a virtual recapitulation of the entire exposition, sometimes capped by yet another entry of the subject in the main key.

All these fugues end with a coda, which can vary greatly in length.

I.3: FUGUE IN C♯ MAJOR

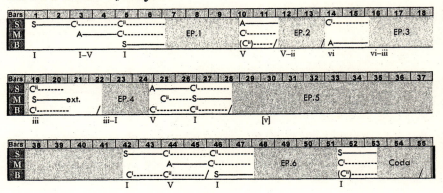

Exposition

1–3: subject in soprano
3–5: answer [tonal] in middle voice with first countersubject
5–7: subject in bass with first and second countersubjects

Extension of exposition

7–10: episode 1
10–12: redundant entry of answer in soprano

Entries in other keys linked by episodes

12–14: episode 2, modulating from V to ii
14–16: answer in bass, vi

16–19: episode 3, modulating from vi to iii
19–21: subject in middle, iii
21–22: phrase extension to cadence in iii

Entries in the keys of the exposition

22–24: episode 4, modulating from iii to I
24–26: answer in soprano, V
26–26: subject in middle, I
Episode 5 (28–42)

Final section

42–48: recapitulation of exposition
48–51: episode 6
51–53: subject in soprano, I
53–55: coda

The subject ends at the first note of bar 3. Since it begins with the dominant, the answer begins with the tonic, moving into the dominant key from its second note onward. (This is a tonal answer, similar to that in **I.Pr.14.**) The distinctive shape of the answer recurs in bar 14 but is partially concealed by the additional notes in the entries at bars 24 and 44. At bar 10 there is a redundant entry of the answer (we have not yet modulated from the keys of the exposition),[1] but its shape is that of an ornamented subject. The same ornamentation is used for the final entry of the subject in bar 51.

This fugue has two countersubjects.[2] The subject leads at once into the first countersubject, which recurs along with every entry throughout the fugue.[3] It is always recognizable, even though it is never exactly the same as in bar 3. It is varied in the following ways:

1. its opening run is altered (bars 5, 14, 19, 24, 26, 42 and 46);
2. its opening run is absent (bars 10 and 51).

Where the third and fourth beats of bar 3 step down by a semitone and then a tone ($g\#''$–$f^{\times}''$, $g\#''$–$f\#''$), each of these steps is made into a tone (bars 14, 19, and 44) or into a semitone (bars 5, 25, 27, 46 and 52).

The last figure of the countersubject matches the previous two beats (bars 26, 28 and 53).

All these may seem like fussy details, but they do add up to a long list of variants. Most of such changes are largely unnoticeable in performance unless the listener's attention is drawn toward them, because in every case Bach is using the main shape of the countersubject, adapting it in a completely natural-sounding way to changing circumstances of tonality.

The second countersubject is the syncopated theme in the soprano of bars 5–6. This is reproduced in the same form in four of its seven other appearances. With one entry (bar 25) it loses its first note; in two entries (bars 10–12 and 51–53) its rhythm is altered, losing the syncopation.

Notes on the Episodes

More than half of this fugue (about 56%) is occupied by the six episodes. They develop figures from the subject and the countersubject, and are all interrelated.

Episode 1 (bars 7–10) is part of the extended exposition, leading to the redundant entry of the answer in bar 10. The bass first repeats the middle part of bar 5, then repeats the semiquaver figure (which is also an inversion of the main countersubject figure of bar 4) in falling sequence, with the whole bar repeated a step lower each time. Meanwhile, the soprano and middle voice treat by imitation a leaping figure, which refers to the leaps of the subject, with some ornamentation before the end of bar 9. The episode modulates from I to V.

Episode 2 (bars 12–14) is a free interchange of the material of episode 1. The soprano adapts the previous bass (now using the countersubject figure direct), while the middle voice and bass adapt the previous upper parts. The episode modulates from V to ii [G#→d#].

Episode 3 (bars 16–19) is virtually a repeat of episode 1. It has the same bass, while the upper voices now ornament continuously as at the end of bar 9. It modulates from vi to iii [a#→e#].

Bar 21 is not the start of an episode but a free interchange of the previous bar, with extension of the phrase toward the cadence in bar 22.

Episode 4 (bars 22–24) uses the first half of the subject in falling sequence in the soprano, while the middle voice develops the bass of episode 1.

Episode 5 (bars 28–42) has four distinct divisions:

28–30: interchange of episode 2, together with allusion to the end of the subject, modulating to v [g#];
30–34: free interchange and development of episode 1;
34–38: repetition of the first half of the subject in sequence (as in episode 4) above tonic and dominant pedals in the main key;
38–42: interchange of bars 34–38.

Episode 6 (bars 48–51): a new point of imitation leads in bar 49 to a recapitulation of episode 1.

I.7: FUGUE IN E♭ MAJOR

Bars	1	2	3	4	5	6	7	8	9	10	11	12	13	14	15	16	17	18
S	S	cod C------										A------					C--------	
M		A------		EP.1	C--------			EP.2							EP.3		A------	
B					S------						C--------						/	
	I–V		I			I–V					I		I–vi				vi	

Bars	19	20	21	22	23	24	25	26	27	28	29	30	31	32	33	34	35	36	37
S								C-------			S------								
M	EP.4	(C)------		EP.5						EP.6	C-------		EP.7			A------		Coda	
B		S------						A------				/							/
	vi–iii	iii–I			I					I–V					I				

Exposition	
1–2: subject in soprano	19–20: episode 4
3–4: answer [tonal] in middle voice	20–22: subject in bass, modulating from
4–5: episode 1	vi to iii
6–7: subject in bass	22–25: episode 5, modulating from iii to I
Extension of exposition	**Final section**
7–10: episode 2	25–27: answer in bass, I
10–12: redundant entry of answer in	27–28: episode 6
soprano	28–30: subject in soprano, modulating
Entries in other keys, linked by episodes	from I to V
	30–33: episode 7
12–17: episode 3, modulating from I to vi	33–35: answer in middle, I
17–19: answer in middle, vi	35–37: coda

The subject ends at the fourth note of bar 2. It starts on the dominant and is therefore given a tonal answer. More important is the fact that the subject modulates from I to V, so that the answer must be modified in order not to lead from V to II. At some point in the answer there must be a drop of a tone, and Bach decided that the rest was the most suitable moment.

A modulating subject (I to V) can sometimes be answered by the opposite modulation (V to I), but the complete answer in this fugue is in the tonic key. Modulation from V to I was made by the codetta in the second half of bar 2. The sense of the tonic key is reinforced by the A♭ in the countersubject.

Since a subject of this type implies a modulation from tonic to dominant, whereas the answer can be harmonized in one key, it is evident that the control of tonality during such a fugue will depend to some extent on whether the subject or answer form is chosen for the various entries. Thus, the redundant entry of the answer in bar 10 (last note of the soprano) retains the original tonality. The third episode (bars 12–17) modulates into the relative minor, and the entry of the answer in bar 17 remains in this key. But the choice of the subject form at bar 20 provides a modulation from vi to iii [c→g]. The entry at the last note of bar 25 is that of the answer, restoring the tonic key after this modulation. The entry at the end of bar 28 begins as if it were the answer in IV [A♭]. After the rest in bar 29 the entry proves to be that of the subject in I (in spite of its first note) modulating to V. The final entry at the end of bar 33 is that of the answer in I.

The countersubject in the soprano begins at the second note of bar 3 and ends with the last note of the answer. Since the answer dropped a tone down after the rest, the countersubject, which has been designed to fit the answer, must be moved up a tone at some point in order to fit the subject. The middle voice makes this change during the semiquaver run in bar 6, with a completely natural-sounding effect. One or the other form of the countersubject is used along with all but two of the later entries. The entry at bar 20 is so harmonized that the beginning of the countersubject in the middle voice has to be slightly varied.

Variety, in all its aspects, is a necessary ingredient of composition. Bach never uses variety merely for the sake of variety; he controls it in such a way that it never disturbs an overall unity. For example, the subject and answer have a different shape during most of this fugue, but the entry at bar 28 seems to combine the shape of both. The same entry even incorporates into the beginning of the subject the tied note, which until this point had been a feature of the countersubject. Paradoxically, while the final section of a fugue is generally more concerned with unity than with variety, it is often toward the end that Bach inserts some new and telling detail, such as the chromatic adornment of the answer in bar 34.

At the first bass entry in bar 6 the continuation of the soprano part is not a second countersubject (as it was at the corresponding moment of the fugue I.3) but a free part. Such a free part is not a mere filling up with any notes that help to make the harmony clear but is almost always an interesting melodic line. In the four other entries, which include subject (or answer), countersubject, and a free part, the free part is always slightly different.

A large proportion of this fugue (about 65%) is not concerned directly with subject or answer but with the development of figures drawn from the subject, the countersubject, or, more particularly, the codetta of bar 2.

Notes on the Episodes and Coda[4]

Episode 1 (bars 4–5) repeats in a falling sequence the main idea (but not the exact notes) of the codetta, while the soprano alludes to the upward leaps of the subject, together with the tied note rhythm of the countersubject.

Episode 2 (bars 7–10) grows naturally out of the previous subject entry, which leads straight into the codetta figure in the bass (as in the soprano of bar 2). Bass and soprano now use the codetta figure by imitation in a falling sequence. The middle voice adds the same figure by augmentation. In bar 10 the bass develops the codetta figure, while the upper voices allude to the beginning of the countersubject by diminution.

Episode 3 (bars 12–17) starts with an interchange of most of episode 2; the bass now has the original middle part, the middle voice has the original soprano part, the soprano has the original bass part. From bar 15 the soprano develops the codetta figure in a variant of the bass in bar 10. The episode modulates from I to vi [E♭→c].

Episode 4 (bars 19–20) is a free interchange of episode 1.

Episode 5 (bars 22–25) first repeats a variant of the first half of the subject in the soprano, in falling sequence, accompanied by allusions to the subject and to the codetta figure. At bar 21 the pattern changes to a rising sequence, which seems to include new variants of the codetta figure. It is also clear that the countersubject has provided material for bars 24 and 25; the ascending quavers in the bass are an inversion of the first figure of the countersubject, while the combination of soprano and middle voice may be an echo of the countersubject at the beginning of bar 4.

Episode 6 (bars 27–28) continues the pattern of the second half of episode 5.

Episode 7 (bars 30–33) is a varied repetition of episode 2, with the upper voices interchanged.

The **coda** (bars 35–37) makes a final allusion to the codetta figure, extending its intervals as in the soprano of bar 19, with imitation in a falling sequence.

I.9: FUGUE IN E MAJOR

```
Bars  1    2    3    4    5    6    7    8    9    10   11   12   13   14   15
 S          A------cod C--------           S------C---------      C-------
 M     S----C--------           EP.1       A-------cod                 EP.2
 B               S------ext          C---   /        A------
       I    I-V  I                   I    V         I         vi
```

```
Bars  16   17   18   19   20   21   22   23   24   25   26   27   28   29
 S
 M     S----  /    EP.3        A--------C-------  S------    EP.4   S------        Coda
 B          /           S------C-----       S------  C---------         [S----]/
       vi   vi-I       I    I-V   I                        I
```

Exposition	Development
1–2: subject in middle	11–16: episode 2 in vi
2–3: answer [real] in soprano	16–17: subject in middle, vi
and countersubject in middle	17–19: episode 3, modulating from vi to I
3–5: subject in bass	**Final section**
Extension of exposition	19–22: recapitulation of exposition
5–6: episode 1	22–25: episode 4
6–10: counterexposition	25–26: subject in soprano, I
	26–29: coda

From its third note onward this fugue is a *moto perpetuo*, with semiquavers in one or another voice until the very end. There is no obvious ending to the subject, which presumably is overlapped by the answer in bar 2. The subject, announced by the middle voice, merges into the countersubject at the third beat of bar 2.[5] With later entries the countersubject consists of the repeated figure [♪♫♪] alone or the repeated figure and some of the following rising scale passage. The answer in bars 2–3 appears to go straight on to the countersubject[6]; the third and fourth beats of bar 3 are in fact a codetta, leading to the countersubject at the beginning of bar 4. In choosing for the codetta so simple a variant of the countersubject (a step of a tone instead of a semitone), Bach has started a sequence that in one form or another will pervade the entire fugue. He has also made our analysis rather more difficult!

The bass entry of the subject is extended toward the inverted cadence in the middle of bar 5, which is the end of the exposition. After an episode the counterexposition begins, with subject in the soprano at the end of bar 6, answer in the middle voice at the end of bar 7, and answer once more (with a♮ instead of a♯) in the bass at the end of bar 9. The counterexposition leads without break into the episode at bar 11. From now on it should be easier to follow the main events.

Before studying how the episodes are made, it may be helpful to trace the different patterns of the subject and answer at their various entries. The subject, when it is to be closely followed by the answer, leads directly to the countersubject (bars 1–2, middle voice; bars 6–8, soprano; bars 19–21 bass). The subject also leads into the countersubject as part of the following episode (bars 3–5, bass; and bars 21–23, middle voice). The subject also leads into the countersubject (albeit at altered pitch) as part of the coda (bars 25–26, soprano). The answer, when it is to be closely followed by the subject, leads to the countersubject via the codetta (bars 2–4, soprano; bars 20–21, soprano). The answer behaves in a similar way in bars 7–9, apparently preparing for a subject entry, which turns out to be another entry of the answer. The answer also leads to the countersubject as part of the following episode, via a varied or lengthened form of the codetta (bars 9–11, bass). The subject behaves in a similar way in bars 16–18.[7]

Notes on the Episodes[8]

Episode 1 (bars 5–6) leads the bass from the countersubject figure into a rising sequence based on figures from the subject, accompanied by a new leaping figure in two-part imitation.

Episode 2 (bars 11–16) is in two sections:

11–12: the bass develops the bass of episode 1, with alternating figures from subject and countersubject, while the upper voices allude to the descending scale of bar 7 and the leaping figures of episode 1.[9]

13–16: a free interchange of bars 11–12.[10]

Episode 3 (bars 17–19) begins before the middle voice has finished its entry. The middle voice continues with the same alternation of figures from subject and countersubject as in episodes 1 and 2, while the soprano develops the leaping figure of episode 1 by inversion.

Episode 4 (bars 22–25) begins before the end of bar 22 and is virtually a repeat of the latter part of episode 2, with its upper voices interchanged.

I.21: FUGUE IN B♭ MAJOR

Exposition	Entries in other keys, linked by episodes
1–5: subject in soprano	17–22: episode 1, modulating from V to vi
5–9: answer [tonal] in middle with first countersubject	22–26: subject in middle, vi
9–13: subject in bass with first and second countersubjects	26–30: answer in bass, modulating from vi to ii
Extension of exposition[11]	30–35: episode 2
13–17: redundant entry of answer in soprano with countersubjects below	35–37: answer (incomplete) in middle, modulating from ii to IV
	37–41: subject in soprano, IV
	Final section[12]
	41–44: answer in middle, modulating from IV to I
	45–48: coda

The subject starts on the dominant and also has the dominant as its third note. Both these notes are answered tonally, with the result that the answer remains in the tonic key for the whole of bar 5, modulating to the dominant with the e♮' and e♮" of bar 6.[13] This has an interesting bearing on later entries.

The redundant entry of the answer (bar 13, soprano) follows immediately after the previous subject entry, without any intervening episode, giving at first the impression that it is the entry of a fourth voice.

After the first episode the middle voice enters with the subject in vi [g] (bar 22). The bass of bar 26 starts as if it were an answer, which we should expect to modulate from vi to iii (the equivalent of the modulation from I to V in bars 5–6): instead, it modulates from vi to ii [g→c] by continuing with the intervals of the subject.

The key of supertonic is retained at the end of the following episode, so that the entry of the answer in the middle voice at bar 35 starts in this key and would be expected to modulate back to vi. Instead, it modulates to IV, with the a♭ of bar 36 leaping up to d' where we might have expected a♮ leaping up to f♯'. The entry in the soprano of bar 37 is a straightforward subject in this new key. The final entry, which immediately follows, is that of the answer, starting in IV and modulating to I.

The first countersubject always has the same form from its second bar onward. Its first bar is unaltered in two later appearances with the answer, in bars 13 and 41. When it is used with the subject its first bar is modified, as in bar 9. With the other entries of the subject, it is altered even further. In bar 22 it seems to combine the shapes of bars 5 and 9. In bars 26 and 37 it is completely different.

The soprano from bar 9 is not a free part but a second countersubject. Since it begins after the answer has made the tonal change, one would assume that no further modification is needed for other entries. It has the same form in bar 13 and bar 26. But in these cases it has been in one of the upper voices; when it is used in the bass (bars 22, 35, 37, and 41), its first two figures would not produce good harmony without some alteration. (In addition the two hands could not have managed these figures in their original form.)

This fugue displays the greatest economy in the use of material. Of its forty-eight bars no less than thirty four are occupied by the subject or answer together with the two countersubjects.

Notes on Episodes and Coda

Episode 1 (bars 17–22) is in two sections:

17–18: virtually a repeat of bars 15–16 a second higher, in vi, with the lower voices interchanged[14];
19–22: a variant of the fourth bar of the subject along with a free inversion of the first bar of the subject, in falling sequence.

Episode 2 (bars 30–35) is also in two sections:

30–32: a free interchange of bars 19–21, with an added third part;
33–35: an interchange of bars 30–32, with additions to the third part.

The **coda** (bars 45–48) is formed by repetition of bars 43 and 44, with interchange of outer voices.[15]

II.13: FUGUE IN F♯ MAJOR

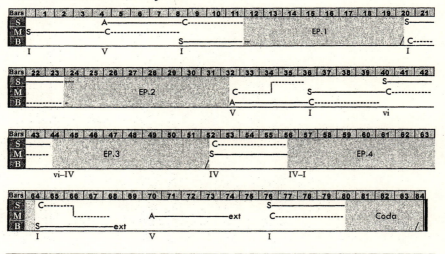

Exposition	Counterexposition (20–40)[16]
0–4: subject in middle voice	20–24: subject in soprano
4–8: answer [real] in soprano	24–32: episode 2
8–12: subject in bass	32–36: answer in bass
Extension of exposition	36–40: subject in middle voice
12–20: episode 1	

cont.

Entries in other keys, linked by episodes	Final section

40–44: subject in soprano, vi
44–52: episode 3, modulating from vi to IV
52–56: subject in middle, IV
56–64: episode 4, modulating from IV to I
	64–70: subject in bass, with two-bar
	    extension
	70–76: answer in middle, with two-bar
	    extension
	76–80: subject in soprano
	80–84: coda

In its rhythm and style the opening subject immediately suggests a gavotte. The dancelike character is continued throughout the fugue, subtly masking the extraordinary skill of its construction. The gavotte rhythm is maintained in measured phrases of four bars length, with two exceptions in the final section of the fugue.

The subject is unique among the "48" in starting on the leading-note. The real answer, therefore, starts at once in the dominant key.[17] We have already noticed that Bach preferred, whenever possible, to retain the tonic key at least for the first few notes of the answer. In this fugue the unusual sudden change to the dominant key is made even more noticeable because of the subdominant implication of bar 2. Every entry is exactly like the opening except for bar 20 and bar 76, where the subject is decorated with a written-out turn [♪♫♩♩] instead of a trill [⁓].

The countersubject is joined directly to the subject by an octave leap in bar 4 and by the leap of a seventh in bars 8 and 20. The leap of a seventh is decorated with an arpeggio in bar 36. The first down-stepping figure [♩|♩♩] is made more prominent in bars 32, 40, 64 and 76, where it is approached from a rest instead of an upward leap. The decorative notes in bar 52 achieve the opposite effect.

On four occasions the countersubject is given a different ending. From the last note of bar 4 to the first note of bar 7, the intervals between answer and countersubject lie within an octave, so that the two voices are interchangeable at the octave. But the other intervals in bar 7 exceed an octave; consequently, the interchange must all be at the fifteenth (as in bars 8–12), or else there must be some modification made at this point of the countersubject, if the interchange has so far been at the octave. The slight changes that Bach makes in bars 35 and 55 keep the two voices clear and avoid an awkward crossing of parts. In bar 79 Bach evidently altered the countersubject in order to avoid a very difficult stretch between the hands or the necessity for bringing his bass higher up for this passage. At bar 67 the same reasons do not apply, and bar 67 could have been like bar 10.

The continuation of the middle voice at bar 8 is a rhythmical and shapely tune that might well have been used as a second countersubject. It does in fact return in the soprano in bars 33–36 and in the middle voice in bars 65–68 but is never used as a bass.[18]

The extension of the subject entry at bar 68 is made in similar fashion to the beginning of episodes 2 and 4, but with a rising sequence. (The middle voice in bar 69 seems to suggest a falling sequence, but the bass is the main factor in determining the nature of the sequence.) The extension of the answer entry at bar 74 recalls the falling sequence of the episodes. The rising sequence is again used in bar 80 to make the coda.

Notes on the Episodes

Episode 1 (bars 12–20) uses the rising scale steps of bars 1–2 by augmentation, along with other figures from the subject, direct and inverted, in a special type of three-part interchangeable counterpoint.[19] The three voices of bar 13 are interchangeable in cyclic order to form bar 15. (The rising steps are now in the soprano.) They are interchanged again for bar 17. (The rising steps are now in the bass.) They are interchanged again for bar 19. (This restores the pattern of bar 13, with the rising steps in the middle voice.) The even-numbered bars continue the general sense of interchange, without being strictly bound by it. It is noticeable that in spite of the difference of register, the rising steps convey the sense of a complete rising scale of an octave and a fifth from bar 13 to bar 20.[20]

Episode 2 (bars 24–32) repeats the end of the subject entry in falling sequence, the middle voice now adding thirds below the repeated-note figure. At bar 26 the middle voice repeats the pattern of the soprano, a fifth lower, while the soprano now adds sixths above the repeated notes. The first half of the episode is then repeated a tone higher. All this process is accompanied by a continuously running bass that incorporates some figures from the subject and also recalls some of the running counterpoint of episode 1. What is not immediately obvious is that this bass is formed primarily from the rising steps of episode 1. Again, in spite of changes of register, the effect is that of a rising scale (i.e., bars 25–26: *b–c×′–d♯′*; bars 27–28: *e–f×–g♯*, etc.) The pattern is broken at bar 28 but then returns (*c♯′–d×′–e♯′*; *f♯–g×–a♯*). Whereas the scale steps of episode 1 are those of major or melodic minor, those of episode 2 are those of the harmonic minor.[21]

Episode 3 (bars 44–52) is a complex interchange of episode 1. The triple counterpoint of bar 45 is interchanged to form bar 47 (the long notes now moving from the soprano to the middle voice). It is interchanged again to form bar 49 (where the long notes are now in the bass). The original position is restored in bar 51. Cyclic order has been used, but in the opposite direction from episode 1. The connection between episode 1 and episode 3 can also be traced in a different way. Episode 3 uses virtually the same bass as episode 1, while interchanging its upper voices.[22]

Episode 4 (bars 56–64) is a repeat of episode 2, with almost the same bass and with its upper voices interchanged.[23]

I.2: FUGUE IN C MINOR

Bars	1	2	3	4	5	6	7	8	9	10	11	12	13	14	15
S			A————————————				C'————————				S—————————				C'———
M	S———————————			C'—————————		EP.1	C''—————		EP.2		C''—————		EP.3		A———
B							S—————————				C'—————				C''—
	i		i–v				i		i–III		III		III–i		v

Bars	16	17	18	19	20	21	22	23	24	25	26	27	28	29	30	31
S	———————				S—————————						C'———C''—————			S———————		
M			EP.4		C'—————————			EP.5			⌈————————			Coda		
B	———————/				C''—————————/						S———————		ext /	(ton.ped)··········		
	v–i				i						i			i		

Exposition	13–15: episode 3, modulating from III to v
1–3: subject in middle voice	15–17: answer in middle, v
3–5: answer [tonal] in soprano, with first countersubject	17–20: episode 4, modulating from v to i
	20–22: subject in soprano, i
5–7: episode 1	22–26: episode 5
7–9: subject in bass, with first and second countersubjects	**Final section**[24]
	26–29: subject in bass, extended to cadence
Development	29–31: coda on tonic pedal, with subject in soprano
9–11: episode 2, modulating from i to III	
11–13: subject in soprano, III	

This is a fugue with the very minimum of modulation; apart from two bars in the relative major everything else is in the tonic or dominant key.

The subject (which is unvaried in all its six entries) has the dominant note shortly after its opening. The answer has the tonic note at the corresponding point, preserving the sense of the tonic key and modulating gradually into the dominant. The sense of the tonic key is further strengthened by the downward scale of the first countersubject.

Because the first countersubject runs down to c', a tenth below eb'' in the answer, the combination is interchangeable at the fifteenth. Alternatively, since the remaining intervals stay within the octave, the latter part of the combination can be interchanged at the octave. This is what happens at bar 15, where the countersubject leaps up a third instead of a tenth, so making the passage playable.

The descending scale of the first countersubject has a very important bearing on the tonality of every passage where it occurs. (This turns out to be every entry of subject or answer.) At its first appearance in bar 3, where it is a scale of C melodic minor (descending by the normal ascending form) it serves to strengthen the feeling that we have not yet left the key of C minor. The key of G minor is reached via its subdominant. The episode in bars 13–14 begins in E♭ but ends in C minor, so that the downward scale in bar 15 has the same effect as in bar 3. With the subject entry of bar 7 the countersubject uses the other form of C melodic minor, and the whole passage of bars 7–9 is firmly in the key of C minor. The only major-key entry of the fugue is at bar 11; here the use of $d\flat$ in the descending scale colors the key of E♭ with its subdominant key, A♭. At bar 20 we have an interchange of bar 7, but the addition of e♮ in the bass adds a subdominant color to this entry also.

The final entry of the subject (apart from its use in the coda) is in the bass of bar 26; here the use of a♮′ in the descending scale (recalling the original scale in bar 3) avoids the subdominant effect, and the first chord of bar 27 is VI, where previously it had been iv. The first countersubject in this passage leaps up to c″ at the end of the scale and then moves from the soprano into the middle voice.

The second countersubject at its first appearance in the middle voice of bars 7–8 has little apparent significance and could be mistaken for a free part.[25] When it returns, again in the middle voice, before the end of bar 11, its second figure is altered for harmonic reasons. It provides a good bass to the entry of bars 15–16, where by changing register after the rest, a more effective melodic line is produced. The same effect is noticeable in the bass of bars 20–22. Here the ending is slightly altered for the sake of the cadence. With the entry of bars 27–28 the second countersubject is in the soprano, in its additional form.

We have seen that the combination of subject (or answer) and two countersubjects is so written that the three lines of melody can be interchanged. This means that any one melody must be capable of acting as a good bass to the other two and also that each one must be of sufficient melodic interest to be heard on occasions in the soprano. In theory there are six permutations of three melodic lines, but it is rare to find all six being used. Bach in this case uses five out of the six (sometimes modifying one or another voice). The one that he did not use (first countersubject in the bass, subject in the middle voice, second countersubject in the soprano) is not quite as effective as the other permutations.

Notes on the Episodes

Episode 1 (bars 5–7) uses the first five notes of the subject [♫♩♪], changing the falling fourth into a falling sixth) and repeats it in rising sequence along with an upward scale that is clearly an inversion of the beginning of the first countersubject.[26]

Episode 2 (bars 9–11) is a two-part canon in falling sequence, based on the opening figure of the subject, accompanied by a running bass that develops the falling scale of the first countersubject.[27]

Episode 3 (bars 13–15) inverts the bass of episode 2 for its soprano now producing a rising sequence. The thirds in the lower voices are a repetition of the figure in the second countersubject (bar 8, middle voice). The episode modulates from the relative major back to the home key, with a suggestion of ♭VII and iv [B♭, f] on the way [E♭→B♭→f→c].

Episode 4 (bars 17–20) is in two sections:

17–18: an interchange at the twelfth of episode 1, with the first figure of the
         subject doubled in tenths by the soprano;

18–20: an interchange at the fifteenth of the foregoing passage, the soprano continuing to double the subject figures, but now in thirds with the middle voice. In spite of the change of register, the soprano in effect rises through seven notes of a scale to reach the next subject entry as part of its sequence. Most of the episode is in v, modulating to i.

Episode 5 (bars 22–26) is also in two sections:

22–25: a repeat of episode 2 (from halfway through bar 9) with the upper voices interchanged. While the bass continues the pattern of falling sequence in bar 24, the upper voices vary the pattern of the canon[28];
25–26: an allusion to episode 1 (but with the soprano figure now stepping down instead of up). The bass recalls the soprano run of episode 3 and the bass run of episode 2. The soprano at bar 25 is also continuing a rising sequence that began with the subject figure in bar 23 and continued (in different rhythm) in bar 24, this rising sequence intersecting the falling sequence of the bass.

The **coda** (bars 29–31) uses a tonic pedal, with added harmony (strict part writing not being maintained) and a final *tierce de Picardie* at the end of the subject.

II.10: FUGUE IN E MINOR

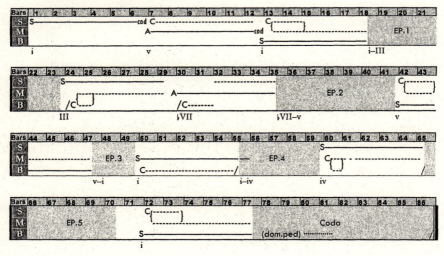

Exposition	Entries in other keys, linked by episodes
1–6: subject in soprano	18–23: episode 1, modulating from i to III
7–12: answer [real] in middle voice	23–29: subject in soprano, III
13–17: subject in bass	29–35: answer in middle, ♭VII
	35–41: episode 2, modulating from ♭VII to V

The dominant occurs relatively early in this long subject and is strongly accented at the beginning of bar 2.[30] But its approach by upward steps makes a tonal answer impossible.

The subject ends at the seventh note of bar 6. It is joined onto the countersubject by a codetta, formed by repeating the end of bar 5 a third higher.[31] The same codetta is used at the end of the answer in bar 12, now approached by a leap of a seventh instead of an octave. Since the entries at bar 23 and bar 29 are also in a subject–answer relationship (keys III and ♭VII [G, D]) the codetta is again approached by an octave leap in bar 29.

All other entries of subject or answer continue with the some codetta in order to lead into episodes, in most cases using the leap of a seventh as in bar 12 (bars 18, 35, 47 and 65). Episode 4 (bar 55) is of special significance and is approached through the same codetta at the end of an entry by the leap of a minor ninth (the codetta figure is in the soprano). The leap of an octave is used at the end of the final entry (bar 77) in order to lead through the codetta to a dominant pedal.

The countersubject adds two new ideas: the four-note figure of bar 7 [♩♪♩], repeated in rising sequence, and the falling and rising steps of bars 9–12.[32] The repeated figure is joined to the downward steps by the codetta figure, and the countersubject ends with an allusion to the jerky rhythm of bar 10 in the subject. The countersubject does not occur again in its original form until bar 50, and even then its ending is altered (bars 54–55). In its six other appearances its form is drastically changed:

13: the upward leaps are the same as in bar 7 (through minor, diminished, and augmented triads) but are made by soprano and middle voice in joint harness. Before the end of bar 14 the middle voice asserts its right to the downward and upward steps. It develops the jerky rhythm of bar 12 into the beginning of the following episode.

24: here the countersubject is accompanying the first major key entry. It makes the appropriate changes to suit the new key, once more sharing the leaping figure between two voices. In bar 25 the tied note and codetta figure of bar 8 are changed into more upward leaps and an upward scale. In bar 27 the last of the four minims is decorated, and the jerky ending is further altered.

30: even more surprising changes are made in the countersubject with the second major key entry. The first two figures are intact in the bass part, but the third one is curiously altered.[33] A variant of the codetta theme now leads to the descending minims, but they are transferred from the bass to the soprano. The jerky ending is like that of bar 18.

42: here the countersubject inverts or partly inverts its repeated figure, again sharing it between two voices. The codetta figure in the middle voice leads to the descending minims; the jerky ending is like that of bars 18 and 35.

60: here the countersubject loses its first figure (apart from the rhythm), shares its repeat between two voices, and substitutes an ascending scale for both the next repeat and the codetta figure; it then transfers its descending minims into the middle voice and provides a variant of the ending of bars 18, 35, and 47.

72: several factors combine to mark the bass entry of bar 71 as the final and the most important entry of the fugue. Not least important is the new treatment of the countersubject, with its bold upward leaps of a tenth, its descending instead of ascending repeated figures, and its complete transformation of the codetta link toward the descending minims.

Notes on the Episodes and Coda

Episode 1 (bars 18–23) is in two sections:

18–20: the last bar of the subject is repeated in rising sequence by the bass, accompanied by the jerky ending of the countersubject in two-part imitation modulating from the tonic to the relative major.

20–23: the bass repeats a new version of the first countersubject figure in falling sequence, accompanied by rising and falling scales leading directly into the beginning of the subject in III [G].

Episode 2 (bars 35–41) is also in two sections:

35–37: this is a new version of the first section of episode 1. The rising sequence formed from the end of the answer is now in the middle voice; the soprano repeats the middle voice of episode 1; the bass has rising chromatic steps, modulating from ♭VII to III [D→G].

37–41: the bass repeats the codetta figure in a sequence falling by thirds, freely imitated by the upper voices.

Episode 3 (bars 47–49) repeats the first section of episode 1, modulating from v to i.

Episode 4 (bars 55–59): the bass continues the altered ending of the countersubject in a partly chromatic rising scale; the soprano repeats the bass of episode 1 in a new form, now rising by ninths instead of sevenths (changing the ninth to a second in the middle of bar 57); the middle voice has a new version of the jerky rhythm of episode 1, alternately rising and falling, taking over the soprano figure in bar 58. The episode modulates from i to iv [e→a].

Episode 5 (bars 65–70): the last bar of the subject is repeated by the middle voice (bar 65) and by the bass (bar 66), linked by falling seconds. (This is a distribution between the three voices of the bass of episode 1.) The accompanying voices allude to the jerky rhythms of episode 1, the codetta figure, and the first countersubject figure. The episode stops abruptly at a pause on the dominant (bar 70).

Coda (bars 77–86): the end of the subject is linked by an octave to the codetta (as in bar 6), culminating in a dominant pedal. The upper voices allude to figures from the subject or countersubject.

II.20: FUGUE IN A MINOR

Exposition

1–3: subject in bass
3–5: answer [tonal] in middle voice, with first countersubject
5–6: episode 1
6–8: subject in soprano, with first and second countersjbejcts

Entries in other keys, linked by episodes

8–9: episode 2, modulating from i to III
9–11: subject (answer) in bass, III

Entries in the keys of the exposition

11–13: episode 3, modulating from III to v
13–15: answer in soprano, v
15–17: episode 4, modulating from v to i
17–19: subject (answer) in middle, i

Entries in other keys, continued

19–21: episode 5, modulating from i to iv
21–23: subject in soprano, iv
23–25: episode 6, modulating from iv to i

Final section

25–27: subject (answer) in bass, i
27–28: coda

The subject ends at the first note of bar 3.[34] A four-note codetta links it with the first countersubject.[35] Since the subject begins on the dominant, the answer begins on the tonic. Most tonal answers retain the tonic key at their opening, but the codetta forces this answer immediately into the dominant key.

The bass entry before the end of bar 9 leaves doubt as to whether it is the subject form with an inserted passing note or the answer form with a shortened first note.[36] Either of these could be made clear in performance. At bar 13 the soprano clearly has the answer, an octave above the original answer. The next entry, in the middle voice at bar 17, is in the tonic key but also has the form of the answer. (An alternative text gives *e'* instead of *b* in the middle voice, which makes the passage like that of bar 9.)[37] At bar 21 the soprano has the subject in the subdominant. The final entry in the bass of bar 25 repeats the doubtful form of bar 9.

The first countersubject starts with the downward run [♫♫♪] in bar 3 and ends at the first note of bar 5. It is used in the same form with every entry until that of bar 21, when extra notes join its first and second downward runs. With the final entry of bar 25 it is completely transformed by the continuously running semiquavers; they do, however, preserve the main sense of the rising and falling curve of the original in bars 3 and 4. [38] The final figure [♩. ♪♩. ♪♪] returns almost unaltered in bar 27 [♮♮♫♩. ♫♩], where it provides the start of the coda.

The second countersubject is in the bass in bars 7–8. [39] It reappears in the bass of bars 14–15. Its ending is altered in three other passages: in the middle voice of bars 10–11, in the soprano of bar 18, and in the middle voice of bar 22.

Analysis of this fugue is made more difficult because of the basic similarity of shape between the first figure of the subject, the second figure of the subject (which is a free diminution of the first figure), the codetta, and the beginning of the second countersubject.

Notes on the Episodes and Coda

Episode 1 (bars 5–6) grows out of the final figure of the answer, combining the shape of subject and codetta figures in falling sequence, accompanied by rising and falling runs derived from the first countersubject. [40]

Episode 2 (bars 8–10) first repeats episode 1 with added bass-notes, then develops the rising and falling runs of episode 1 in two-part imitation overlapping the bass entry.

Episode 3 (bars 11–13): the final figure of the bass entry is joined to the final figure of the first countersubject and imitated a fifth higher by upper voices, with the effect of a three-part canon. The last three notes of bar 12 enter as if they were adding a fourth part to the canon but move to the codetta instead of to the countersubject figure, overlapping the soprano entry.

Episode 4 (bars 15–17) repeats the first half of episode 1 (starting at three octaves distance), [41] then interchanges the voices. From bar 16 there is three-part imitative treatment of the material of bar 9, again overlapping the following entry.

Episode 5 (bars 19–21): the end of the first countersubject is repeated five times, with the effect of an ornamented scale rising for most of three octaves. The upper voices develop the first figure of the first countersubject in two-part imitation. The bass appears to be using some kind of rising sequence; the upper voices make it clear that the total effect is that of a falling sequence.

Episode 6 (bars 23–25) starts by repeating episode 1, with added sixths in the middle voice. Bar 25 develops the beginning of bar 13, with imitative use of both rising and falling scales, merging into the transformed first countersubject in the soprano.

This **coda** (bars 27–28) is a model of economy! The end of the first countersubject is imitated by the middle voice; the new rhythmic figure [♪♩♪]

in the bass recalls by inversion the first three notes of bar 4; there are also allusions to the end of the subject.

COUNTERSUBJECTS OR FREE COUNTERPOINT?

The eight three-voice fugues that we have analyzed so far all have a regular countersubject. Four of them have two countersubjects. From the study of these fugues it must now be evident that the theorists are right in stressing the importance of countersubjects in fugal composition. They are important for several reasons:

1. they afford contrast with the subject.
2. they provide material for episodes.
3. they help to strengthen the overall sense of formal unity.

For any one subject it is often possible to devise many alternative countersubjects. In this initial choice the composer finds his main opportunity for giving a unique character to a particular fugue. (This was perhaps especially true of the A minor fugue recently examined.) A fugue without a regular countersubject must depend on the subject itself to achieve a definite character.

In using free counterpoint with every recurring entry of subject or answer, there is obviously scope for obtaining variety of mood within a fugue. But too much variety will lessen the sense of overall unity. It is in fact a good deal harder to write a successful fugue without using a regular countersubject. In the next five fugues of this group we shall see how Bach himself faced this problem.

II.1: FUGUE IN C MAJOR

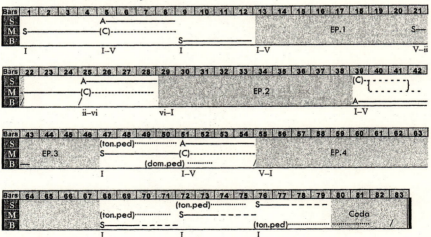

Exposition	Entries in the keys of the exposition
1–5: subject in middle voice	39–43: answer in bass, modulating from I to V
5–9: answer [tonal] in soprano	
9–13: subject in bass	43–47: episode 3, modulating from V to I
Entries in other keys, linked by episodes	47–51: subject in middle, I
	51–55: answer in soprano, modulating from I to V
13–22: episode 1, modulating from I to V	Episode 4 (55–68), modulating from V to I
21–25: subject in middle, modulating from V to ii	Final section[42]
25–29: answer in soprano, modulating from ii to vi	68–72: subject in bass, I
29–39: episode 2, modulating from vi to I	72–76: subject in middle voice
	76–80: subject in soprano
	80–83: coda

The first three notes of the subject decorate the dominant by lower diatonic mordent (a tone). The answer therefore starts with the tonic, also decorated by a lower diatonic mordent (in this case a semitone). Consequently, there is a very striking difference between subject and answer forms.

The answer is harmonized at first in I, modulating to V in bar 7, and is treated the same way in the entries of bars 39 and 51. The first bass entry of the subject (bar 9) is also given a subdominant coloring by the *b♭′* of the soprano in bar 10. The same subdominant coloring is provided at an earlier point of the subject by the bass of bar 47.

The subject entry in the middle voice at bar 21 is unusual in several respects. Melodically, it is in the key of D major at its opening but in D minor from bar 23 onward. Harmonically, however, it begins in the key of G major (entering on chord V in that key), modulating to D minor from bar 22 onward. We have here an apparent contradiction of keys; the subject in itself implies one key, while its harmonic context implies another. Also remarkable is the timing of this subject entry, overlapping the end of the previous episode and arriving as part of the perfect cadence in V.[43]

The final section, starting at bar 68, includes three entries of the subject, none of which are completed in their original form.[44] The bass entry at bar 68 substitutes a sequential-like second half for the original running passage.[45] The middle voice entry at bar 72 alters the ending even further. The final soprano entry at bar 76 repeats the form of the bass entry.

The opening subject seems to last until the first note of bar 5, where there is a feeling of implied cadence. But in continuing its run under the entry of the answer and in its use of figures from the subject, the middle voice does not become a recognizable theme until the rising scale of bar 7. In bar 8 the parallel fourths are harmless at a reasonable speed but cannot sound well if the voices are interchanged, when they become parallel fifths. Consequently, this "countersubject" is hardly a regular one, in spite of its recurrences below entries of the answer in bars 25 and 51; when it is to be used above the subject or answer, it has to be so drastically modified that it is evidently regarded as a free part (bars 39–41, soprano and middle voice).[46] This fugue is generally classified as one without a countersubject, though it can be regarded as being of a hybrid type.[47]

Tonic and dominant pedals appear frequently during the second half of the fugue in every one of the voices. The final section has a most effectively decorated tonic pedal, from bar 76 to bar 80.

Notes on the Episodes

Episode 1 (bars 13–22): the bass repeats the end of the subject and the beginning of the "countersubject" in a rising sequence, while the upper voices use the beginning of the subject in two-part imitation. The episode is led up to a strong perfect cadence at bar 22, overlapping the subject entry at bar 21. It modulates from I to V.

Episode 2 (bars 29–39) is in two sections:

29–33: the middle voice uses the bass figures of episode 1, but now in falling sequence, while the soprano repeats a variant of the beginning of the subject;

33–39: the figures of bar 3 and bar 5 are combined, with interchange at every bar. The episode modulates from vi to ii.

Episode 3 (bars 43–47): the bass repeats the final figure of the answer in rising sequence, while the upper voices repeat a leaping figure that alternately rises and falls.

Episode 4 (bars 55–68) is in two sections:

55–60: a repeat of the rising sequence of episode 1;

60–68: the bass continues its sequence for one more bar, then breaks the pattern to resume it in a varied form. The upper voices allude to the suspension of bar 19, repeating it in falling sequence toward an interrupted cadence at bar 68.

II.11: FUGUE IN F MAJOR

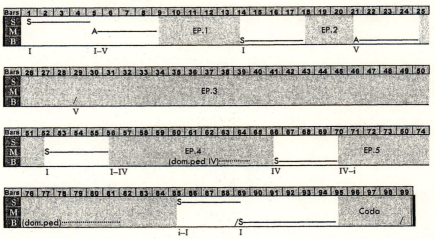

Exposition	Development
1–5: subject in soprano	25–52: episode 3 (with transient modulations to vi, ii and v)
5–9: answer [tonal] in middle voice	52–56: subject in middle, I
9–14: episode 1	56–66: episode 4, modulating from I to IV
14–18: subject in bass	66–70: subject in bass, IV
Extension of exposition	70–85: episode 5, modulating from IV to i
18–21: episode 2	**Final section**
21–25: redundant entry of answer	85–89: subject in soprano, I
	89–95: subject in bass, I
	95–99: coda

At the beginning of the subject and answer [♩♪♪ ♩], we can find the same principle at work as in the C major fugue (II.1) but in reverse. Here, the subject begins with the tonic, ornamented by a lower diatonic auxiliary (a semitone), while the answer begins with the dominant, also ornamented by a lower diatonic auxiliary (a tone). The fourth note of the subject is the dominant, so that the fourth note of the answer is the tonic.

The sense of the tonic key is retained until the second half of bar 7. But in the redundant answer of bar 21 Bach has used B♮, so that the answer at this point is entirely in the dominant key. We might expect to be kept guessing as to which form of answer would recur in later entries; in fact, all the other entries are those of the subject. (The final entry of bar 89 suggests the answer at its beginning but turns out to be an extended version of the subject.)[48]

There is no regular countersubject. The accompaniment of every entry is different, but certain figures of accompaniment tend to recur. The only recognizable melodic line is the soprano of bars 16–18 [e″–f″–g″–c′–f″–f″–e″–f″], which is used again in bars 23–25. Otherwise, the figures are mainly rhythmic. The answer in bar 5 is accompanied by a figure of leaping fifths and fourths ([♩♪ ♪], derived from the subject) whose rhythmic outline recurs in some form during every entry except the final one. The subject entry of bar 14 is at first accompanied by the figure of the first episode [♪ ♪♪♪] which is used in two-part imitation. The same figure, but in a single voice, is used with the entry of bar 52. The entry at bar 21 adds a syncopated figure, which reappears briefly with the entry of bar 66. For the final entry in the bass at bar 89, Bach extends the subject by sequence to make it six bars long instead of four and adds a new and completely unforeseen accompaniment, in a whirl of demisemiquavers. It is unlike his usual practice to introduce entirely fresh material into the last few bars of a long fugue; the final brilliant accompaniment was in fact foreshadowed by the run in bar 45 in the long central episode.

Of the eight entries only one is in a key outside those of the exposition, and it is IV rather than the expected vi. This is the only fugue of this group that does not use the relative minor or major for an entry. But in spite of its apparently restricted key scheme, it manages to suggest a large number of keys as it goes on, notably, during the long central episode of bars 25–52.

Notes on the Episodes

Episode 1 (bars 9–14): melodically, this episode is formed from the second figure of bar 3 and the first figure of bar 4, linked by a tied note [♫ ♪ ⌐♫]. It is a two-part canon, in which the soprano leads on the first beat of bar 9, followed by the middle voice a fourth below after one bar's interval. Alternatively, the middle voice may be considered the leader on the first beat of bar 9, followed by the soprano a sixth above after one beat's interval. However you choose to explain this canon, you cannot fail to notice another significant fact about it, namely, that it is only by the combination of the two voices that the gigue rhythm is maintained. For if the soprano part is considered by itself, it is in three-time from bar 9 to bar 14 inclusive, the bass entry of bar 14 entering as if on the third beat of a bar of $\frac{9}{16}$. The tied dotted quaver recurs throughout the fugue, but this particular cross-rhythm is not used a second time.

Episode 2 (bars 18–21) is formed from bar 4 in three-part imitation, together with the jerky rhythm [♩♪] of bars 6–7.

Episode 3 (bars 25–52) is in four sections:

25–29: the bass repeats bar 25 in rising sequence, while the upper voices develop material from episode 2 in two-part imitation;

29–37: this develops episode 2, with allusions to the jerky figures of episode 1, modulating from V to vi and ii [C→d→g];

37–45: the canon of episode 1 appears in a new version, now in duple time, mainly in I;

45–52: this is a return to the material of bars 25–29, with transient modulations to V minor, ii, and IV [c→g→B♭].

Episode 4 (bars 56–66) is in two sections:

56–61: this is a development of episode 1, with allusion to the jerky theme of bars 5–7 becoming a new canon from bar 57 (the middle voice leading, the soprano following at the sixth above, at one beat's interval), modulating from vi to IV [d→B♭];

61–66: the rhythm of the canon continues with decorated suspensions above a dominant pedal in IV [B♭].

Episode 5 (bars 70–85) is in two sections:

70–76: after repeating the end of the subject entry, it settles into a new canon in the rhythm of that in episode 4, the soprano leading, the middle voice following a seventh below, modulating from IV to ♭VII to the dominant of I [B♭→E♭→C];

76–85: this section recalls the material of bars 61–65, above a dominant pedal in I minor. It also alludes to the main figure of episode 2, the jerky rhythm of bars 6–7, and the syncopated accompaniment to the answer in bar 22.

II.15: FUGUE IN G MAJOR

Exposition

1–6: subject in soprano, with codetta

8–13: answer [tonal] in middle voice, with codetta

15–20: subject in bass, with extension

Entries in other keys, linked by episodes

23–33: episode 1, modulating from V to vi

33–38: subject in bass, vi

40–45: answer in soprano, iii

45–62: episode 2, modulating from iii to dominant of I

Final section[49]

65–70: subject in middle voice, I

70–72: coda

The subject ends at the first note of bar 6[50] and is extended by a codetta of two bars, modulating to the dominant key. Since the subject begins on the dominant, the answer begins on the tonic. The chordal center of bar 8 is chord I in key V; the answer, therefore, starts with the effect of an unessential note. The codetta of bars 6–8 is modified in bars 13–15 to lead back to the tonic key for the subject entry in the bass. The end of this entry is extended toward a cadence in V by a development of the codetta. The original codetta is used again at the end of the entry of bars 33–38 to modulate from vi to iii [e→b] for the answer in bar 40. The final entry of the subject in the middle voice at bar 65 is preceded by a rapid three-octave scale, whose ornamental curves recall the shape of the first codetta.

The accompaniment of the first entry of the answer in bars 8–13 appears to be a countersubject, to judge from its melodic and rhythmic character.[51] It cannot, however, be a countersubject because an interchange would produce several disconnected six-four chords.[52] The subject at bar 15 is accompanied by a sequential pattern of 7–6 suspensions, which is used again above the entry of bar 33 and again in interchanged form below the entry of bar 40. This suspension pattern can be regarded as a combination of first and second countersubjects.

Notes on the Episodes and Coda

Episode 1 (bars 23–33) is formed from the first two bars of the subject in two-part imitation, with added harmony, modulating from V to vi [D→(G→a→)e].

Episode 2 (bars 45–62): an arpeggio figure derived from the subject is treated imitatively by the three voices in falling sequence with further repetition of the figure by the bass, to lead to a dominant pedal on which the soprano repeats the same figure.

This **coda** (bars 70–72) must be one of the most simple and effective of all codas! The soprano adds a short descending version of the ascending run that preceded the final entry, recalling the general shape of the first codetta by inversion.

II.19: FUGUE IN A MAJOR

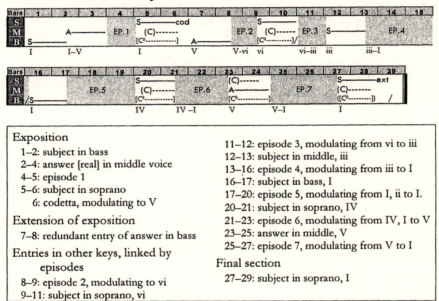

Exposition
1–2: subject in bass
2–4: answer [real] in middle voice
4–5: episode 1
5–6: subject in soprano
  6: codetta, modulating to V

Extension of exposition
7–8: redundant entry of answer in bass

Entries in other keys, linked by
  episodes
8–9: episode 2, modulating to vi
9–11: subject in soprano, vi

11–12: episode 3, modulating from vi to iii
12–13: subject in middle, iii
13–16: episode 4, modulating from iii to I
16–17: subject in bass, I
17–20: episode 5, modulating from I, ii to I.
20–21: subject in soprano, IV
21–23: episode 6, modulating from IV, I to V
23–25: answer in middle, V
25–27: episode 7, modulating from V to I

Final section
27–29: subject in soprano, I

The forward-driving rhythm of the subject is even more noticeable in the entries that begin with an extra step (bars 9, 20, and 27) or with a leap to the first note (bars 12, 16, and 23).[53] The rhythmic impetus is further increased in four of the nine accompanied entries by the fact that they start as resolutions of a suspension. The answer in bar 2 is so harmonized that the tonic key is maintained until the final figure, when it modulates to the dominant. This, as we have seen in other fugues of this group, is common practice with tonal answers but not always possible with real answers. The harmonization of the subject in bar 5 is entirely in the tonic key.

The subject uses every note of the scale except the leading-note; this fact makes it possible to harmonize it with a subdominant coloring. This is done at the end of the entry of bars 7–8, where the redundant answer has started in E but ended with the implication of A. It is also done in the entry of bars 16–17 (keys I–IV).

In the last four entries Bach has decorated the subject with a chromatic note. In the entries of bars 16–17, [20–21] and 27–29 it is clearly decorated even in the melodic context of the subject itself, supported in bar 17 by the harmonic context.[54] The $g \natural '$ in the entry of bars 23–25 is a most effective chromatic decoration, supported by the chromatic steps of the soprano. If this particular passage is reckoned to be in the key of E major, then not only the A$\sharp$ but also the D$\natural$s of the bass are chromatic notes. The overall effect of this entry is that it is not just the key of E but part of an extended dominant preparation for the final entry of bar 27.

The continuation of the opening subject toward the cadence in V at bar 4 is melodically and rhythmically interesting but does not constitute a countersubject.[55] Its main rising scale steps, however, are felt within the middle voice in bars 5–6 and there may be regarded as a countersubject. That it is so intended becomes increasingly clear with the entries of bar 9, bar 20 (with chromatic decoration), bar 23 (with even more chromatic decoration), and bar 27 (finally diatonic).

Notes on the Episodes[56]

Episode 1 (bars 4–5): the middle voice repeats the last figure of the answer in falling sequence, accompanied by a figure that introduces a jerky rhythm [♩. ♪ ♫].

Episode 2 (bars 8–9): the bass repeats the last figure of the answer, while the upper voices allude to the bass of episode 1 in two-part imitation.

Episode 3 (bars 11–12): the upper voices treat the last figure of the subject in two-part imitation, while the bass develops the bass of episode 1.

Episode 4 (bars 13–16) develops the material of episode 3, now including the inversion of the last figure of the subject in two-part imitation.

Episode 5 (bars 17–20) is in two sections:

17–18: a repeat of episode 2, with the upper voices interchanged;
18–20: the last figure of the subject repeated in two voices, both direct and inverted.

Episode 6 (bars 21–23) repeats the last figure of the subject in two-part imitation, with added sixths or tenths.

Episode 7 (bars 25–27) repeats the last figure of the subject, simultaneously direct and inverted.

II.12: FUGUE IN F MINOR

Bars	1	2	3	4	5	6	7	8	9	10	11	12	13	14	15	16	17	18	19	20	21
S	S————cod																			EP.2	
M				A————				EP.1													
B											S————ext										
	i				v						i						i–III				

Bars	22	23	24	25	26	27	28	29	30	31	32	33	34	35	36	37	38	39	40	41	42	43
S				S————cod										EP.3							
M							A————ext														
B																			/ S————			
			III				♭VII					♭VII–v							i			

Bars	44	45	46	47	48	49	50	51	52	53	54	55	56	57	58	59	60	61	62	63	64	65
S			EP.4					S————							EP.5							
M																						
B							(dom.ped)··········															
				i				i–iv														

Bars	66	67	68	69	70	71	72	73	74	75	76	77	78	79	80	81	82	83	84	85
S						S————														
M									S————				Coda							
B																				/
			iv					i												

Exposition	**Entries in the tonic key**
0–4: subject in soprano[57]	40–44: subject in bass, i
4–8: answer [tonal] in middle voice	44–50: episode 4
8–11: episode 1	50–54: subject in middle, i, mainly on a
11–15: subject in bass	dominant pedal
15–17: extension of subject	**Entries in other keys, continued**
Entries in other keys, linked by	54–71: episode 5, modulating to iv
episodes	71–75: subject in soprano, iv
17–24: episode 2, modulating from i to III	**Final section**
24–28: subject in soprano, III	74–78: subject in middle, i (overlapping
28–32: answer in middle, ♭VII	previous entry)
32–33: extension of answer	78–85: coda
33–40: episode 3, in v	

The first note of the subject is the dominant; the answer, therefore, starts on the tonic and is in the dominant key from its beginning. The answer occurs only once more, at bar 28, when it is the second of a pair of entries in keys III and ♭VII [A♭ and E♭]. All the other entries use the subject form without ornamentation.[58] In the final section the entry of the middle voice in bar 74 overlaps by one bar the end of the previous entry in iv [b♭].[59]

At the first entry of the answer in the middle voice in bar 4, the soprano first repeats bar 3 at a different pitch, then extends the falling steps into a complete scale, and finishes with an arpeggio of the diminished seventh. Though not a countersubject, the soprano of bars 5–8 provides material for later development. In addition, its basic shape of e♭"–d"–b♮'–c" can be traced in the accompaniment of some later entries. This basic shape is shared between the upper voices above the subject entry in bar 11. The upper voices also share a new version of the falling scale. The basic steps below the entry in bar 24 are now $c'-bb-g-ab$. The bass here develops further the falling scale and also adds a figure from episode 2 (the bass of bar 19) by diminution. The accompaniment of the answer in bar 28 consists of two-part imitation, based on a variant of the subject figure of bar 3, with a falling scale. The subject entry at bar 40 is accompanied by a variant of the upper voices of bars 11–15. The entry at bar 50 is on a dominant pedal; the soprano accompanies it with a variant of the bass of bars 24–28 (the arpeggio figure now being inverted). The entries of bars 71 and 74 are accompanied mainly by scale figures, including an inversion of bar 4.

Notes on the Episodes and Coda

Episode 1 (bars 8–11) is a development of the material of bar 7, with figures from the subject in the middle voice and a quasi-sequential repetition of the quaver figure of bar 7 in the soprano.[60]

Episode 2 (bars 17–24): the upper voices use the repeated-note figure of bar 1, in thirds decorated by suspensions, adding to it a repeated inversion of the first figure of bar 3, while the bass develops, partly by diminution, the quaver figures of bars 8 and 9 in a more evident falling sequence. The episode modulates from i to the dominant of III [i.e. Eb].

Episode 3 (bars 33–40) is basically a repeat of episode 2, with varied ending and with the upper voices of episode 2 interchanged.

Episode 4 (bars 44–50) is in two sections:

44–47: a variant of episode 1;

47–50: with further allusions to figures from the subject, the bass repeats bar 47 twice at lower pitch, with the effect of a decorated falling scale, leading to a dominant pedal. The upper voices mainly double the bass in tenths.

Episode 5 (bars 54–71) is in five sections:

54–55: two-part imitation of a figure from the end of episode 4;

56–59: the bass repeats the first figure of the subject at various pitches, accompanied by suspensions;

58–62: figures from bars 3 and 4 in three-part imitation;

62–65: a variant of bars 56–59;

66–71: a repeat of episode 3.

The **coda** (bars 78–85) is basically a repeat of episode 2.

THE KEY SCHEMES OF THE FUGUES IN GROUP 2

	Exposition	Counterexposition (or redundant entries)	Development	Final Section
With countersubject:				
Major:				
I.3	I V I	EP V	EP vi EP iii EP V I	EP I V I EP I
I.7	I-V I EP I-V	EP I	EP vi EP vi-iii	EP I EP I-V EP I
I.9	I V I	EP I V I	EP vi	EP I V I EP I
I.21	I V I	V	EP vi ii EP IV IV	I
II.13	I V I	EP I EP V I	vi EP IV	EP I V I
Minor:				
I.2	i v EP i		EP III · EP v EP i	EP iii
II.10	i v i		EP III ♭VII EP v EP i EP iv	EP i
II.20	i v EP i		EP III · EP v EP i EP iv	EP i
Without countersubject:				
Major:				
II.1	I V I		EP ii vi EP V EP I V	EP I I I
II.11	I V EP I	EP V	EP I EP IV	EP I I
II.15	I V I		EP vi iii	EP I
II.19	I V EP I	V	EP vi EP iii EP vi EP IV EP V	EP I
Minor:				
II.12	i v EP i		EP III ♭VII EP i EP i EP iv	i
Common basic forms:				
Major:	I V I		EP vi	EP I
Minor:	i v i		EP III	EP i

8

Episodes (1)

The fugues in Group 1 and Group 2 between them have more than seventy episodes. The importance of episodes is obvious when we realize that they can occupy anything from one-third to two-thirds of the total length of a fugue (see Appendix A). Before going on to study more complex fugues, it may be helpful at this point to try to sum up the general characteristics of episodes, as revealed by the fugues so far studied.

MELODIC CONTENT

All episodes, of whatever length, are concerned with the development of thematic material. This usually consists of figures derived from the subject, the countersubject (if there is one), or the codetta. To a lesser extent, new melodic figures are used, apparently having no connection with anything in the exposition but in a subordinate role.

Development can occur in different ways. A figure can be used in its original form, inverted, or with altered melodic intervals or with altered rhythm. Figures that were previously heard in succession can be used simultaneously in two voices; as the episode proceeds, the two voices can be interchanged. Or two voices can be connected by the use of canon. In almost all episodes some form of melodic sequence, either rising or falling, is virtually a necessity.

CHORD PROGRESSIONS

A melodic sequence usually, though not necessarily, implies a harmonic sequence. The harmonic sequences of the episodes so far examined have used a wide variety of chord progressions, including the following:

- roots falling a third and rising a second;

- roots rising a second and falling a fifth;
- roots falling a third.

But these are less frequent progressions. More frequent, in rising sequences, is the progression roots rising a fourth and falling a third.

By far the greater number of the sequences (about four in five) are falling sequences, based on the progression roots falling a fifth and rising a fourth.

RELATIONSHIP OF EPISODES WITHIN A FUGUE

If there are only two episodes in a fugue, overall unity is more important than complete contrast. Therefore, the second of two episodes is normally either a development of the first or a restatement (often longer) with voices interchanged.

With more then two episodes there is more opportunity for contrast. But any fresh material is likely to be repeated, either in a later episode or in the coda.

Complete contrast is less common than partial contrast. Besides the use of interchange, we find episodes repeating previous material in another key or with change of mode; continuing a process of development that was interrupted by an entry; or using one voice part of a previous episode and grafting new counterpoint onto it.

Episodes can fulfill several functions; besides their main use as passages of figure-development, they are the chief means of modulation. They give relief from what would otherwise be an uninterrupted succession of entries. Episodes can be viewed from two angles; they keep two entries apart, but they also join them together, particularly by dovetailing the material of an episode into the end of one entry and the beginning of the next.

A fuller discussion of episodes is reserved for Chapter 16.

9

Group 3: Fugues for Three Voices, with Stretto

With countersubject:
(Major)   **I.11, 15**
(Minor)   **I.6; II.6**

Without countersubject:
II.3, Pr.3
I.8

The fugues so for examined have included a few isolated instances of two entries overlapping by a few notes. While these fugues hinted at the stretto principle, they did not develop it as do the fugues of the following group, in which stretto becomes an important element of formal organization. The fuller use of stretto, however, does not mean that fugues will now cease to have episodes, though episodes may now be fewer in number and may sometimes be of second importance in the scheme.

The fugues of Group 3 vary in order of voice entry in the exposition; in three fugues the order is middle–soprano–bass; in three fugues the order is soprano–middle–bass; and in one fugue the order is bass–soprano–middle.

I.11: FUGUE IN F MAJOR

Bars	1	2	3	4	5	6	7	8	9	10	11	12	13	14	15	16	17	18

S　　　　　　A————————cod　　C------------------　　　　　　　　　　　　　　　S———
M　S———————————cod　C--------------------　　　　　　　　EP.1　　　　
B　　　　　　　　　　　　　　　　　　　S———————cod　C------------------　　C----

I　　　　　I–V　　　　　I　　　　I–V　　　　　I

Bars	19	20	21	22	23	24	25	26	27	28	29	30	31	32	33	34	35	36

S　——————cod　C--------------------　　C- - - --------------　　　　　　　　　
M　--┐　　　　　A———————cod　　S——————　　EP.2
B　┘-------------　　　　　　S———————C-------------　　　　(dom.

I–V　　　　I　　　　I　　　I–vi

Bars	37	38	39	40	41	42	43	44	45	46	47	48	49	50	51	52	53	54

S　S———————C------------　　　　　　　　　　　　S————————ext
M　　　S———————　　　　　　　　　　　S—————C------------
B　ped)··S———————ext　/　S———————

vi　　vi　　vi　　　　　ii　　　ii　　　ii

Bars	55	56	57	58	59	60	61	62	63	64	65	66	67	68	69	70	71	72

S　　　　　　　　　　　　　　　S————————
M　　　　EP.3　　　　[S———————]　　Coda
B　/　　　　　　　　　　　　　　　　　　　　　　　　　/

ii–I　　　　　　　I

Exposition
　0–4: subject in middle voice
　4–8: answer [tonal] in soprano
　9–13: subject in bass

Counterexposition and first stretto
　13–17: episode 1
　17–21: subject in soprano
　21–25: answer in middle voice
　25–29: subject in bass ⎤
　27–31: subject in middle voice ⎦ Stretto 1

Entries in other keys
　31–36: episode 2, modulating from I to vi
　36–40: subject in soprano, in vi ⎤
　38–42: subject in middle voice ⎬ Stretto 2
　40–44: subject in bass ⎦
　44–46: extension toward cadence
　46–50: subject in bass, in ii ⎤
　48–52: subject in middle voice ⎬ Stretto 3
　50–54: subject in soprano ⎦
　54–56: extension toward cadence
　56–64: episode 3, modulating from ii to I

Final section
　64–68: subject in soprano
　68–72: coda

The subject ends at the first note of bar 4.[1] A codetta, incorporating the rising scale of bar 2, leads to the countersubject in bar 5.[2] The codetta is used again at the end of the answer (bar 8) along with the first figure of the subject (with interchange in bar 9). The codetta again links the subject with the countersubject in bar 21 and is used in a varied form in bar 25.

The subject begins on the dominant; the answer therefore begins on the tonic and is harmonized in the tonic key until bar 6, when it modulates to the dominant key. The answer at bar 21 is treated in a similar way. Of the fourteen entries in this fugue these two are the only ones to use the form of the answer.[3]

The countersubject, beginning at bar 5,[4] first repeats the codetta of bar 4 a third higher, then accompanies the answer with an inversion of its rising scale.

In doing so, it crosses over the answer, so that a complete interchange is impossible. The countersubject is used in full in the soprano of bars 10–13. With the subject entry at the end of bar 17, the countersubject appears first in the middle voice; then in bar 19 it is transferred to the bass (thus avoiding the original crossing of parts). It is used in full in the soprano of bars 22–25. With the subject entry in the bass of bar 25, the countersubject appears in altered form in the soprano, resuming its original shape at bar 27 (with an additional decorative note toward its cadence). The same bass entry leads straight into an abbreviated countersubject in bars 29–31. The soprano entry of bars 36–40 does the same thing, as does the middle voice entry of bars 48–52 (♪ ♪ ♪ f♯ in bar 53 corresponding to the trilled ♩. b♮ of bar 7).

The subject is so made that it can be used in canon with itself at the octave after an interval of two bars. All three stretti are of the same type, but with interesting differences. The first stretto prolongs the counterexposition (which started with the subject entry in bar 17) by repeating the bass entry of bar 25 in the middle voice in bar 27. The second stretto includes an entry in vi [d] by all three voices: soprano, bar 36; middle voice, bar 38; bass, bar 40. The third stretto treats the three voices in the reverse order, in ii [g]: bass, bar 46; middle voice, bar 48; soprano, bar 50. Both the second and third stretti are extended toward cadences in vi and ii, respectively.

Notes on the Episodes and Coda

Episode 1 (bars 13–17): the bass, having finished the subject at bar 13, continues with the codetta and the countersubject. The upper voices use a new leaping figure in two-part imitation. The episode modulates from I to V.

Episode 2 (bars 31–36): the middle voice repeats the last figure of the subject [♪♪♪ |♪] in falling sequence, imitated by the soprano (which now makes that figure identical with the countersubject figure of bar 6). The bass develops the first part of the subject [inverted]. The episode modulates from I to the dominant of vi [F→A(→d)].

Episode 3 (bars 56–64) is in three sections:

56–59: the upper voices treat in two-part imitation (or a canon at the fourth) a variant of the last figure of the subject, while the bass develops the inverted subject figure of bar 31 into a rising scale.
60–63: free interchange of the material of bars 56–59.
63–65: virtually a repeat of bars 56–59, with interchange of the upper voices.

Coda (bars 68–72): the bass extends the scale steps of bars 64–65 accompanied by the soprano in thirds, ornamented with *échappées* like the final figure of the previous entries (i.e., bars 45 and 55).

I.15: FUGUE IN G MAJOR

Bars	1	2	3	4	5	6	7	8	9	10	11	12	13	14	15	16	17	18	19	20	21	22
S	S		C----------------------																EP.1	S(inv)-------		
M			A----------------cod						C-------------												
B									S------------------cod										C(inv)----------		
	I				V					I									I			

Bars	23	24	25	26	27	28	29	30	31	32	33	34	35	36	37	38	39	40	41	42	43	44
S	A(inv)-------					C(inv)----										S-------				---cod C(inv)----		
M	C(inv)-----------------								EP.2							C----------			S(inv)-----		
B	----						S(inv)-------								/						
	V			I			I--vi						vi					vi			

Bars	45	46	47	48	49	50	51	52	53	54	55	56	57	58	59	60	61	62	63	64	65	66
S	-----------						S-------										A-------				
M	---cod		EP.3								EP.4					A-------					EP.5
B							S-------									(dom.ped)-----					
	vi--iii			iii		iii		iii--V							V	V					

Bars	67	68	69	70	71	72	73	74	75	76	77	78	79	80	81	82	83	84	85	86
S	(dom.ped)										S-------									
M		C(inv)------				EP.6				S(inv)--- [S-------]						Coda			
B	/S(inv)-------									S(inv)-- --						/(ton.ped)-------			

Exposition

　　1–5: subject in soprano
　　5–9: answer [real] in middle voice
　　9–10: codetta
　　11–15: subject in bass

Extension of exposition

　　15–16: codetta
　　17–19: episode 1
　　Counterexposition (20–31)
　　20–24: subject (inverted) in middle voice
　　24–28: answer (inverted) in soprano
　　28–31: subject (inverted) in bass (lacking
　　　　　final bar)

Development

　　31–37: episode 2, modulating from I to vi
　　38–42: subject in soprano, in vi
　　42: codetta

　　43–47: subject (inverted) in middle, in vi
　　47: codetta
　　48–50: episode 3, modulating from vi to iii
　　51–54: subject in soprano, in iii (abbr) } Str.1
　　52–54: subject in bass, in iii (abbr)
　　54–60: episode 4, modulating from iii to V
　　60–63: answer in middle, in V (abbr) } Str.2
　　61–64: answer in soprano, in V (abbr)
　　65–69: episode 5
　　69–72: subject (inverted) in bass
　　73–76: episode 6

Final section[5]

　　77–78: subject (inverted) in middle
　　78–79: subject (inverted) in bass } Str.3
　　79–83: subject (altered) in soprano)
　　83–86: coda

The subject ends at the first note of bar 5, leading straight into the countersubject.[6] Although the subject ends on the leading-note, and the answer begins immediately in the dominant key, the subject is not treated as a modulating one and is given a real answer. The harmony at the end of the answer (bars 8–9) makes the matter plain.

The exposition is a straightforward one, including a codetta (bars 9–10) before the bass entry of the subject in bar 11. This codetta, as we shall see, proves to be of enormous importance in the development of the fugue. An episode leads to a counterexposition (bars 20–31), using the inverted form of both subject and answer. The inverted subject entry of bar 28 lacks its final bar, joining itself instead into the following episode. At bar 38 the direct subject appears in the soprano, in vi, leading via an interchange of bar 9 into the inverted subject in the middle voice (bar 43), also in vi, with alteration of its final bar.

The ear accepts the entries of bar 51 and bar 52 as a two-part stretto, the bass entering two octaves below the soprano. Both these entries, in fact, omit the second bar of the subject, as do the pair of entries in bars 60 and 61. The bass entry of the inverted subject in bar 69 behaves like that of bar 28, joining itself to the following episode. The final section (bar 77) is a three-part stretto, with entries of the inverted subject in the middle voice at bar 77 and the bass at bar 78, the entries being, respectively, two bars and one bar long and giving place to the transformed version of the subject in the soprano at bar 79.[7]

The countersubject (bars 5–8) is altered on its second appearance (bar 11). Its first bar is now in outline only, and it is not really recognizable until the beginning of the semiquavers in bar 12.[8] With the entries of the inverted subject (bar 20) and the inverted answer (bar 24), the countersubject is complete and is also inverted. With the entry of the subject in bar 38, the countersubject is at first missing but is represented by the semiquaver run in bar 40. It is used in full, inverted, with the inverted entry of bar 43, with a most effective octave leap in bar 44, which keeps it clear of the pitch area of the subject. It makes a final appearance with the inverted subject entry of bar 69, starting with the semiquavers in bar 70.

Notes on the Codettas, Episodes, and Coda

Codetta (bars 9–10): scale steps are such common property that it seems absurd to attach much importance to them. Nevertheless, the falling steps in the middle of the subject (bars 2–3) and again at the end of the subject (bars 4–5) are a fifth in range, and so are the falling steps of the middle voice in the codetta of bar 9, though their effect is now quite different owing to the displacement of accent. The soprano adds parallel sixths, alternating with an upper pedal. In bar 10 there are both an inversion of each voice of bar 9 and also an interchange of the two voices, so that the rising steps are now above the pedal.

Codetta (bars 15–16) is a variant of bars 9–10. The falling quaver steps of bar 9 are now ornamented; and while bar 16 is basically an interchange of bar 15, the bass of bar 15 is not inverted for bar 16.

Episode 1 (bars 17–19): the bass repeats the soprano part of bar 9 in falling sequence. The soprano starts like the middle voice of bar 10, then adds an inversion of a figure from the countersubject (the second half of bar 6, soprano). The middle voice adds falling scale steps. The three voices form triple interchangeable counterpoint, modulating from I to V and back to I.

Episode 2 (bars 31–37) is in two sections:

31–33: an interchange of episode 1;

34–37: a development of figures from the previous codettas, modulating from I to vi [G→e]. In bar 34 the bass repeats the lower part of bar 10, accompanied by a falling scale. Bar 35 is an interchange. In bar 36 the soprano repeats the upper part of bar 9, accompanied by a rising scale. Bar 37 is an interchange.

Codetta (bar 42): the entry of the direct subject in vi is separated from the entry of the inverted subject by a repeat of bar 9, with the voices interchanged.

Codetta (bar 47): the entry of the inverted subject is led into the following episode by an ornamental version of bar 16.

Episode 3 (bars 48–50) is an interchange of episode 1, modulating from vi to iii [e→b]

Episode 4 (bars 54–60) is a development of the codetta figures, modulating from iii to V [b→D].

Episode 5 (bars 65–69) is an interchange of episode 1 extended toward a cadence.

Episode 6 (bars 73–76): bars 73–74 are an interchange of bars 34–35. But whereas the directions were reversed in bar 36, bar 75 repeats the pattern of bar 74, with interchange in bar 76.

Coda (bars 83–86) makes final allusions to the codetta, on a tonic pedal.

I.6: FUGUE IN D MINOR

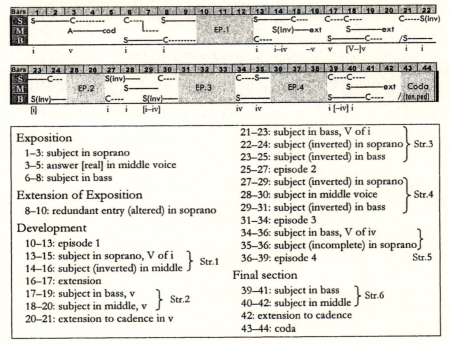

Exposition	21–23: subject in bass, V of i
1–3: subject in soprano	22–24: subject (inverted) in soprano ⎫ Str.3
3–5: answer [real] in middle voice	23–25: subject (inverted) in bass ⎭
6–8: subject in bass	25–27: episode 2
Extension of Exposition	27–29: subject (inverted) in soprano ⎫
8–10: redundant entry (altered) in soprano	28–30: subject in middle voice ⎬ Str.4
Development	29–31: subject (inverted) in bass ⎭
10–13: episode 1	31–34: episode 3
13–15: subject in soprano, V of i ⎫ Str.1	34–36: subject in bass, V of iv ⎫
14–16: subject (inverted) in middle ⎭	35–36: subject (incomplete) in soprano ⎭
16–17: extension	36–39: episode 4 Str.5
17–19: subject in bass, v ⎫ Str.2	Final section
18–20: subject in middle, v ⎭	39–41: subject in bass ⎫ Str.6
20–21: extension to cadence in v	40–42: subject in middle ⎭
	42: extension to cadence
	43–44: coda

The subject, which lasts for two bars,[9] ends on the dominant, but without modulating to the key of the dominant. The answer starts immediately in the dominant key. All sense of subject–answer relationship is lost after the exposition[10]; later entries will therefore be referred to as entries of the subject.[11]

Of the ten entries of the **direct subject** after the exposition, only one (bar 28) is exactly like the opening. In all the other entries the subject is abbreviated, altered in its intervals, ornamented with chromatic notes, or given a new position in the scale. Because the first figure of the subject is used frequently in the episodes, it is sometimes difficult to distinguish real entries from false entries. All the remaining real entries are as follows[12]:

8:          the soprano starts on *e'* as the supertonic in D minor, leaps from *f'* to *bb'* (instead of stepping to *g'*), and includes a most effective flattened supertonic;

13:         the soprano starts on *a'* as the dominant of D minor[13];

17:         the bass starts on *A* as the tonic of A minor but sharpens the third in its second bar;

18:         the middle voice starts on *a* as the dominant of D minor but flattens the third in its second bar;

21:         the bass starts on *A* as the dominant of D minor[14];

34:         the bass starts on *d* as the tonic of D minor, but sharpens the third, with the effect of modulating to G minor.[15] Its ending is also altered[16];

35:         the soprano starts on *f♯'* as the leading-note of G minor. Its ending is altered[17];

39+40:   the same alterations are made as in bars 17 and 18, but starting in each case on D.

The following five entries of the **inverted subject** also have varied positions in the scale, of which two have altered intervals:

14:         the middle voice starts on *e'* as the supertonic in D minor, with a falling fifth instead of a sixth in its second bar;

22:         the soprano starts on *e''* as the supertonic in D minor;

23:         the bass starts on *f* as the mediant in D minor;

27:         the soprano starts on *a''* as the dominant in D minor;

29:         the bass starts on *a* as the dominant in D minor, becoming the supertonic in G minor and using the falling fifth as in the entry of bar 14.

The **countersubject** (bars 3–4) never reappears in its original form.[18] But its presence is felt all through the fugue, in spite of the closely woven stretti, chiefly by allusions to the semiquaver figure either of bar 3 [♩♪♫♫] or of bar 4 [♩♫♫], as follows[19]:

6–7:   the countersubject is transferred from soprano to middle voice;

8–9:   the bass alters the intervals for the first two notes of bar 9;

13:     the bass has the first half of the countersubject;
15:     the soprano has only the first half of the countersubject;
17:     the soprano has only the second half (the first half having been suggested in bar 16)[20];
18–19: the soprano has only the second half (altered), repeated by the bass;
21:     the soprano has only the first half;
24:     the soprano has only the second half[21];
27:     the bass has only the first half;
30:     the soprano has only the second half;
34:     the soprano has only the first half;
39:     the soprano has only the second half (its first half having been suggested in bar 38, as in bar 17)[22];
40:     the soprano has only the first half (altered);
41:     the bass has only the second half.

This is one of the most unified fugues of the "48"; no new thematic material is introduced after bar 4. The four episodes are formed from figures in the subject and countersubject and do not stand out with particular contrast. The only modulation is to v, with the strong approach to the perfect cadence at bars 20–21.[23] Bars 34–37 certainly suggest key iv; otherwise most of the fugue never seems to leave the tonic key. There are no major key entries.

Notes on the Episodes, Stretti, and Coda

Bar 5 is a codetta, formed by freely interchanging the voices of bar 4.

Episode 1 (bars 10–13): the upper voices repeat the end of the subject in falling sequence (mainly in sixths), while the bass repeats the end of the countersubject. In bar 12 the middle voice hints at the inverted subject, while the bass directly quotes the second half of the subject.[24] After this episode almost all the entries are in stretto, always at one bar's distance.

Stretto 1 (bars 13–16): the soprano enters in imitation (by contrary motion) of the middle voice in bar 12; the effect is very nearly that of stretto, but with no actual overlap. Stretto proper begins with the middle voice entry of bar 14. Bar 16 is an extension of the phrase by a quasi sequence.

Stretto 2 (bars 17–20) contains another pair of entries: the bass in bar 17 is followed by the middle voice in bar 18, with an extension toward the cadence in v [a] at bars 20–21.

Stretto 3 (bars 21–25): although only two voices are involved in the stretto, they provide three entries: bar 21, bass; bar 22, soprano; bar 23, bass.

Episode 2 (bars 25–27): the middle voice has the first half of the inverted subject, imitated by the bass, while the soprano makes a rising sequence out of an inversion of the last figure of the subject.

Stretto 4 (bars 27–31) is a stretto of all three voices: bar 27, soprano; bar 28, middle voice; bar 29, bass.

Episode 3 (bars 31–34) arises out of the previous entry of the inverted subject, as episode 1 arose out of the direct subject. This episode is, in fact, a free interchange of episode 1: the soprano of bars 30–33 is a repeat of the bass of bars 9–12 (the same pattern is, in fact, continued for a further two bars), while the upper voices of bars 9–11 with their falling sixths now appear as the lower voices in bars 30–32, with rising thirds. The false entry of the inverted subject in bar 12 is matched by a similar false entry of the direct subject in the middle voice at bar 33.

Stretto 5 (bars 34–35) is a two-part stretto: bar 34, bass; bar 35, soprano. Both entries are radically altered in their second bar.

Episode 4 (bars 36–39) arises out of the altered ending of the previous soprano entry. In a threefold rising sequence (the third bar jumping a third higher than is expected) the soprano repeats the main figure of the first bar of the countersubject, while the lower voices in thirds repeat the first half of the inverted subject.

Stretto 6 (bars 39–42) is an exact repeat of stretto 2 but now in the tonic key instead of the dominant, with the same extension of the phrase toward the cadence.

The **coda** (bars 43–44) makes an allusion to the first bar of the subject, simultaneously both direct and inverted, with added thirds, on a tonic pedal.

The six stretti include eight separate pairs of overlapping voice entries. In them Bach has fully exploited the rich stretto possibilities of his subject:

Direct subject followed by direct subject, an octave higher:	bars 17–18, 39–40
Direct subject followed by direct subject, a tenth higher:	bars 34–35
Direct subject followed by inverted subject, a fourth lower:	bars 13–14, 28–29
Direct subject followed by inverted subject, a twelfth higher:	bars 21–22
Inverted subject followed by direct subject, a twelfth lower:	bars 27–28
Inverted subject followed by inverted subject, a seventh lower:	bars 22–23

II.6: FUGUE IN D MINOR

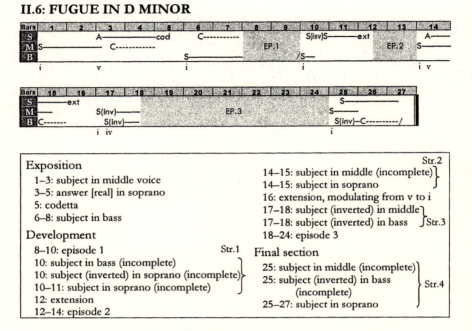

Exposition

1–3: subject in middle voice
3–5: answer [real] in soprano
5: codetta
6–8: subject in bass

Development

8–10: episode 1   Str.1
10: subject in bass (incomplete)
10: subject (inverted) in soprano (incomplete)
10–11: subject in soprano (incomplete)
12: extension
12–14: episode 2

Str.2
14–15: subject in middle (incomplete)
14–15: subject in soprano
16: extension, modulating from v to i
17–18: subject (inverted) in middle
17–18: subject (inverted) in bass   Str.3
18–24: episode 3

Final section

25: subject in middle (incomplete)
25: subject (inverted) in bass
     (incomplete)   Str.4
25–27: subject in soprano

Like **I.6**, this fugue hardly modulates at all. Its two perfect cadences are both in the tonic key. The third episode, however, does touch on other keys (iv, ♭VII, VI [g, C, B♭]) without actual modulation.

The subject presumably ends at the first note of bar 3, being overlapped by the answer for its final note.[25] The leaps at the beginning of bar 3 appear to be the beginning of a countersubject, interrupted by the rests and then continuing with the semiquavers; but in fact the countersubject proper does not begin until the semiquavers. We shall find that the quavers are an important ingredient of episode 3.

The subject in its complete form consists of the opening semiquaver triplets, the leap to the falling chromatic steps, their continuation with diatonic steps, and the cadence. It never appears again in its complete form after the exposition. The entries are:

10	bass:	first half bar only
10 [2bt]	soprano:	first half of the inverted subject[26]
10 [4bt]	soprano:	including the chromatic steps
14	middle voice:	including the chromatic steps
17	middle voice:	the inverted subject, including the chromatic steps[27]
17 [2bt]	bass:	the inverted subject, including the chromatic steps
25	middle voice:	the first half bar
25 [2bt]	bass:	the inverted subject, first half bar
25 [3bt]	soprano:	virtually complete, but with altered ending

Some commentators consider the second half of bar 18 to include entries of bass and soprano (the first half bar of the subject) in key iv.[28] But it seems more likely that this passage is part of an episode, since these apparent entries do not lead to a complete or nearly complete entry of the subject. Furthermore, if they are regarded as entries of the subject, then logically bar 5 ought to be regarded as two entries of the inverted subject, whereas at this point of the exposition bar 5 is clearly a codetta.

The countersubject, beginning after the third beat of bar 3,[29] is heard again with the answer in bars 6–7. Otherwise, its only appearances are with the two virtually complete entries of the soprano in bar 14 and bar 25.

The answer is so very much in A minor throughout that it cannot lead straight on to the bass entry in D minor. The codetta (bar 5) is formed by inverting the last four soprano notes of bar 4, while the middle voice alludes to the first half bar of the inverted subject, with interchange halfway through the bar. The "free part" in the middle voice before the end of bar 7 proves to be of great importance in the episodes.

Notes on the Episodes, Stretti, and Coda

Episode 1 (bars 8–10) originates from the second half of bar 7, which is a combination consisting of the end of the subject, the end of the countersubject, and the "free part," together forming triple interchangeable counterpoint. Interchange is made at every half-bar, varied at the end of bar 9 for the approach to the cadence (with a short allusion to the first subject figure in the bass).

Stretto 1 (bars 10–12): academically speaking, it is a poor sort of stretto, since the soprano has both the inverted subject (second beat) and the direct subject (fourth beat).[30] But in terms of a keyboard fugue Bach often takes liberties, as we have already noted, and the effect here is as if the soprano on the fourth beat is a fresh voice entering with the subject. (If Bach had reversed the direction of his stems from the second quaver of bar 10, continuing as before from the fourth beat of bar 10, it would be orthodox enough, with the middle voice rising for two beats above the soprano.)

Episode 2 (bars 12–14) arises out of a sequential extension at the end of the previous subject group. It is then basically an interchange of the material of episode 1.

Stretto 2 (bars 14–16): the middle voice is followed on the second beat by the soprano, a fifth higher. The bass enters with the countersubject to fit the soprano entry; it also happens to fit the chromatic steps of the middle voice entry as well. The extension of the subject group in bar 16 is a development of the upper voices of bars 11–12, together with a sequential allusion to part of the countersubject in the bass.

Stretto 3 (bars 17–18): the inverted subject is in the middle voice, followed a beat later by the inverted subject a twelfth lower in the bass. The soprano adds allusions to the first figure of the direct and the inverted subject.

Episode 3 (bars 18–25) is in three sections:[31]

18–21: three-part imitative treatment of the beginning of the direct or the inverted subject,[32] together with allusion (by inversion) to the leaping quavers of bar 3[33];

21–24: a free interchange and development of the material of episode 1. (The half-bar combination of episode 1 now appears mostly with reversal of accent);

24–25: a two-part canonic treatment of the "free part" of bars 7–8.

Stretto 4 (bars 25–27): the direct subject in the middle voice is followed a beat later by the inverted subject in the bass and a beat later by the direct subject in the soprano.[34] The countersubject is used in the bass in bar 26.

II.PR.3: PRELUDE IN C♯ MAJOR (FINAL SECTION)

Bars	25	26	27	28	29	30	31	32	33	34	35	36	37	38	39	40	41	42	43	44	45	46	47	48	49	50
S	S————····																	A————								
M	A————····									EP			S————····								Coda					
B			S————————/										A————···/													/

I   I–V   I   V   I   V–I

This prelude ends with a short, three-part fugato. The subject has no definite ending but may be considered to last until bar 28.[35] The answer is in close stretto. The third voice entry in the bass at bar 30 is an altered version of the subject; it starts a note too high in the scale but reverts to the intervals of the subject with the quaver leaps. In bar 31 the upper voices imitate the first figure of the subject, inverted in the soprano at bar 32.

In the single episode (bars 34–37) the bass uses the inverted subject figure, imitated by the upper voices.

At bar 37 the bass has the answer, followed a bar later by the inverted subject figure in the soprano. At bar 41 the subject in the middle voice is followed by the answer in the soprano, in stretto as at the opening, but now with interchanged position. The bass accompanies the stretto with a continuous development of the subject figure. The middle voice entry of bar 41 culminates in an unexpected falling chromatic scale passage (bars 44–46), productive of rich harmony.[36] The coda is made by further allusions to the inverted subject figure.

II.3: FUGUE IN C♯ MAJOR

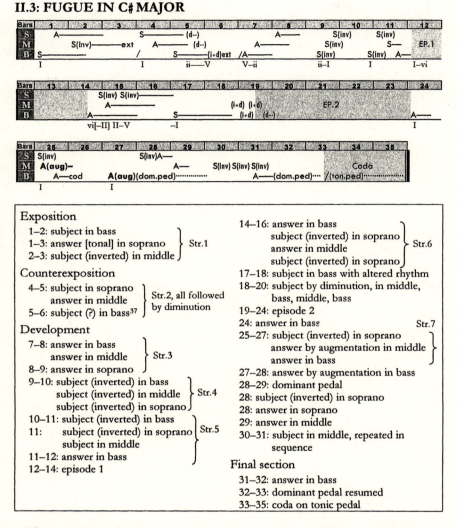

Exposition

1–2: subject in bass
1–3: answer [tonal] in soprano   } Str.1
2–3: subject (inverted) in middle

Counterexposition

4–5: subject in soprano
answer in middle   } Str.2, all followed
5–6: subject (?) in bass[37] } by diminution

Development

7–8: answer in bass
answer in middle   } Str.3
8–9: answer in soprano
9–10: subject (inverted) in bass
subject (inverted) in middle } Str.4
subject (inverted) in soprano
10–11: subject (inverted) in bass
11:    subject (inverted) in soprano } Str.5
subject in middle
11–12: answer in bass
12–14: episode 1

14–16: answer in bass
subject (inverted) in soprano }
answer in middle   } Str.6
subject (inverted) in soprano }
17–18: subject in bass with altered rhythm
18–20: subject by diminution, in middle,
bass, middle, bass
19–24: episode 2
24: answer in bass   Str.7
25–27: subject (inverted) in soprano }
answer by augmentation in middle }
answer in bass   }
27–28: answer by augmentation in bass
28–29: dominant pedal
28: subject (inverted) in soprano
28: answer in soprano
29: answer in middle
30–31: subject in middle, repeated in
sequence

Final section

31–32: answer in bass
32–33: dominant pedal resumed
33–35: coda on tonic pedal

The opening subject is 1½ bars long[38]; the **exposition** is therefore in stretto. The tonal answer continues at its lowered pitch, so that effectively it modulates from I to IV. The middle voice enters with the inverted subject, restoring the tonality of I, which is reinforced by the extension to a cadence at bar 4, the bass alluding to the first figure of the inverted subject, in falling sequence.

The **counterexposition** (bars 4–7) is also in stretto, all voices having the direct subject or answer, with an altered ending for the middle voice and bass. Each voice leads to an entry by diminution, modulating to ii. The phrase is extended to a cadence in V.

Stretto 3 (bars 7–9): all three voices now begin like the tonal answer but continue differently, evolving a "new theme" [♩♪♪♪ ♫♫♫♪], which will become important as the fugue develops.[39]

Stretto 4 (bars 9–10): all three voices now use only the first four notes of the inverted subject, accompanied by the "new theme" both direct and inverted.

Stretto 5 (bars 10–12): at the last note of bar 10 the bass enters with the shortened inverted subject, followed by the soprano (bar 11), also with the inverted subject. The middle voice adds the direct subject, followed by the bass with the direct answer,[40] leading straight into the first episode.

Episode 1 (bars 12–14): the bass develops the main shape of the inverted subject in falling sequence, accompanied by ornamented suspensions, modulating to the dominant of vi.

Stretto 6 (bars 14–16): the bass and middle voice both use the complete answer,[41] and the soprano uses the complete inverted subject (preceded by a "false entry" of the shortened inverted subject). The middle voice entry leads to a sequential allusion (bar 16) to the final figure of the "new theme" of bars 8–9. The end of the soprano entry is extended by falling sequence.

During the following passage there is temporary relief from the pattern of stretto entries. In bar 17 the bass enters with the subject, reproducing its first six notes in varied rhythm and spreading them over two bars, accompanied by continuous reference to the figures from the "new theme" in the soprano. Before the end of bar 18 a series of entries treats the subject by diminution.

Episode 2 (bars 19–24) overlaps the previous group of entries; it uses a figure of the "new theme" by inversion in falling sequence.[42] Bar 21 is a subtle recapitulation of bars 12–13 in the first episode, compressing into one bar the downward steps that first occupied two bars. A rising sequence (bars 22–23) alludes to the subject by diminution.

At bar 24 the tonal answer in the bass is accompanied by the "new theme," which now seems to have taken on the property of a countersubject.[43]

Stretto 7 (bars 25–27): the inverted subject in the soprano is followed by the answer in the middle voice, by augmentation, then by the answer at its original speed in the bass.[44]

The "new theme," direct or inverted, and allusions to the inverted answer form a codetta leading to the augmented answer in the bass (bars 27–28). The end of the bass entry is a dominant pedal on which the upper voices allude to the subject and answer and also to the "new theme" both direct and inverted.

In bar 30 the bass leaves temporarily its dominant pedal and takes over the "new theme," while the middle voice has three repetitions in falling sequence of the inverted subject (the last one partially diminished). Just before this series of entries is finished, the bass brings back the tonal answer by way of final entry (bars 31–32) and then resumes the dominant pedal.

A **coda** begins with the tonic pedal in bar 33; above it the upper voices allude to the subject by diminution.

I.8: FUGUE IN D♯ MINOR

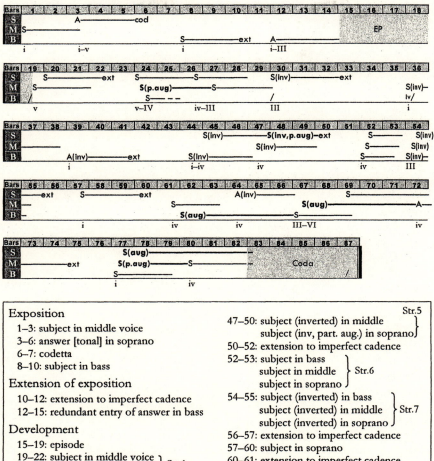

Exposition

1–3: subject in middle voice
3–6: answer [tonal] in soprano
6–7: codetta
8–10: subject in bass

Extension of exposition

10–12: extension to imperfect cadence
12–15: redundant entry of answer in bass

Development

15–19: episode
19–22: subject in middle voice ⎫
20–22: subject in soprano   ⎬ Str.1
22–24: extension to imperfect cadence
24–26: subject in soprano   ⎫
26–27: subject (part. aug.) in middle ⎬ Str.2
24–25: subject (incomplete) in bass   ⎭
27–29: subject in soprano ⎫
27–30: subject in middle ⎬ Str.3
30–33: subject (inverted) in soprano
33–36: extension to perfect cadence
36–38: subject (inverted) in middle voice
39–41: answer (inverted) in bass
41–44: extension
44–47: subject (inverted) in bass   ⎫
45–47: subject (inverted) in soprano ⎬ Str.4

Str.5

47–50: subject (inverted) in middle   ⎫
      subject (inv, part. aug.) in soprano ⎭
50–52: extension to imperfect cadence
52–53: subject in bass   ⎫
      subject in middle   ⎬ Str.6
      subject in soprano ⎭
54–55: subject (inverted) in bass   ⎫
      subject (inverted) in middle   ⎬ Str.7
      subject (inverted) in soprano ⎭
56–57: extension to imperfect cadence
57–60: subject in soprano
60–61: extension to imperfect cadence
61–63: subject in middle
62–66: subject (augmented) in bass ⎫ Str.8
64–67: answer (inverted) in soprano ⎭
67–69: subject in bass
67–72: subject (augmented) in middle ⎬ Str.9
69–72: subject in soprano
72–75: answer in middle voice
75–77: extension to imperfect cadence

Final section[45]

Str.10

77–79: subject in bass
77–80: subject (part. aug.) in middle ⎫
77–83: subject (augmented) in soprano ⎬
80–83: subject in middle   ⎭
83–87: coda

The second note of the subject is the dominant; the subject is therefore given a tonal answer.[46] The continuation of the middle voice in bars 3–6 is not a countersubject but a free counterpoint.[47] The rhythmical figure in the second beat of bar 5 [♫♪] will be used again, as will the syncopated suspension.

Bars 6–7 delay the entry of the subject in the bass. In an episodic fugue this passage might be regarded as the first episode in which case some nine other short passages in this fugue should also be regarded as episodes.[48] But this is anything but an episodic fugue, having only one such passage significant enough to be counted as an episode (bars 15–19). The present analysis refers to bars 6–7 as a codetta and to all the other short passages between entries as extensions, since in almost every case they serve to extend an entry toward a cadence. Thus, the bass entry of bar 8 is extended through bars 10 and 11 toward an imperfect cadence at bar 12. The extension introduces an effective chromatic bass and develops the rhythmic figure of bar 5. It leads to a redundant entry of the answer in bar 12.[49]

Episode (bars 15–19) is made up by a free rising sequence, based on scalic steps, modulating from iv, through i, III to v [g#→d#→F#→a#].[50]

Stretto 1 (bars 19–22) starts with the middle voice, followed by the soprano an octave higher and two beats later. The rhythm is altered before the end of the subject in both voices, and the canon is continued through the extension in bar 23, leading to another imperfect cadence at bar 24.

Stretto 2 (bars 24–27) involves the successive entries in the soprano, middle voice, and bass at one beat's interval. They all start like the answer but go on like the subject (as do most of the thirty-six entries in this fugue). The soprano is altered chromatically; the bass is a mere fragment; the middle voice entry is complete except for its final note and is remarkable in that it presents the subject in altered rhythm, partly augmented.[51]

Stretto 3 (bars 27–30) follows immediately after the previous stretto. Soprano and middle voice are now at two beats' interval.

A succession of single entries is found in bars 30–44, all using the inverted subject. The subject in the soprano (bar 30) is extended through bars 33–35 (with allusion to figures from the subject) to a perfect cadence at bar 36, where the middle voice has the subject. The answer (with ornamented beginning) in the bass at bar 39 is extended to the imperfect cadence at bar 43. A short link (recalling the codetta of bars 6–7) leads to the next stretto.

Stretto 4 (bars 44–47) is an inverted form of the first stretto. The bass is followed by the soprano at two beats' interval.

Stretto 5 (bars 47–50) follows directly the previous stretto. The middle voice is followed by the soprano after one beat's interval. The soprano presents the inverted subject in the same partly augmented form as in stretto 2. The phrase is extended through bars 50–51 to an imperfect cadence at bar 52, with allusion to material from the episode (bars 15–19).

Stretto 6 (bars 52–54) features an abbreviated version of the subject being treated in three-part stretto, starting with the bass, followed by the middle voice and soprano, at one beat's interval.[52]

Stretto 7 (bars 54–56) matches the previous stretto, but with the inverted subject. An extension of the phrase again leads to an imperfect cadence at bar 57.

Immediately after the cadence is there a single entry (bars 57–60) in the soprano; it is extended through bars 60 and 61 to another imperfect cadence, with allusion to the syncopated suspension of the codetta (bar 5).

Stretto 8 (bars 61–67) starts afresh with the middle voice without any accompanying voices (albeit momentarily). The bass entry follows, now using the fully augmented form of the subject. Before it finishes at bar 67, the soprano adds the inverted answer in bar 64.

Stretto 9 (bars 67–72): the last note of the augmented bass entry serves as the first note of a new entry, followed by middle voice with the augmented subject and soprano (before the end of bar 69) with the subject. During the latter part of this stretto the bass alludes to the material of bar 11.

The end of the augmented entry overlaps with a single entry (bars 72–75) in the middle voice; it presents an altered version of the answer, accompanied by a soprano that recalls the chromatic bass of bar 11. The phrase is extended to an imperfect cadence at bar 77, overlapping the following bass entry.

Stretto 10 (bars 77–83) marks the final section of the fugue, involving all three voices; they present the subject in three different octaves, the middle voice with the partly augmented rhythm of bars 24 and 47, the soprano with the fully augmented subject.

The **coda** (bars 83–87) exploits the idea derived from the falling fifths of the subject that are now divided into two intervals of a third, in a falling sequence, which is certainly one of the most telling features of this fugue. The coda ends with allusion to the episode of bars 15–19.

REVIEW OF THE FUGUES IN GROUP 3

Two of the seven fugues in this group are not radically different in form from the fugues of Group 2, except that they use groups of entries in stretto at certain points, instead of single voice entries. In all other respects they follow the general plot of the purely episodic fugues of Group 2:

	Exposition etc.				**Development**									**Final Section**		
I.11	Exp.	EP	Co-Exp	EP	vi		ii					EP	I		Coda	
			(stretto)		(stretto)		(stretto)									
I.15	Exp.	EP	Co-Exp.	EP	vi	EP	iii	EP	V	EP	I	EP	I		Coda	
							(stretto)		(stretto)					(stretto)		

Textbooks sometimes speak of stretto as one of the "devices" of fugal composition, along with inversion, augmentation, and diminution. Obviously, any subject can be inverted (though not always with good effect). Any subject can be augmented (though this can lead to unbearable dullness if the subject is long, or if it has many long notes). Any subject within reason can be diminished (though at the risk of sounding frivolous if it is already short or has many short notes). But stretto can be applied to a subject only if the subject has been designed for stretto or is found to have stretto possibilities. The subjects of fugues **I.11** and **I.15** have one feature in common: each of them can be combined with itself in canon at the octave, and in each of them there is a natural moment of time at which a second voice can enter, either an octave higher or an octave lower than the first voice. Bach has used only this type of stretto, whether any other possibilities existed or not.

In all the other fugues of this group the stretti are more wide-ranging. In the D minor fugue (**II.6**) Bach discovered or invented a subject that has two possibilities of stretto: the subject (or a part of it) will readily combine with itself in canon at the octave or, alternatively, at the upper fifth.

The same possibilities are open to the inverted subject. In addition, it is possible to combine two entries, one with the direct and one with the inverted subject.

For the fugue in D minor (**I.6**) Bach devised a short subject of apparent simplicity that can be combined with itself in many different ways. All four combinations of direct and inverted subject are equally effective. The stretto entries are always after one beat's interval, but the interval of pitch is greatly varied.

The subject of the D♯ minor fugue (**I.8**) can be treated in stretto not only at various intervals of pitch but also at various intervals of time, with both the direct and the inverted forms of the subject. It can also be combined with itself in various rhythms—plain, partly augmented, fully augmented.

Both in the D♯ minor (**I.8**) and the C♯ major fugues (**II.3**), groups of entries in stretto are contrasted with single voice entries. Most stretto fugues start off with an orthodox exposition before revealing their stretto possibilities. Bach, however, starts the C♯ major fugue with an exposition that is in stretto and that includes one entry of the inverted subject. After such a beginning, almost anything could happen! Bach's subject proves to be capable of an apparently endless variety of combinations with itself, including every mixture of direct and inverted forms, plain rhythm, augmented and diminished.

The wide-ranging differences of form in the fugues of this group can now be summarized. The following table shows the groups of entries in stretto (STR), the single voice entries (S), the redundant entry (R), and the episodes (EP) along with the main keys of the entries. The position of perfect cadences is denoted by the sign /.

THE FUGUES OF GROUP 3

	Exposition	Counterexposition	Development	Final Section
I.11	S S EP / I I–V I	S S STR I I–V I	STR / STR / vi ii	EP S / I
I.15	S S S EP I V I	S S S I V I	EP S / S EP STR EP STR EP / S vi vi iii V I	EP STR / i
I.6	S S S R EP i v i i		STR STR / STR EP STR EP STR i v i i iv	EP STR / i
II.6	S S S EP / i v i		STR EP STR STR i i i	EP STR / i
II.Pr.3	STR S / EP I, I–VI		S / V	STR I, V–I
II.3	STR / I	STR / I, ii–V	STR STR STR EP STR S EP S STR S S S S V–ii ii–I I vi–VI I I I I	S / I
I.8	S S SR EP / i i–vi i–III		STR STR / S / S / S STR STR STR STR STR S v IV III III i i i–iv iv III i iv III–VI iv	STR / i, iv i

10

Fugues for Four Voices (General)

THE EXPOSITION

Theoretically, there are now twenty-four ways in which the voices may make their first entry. Bach uses seven of these in the "48":

Cyclic orders:	tenor–bass–soprano–alto	(1)
	tenor–alto–soprano–bass	(4)
	bass–tenor–alto–soprano	(4)
	alto–soprano–bass–tenor	(3)
	alto–tenor–bass–soprano	(2)
Noncyclic orders:	tenor–alto–bass–soprano	(2)
	alto–soprano–tenor–bass	(2)

In a vocal fugue the natural order of entry is usually cyclic, the subject and answer, respectively, suiting the range of adjacent voices. In keyboard fugues, where the original limitation of vocal range no longer applies, Bach still prefers the cyclic order. Though the descending order soprano–middle voice–bass is very common in the three-part fugues, Bach prefers to avoid this order of entry in the four-part fugues.

Whatever the order of voice entry, we would expect the exposition to present the main theme of a fugue in the pattern subject–answer–subject–answer. While this pattern is normally kept, the four-part fugues also show examples of unorthodox behavior, which must be a source of irritation to theorists, because the fugues in question manage to be very good fugues. The very first fugue of the "48" starts with subject–answer–answer–subject. Two others (**I.12** and **I.14**) start with subject–answer–subject–subject.

We already know what wide variety of treatment can be given to a three-voice exposition, through the presence or absence of codetta or of an episode before the third entry. Similar variations are found in the four-part fugues:

Simple exposition without codetta or episode:	I.18, 23	II.7, 9, 16
With codetta before the third entry:	I.5, 16, 17, 20	II.5, 8, 17
With episode before the fourth entry:	I.12, 14.	
With episodes before both the third and fourth entry:	I.24	II.22

THE REST OF THE FUGUE

After the exposition the fugue will not differ basically from a three-part fugue. Indeed, it is important to realize that all four parts need not be kept going continuously after the exposition, and that one source of variety is the reduction of the texture to three or even two voices for certain passages, four voices being reserved for the climaxes. Even the most active four-part fugue (**II.9**) uses all four voices for only four-fifths of its total length. At the other extreme we can find a four-part fugue (**I.24**) in which only one fifth is actual four-part writing.

The following table may be useful for reference. (The calculation is based on the number of bars in each fugue that have four real parts.)

PROPORTION OF FOUR-PART WRITING IN THE FOUR-PART FUGUES

I.24	20%	II.2	34%	I.5	52%
I.16	23%	I.23	36%	I.20	53%
I.14	30%	II.7	46%	II.16	57%
II.17	30%	II.8	48%	I.1	67%
I.12	31%	I.18	51%	II.5	78%
I.17	34%	II.22	51%	II.9	82%

Group 4: Fugues for Four Voices, without Stretto

With countersubject:

(Major)　　**I.23; II.17**
(Minor)　　**I.12, 14, 18, 24; II.8, 16**

Without countersubject:

I.5, 17

I.23: FUGUE IN B MAJOR

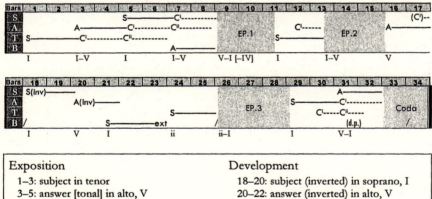

Exposition

1–3: subject in tenor
3–5: answer [tonal] in alto, V
5–7: subject in soprano, I
7–9: answer in bass, V

Extension of exposition

9–11: episode 1, modulating from V to I
11–13: redundant entry of subject in tenor
13–16: episode 2, modulating from I to V
16–18: redundant entry of answer [real] in alto

Development

18–20: subject (inverted) in soprano, I
20–22: answer (inverted) in alto, V
21–23: subject in bass, I
24–26: subject in tenor, ii
26–29: episode 3, modulating from ii to I

Final section

29–31: subject in alto
31–33: answer [tonal] in soprano
33–34: coda

The somewhat unusual answer that Bach gives to his subject received comment in Chapter 2, page 6. In the light of the fugues that we have so far studied, it should now be easier to see why Bach chose this particular answer, rather than a real answer or a tonal answer with a change only at the fifth note. The effect of a real answer is to make an immediate change to the dominant key; this would be unsuitable in the exposition. (A real answer, however, sounds right in bar 16, where the dominant key has already been prepared in the previous episode.) A simple tonal answer would have been equally unsuitable in the exposition, since it does not avoid the sudden key change. Moreover, a change only of the fifth note would have been less effective harmonically than the answer that Bach wrote.

The exposition is a simple one, without codetta or episodes. The tenor harmonizes the answer in bars 3–4 with a first countersubject that is repeated by the alto along with the soprano subject in bars 5–6. The tenor in bars 5–6 continues with a second countersubject.[1] At the bass entry of bar 7 the first countersubject is in the soprano, and the second countersubject (starting from the tied note and slightly ornamented) is in the alto.

After episode 1 (bars 9–11) the redundant entry of the subject in the tenor is accompanied by the latter part of the first countersubject in the alto.[2] After episode 2 (bars 13–16) the real answer in the alto is accompanied in similar fashion by the soprano.[3] The first half of the fugue is now rounded off by a perfect cadence in V at bar 18.

Four entries now follow in close succession; at bar 18 the soprano inverts the subject; at bar 20 the alto also inverts the subject (but starts as if it were the tonal answer)[4]; at bar 21 the bass enters with the subject before the alto entry is quite finished[5]; after a half-bar extension (alluding to figures from the first countersubject), the tenor enters with the subject, starting as if on the first note of E major but harmonized in C♯ minor, so that it ends on the mediant in that key. Both the inverted entries were free in their endings, with a final falling step where a strict inversion would have had a rising step.

After episode 3 (bars 26–29), the final section begins with the subject in the alto at bar 29, with part of the first countersubject in the tenor,[6] and ends with the answer in the soprano at bar 31, with first countersubject in the alto and second countersubject in the tenor. This leads to a short coda.

Notes on the Episodes

Episode 1 (bars 9–11) is made up by a falling sequence, using figures derived from the subject and the first countersubject, in three-part imitation.[7]

Episode 2 (bars 13–16) is an interchange of episode 1, with added fourth part.

Episode 3 (bars 26–29) is mainly a repeat of episode 1, but extended.

II.17: FUGUE IN A♭ MAJOR

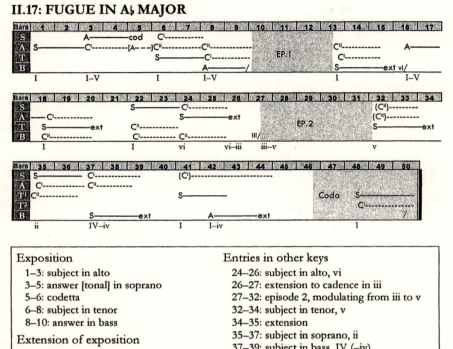

Exposition	Entries in other keys
1–3: subject in alto	24–26: subject in alto, vi
3–5: answer [tonal] in soprano	26–27: extension to cadence in iii
5–6: codetta	27–32: episode 2, modulating from iii to v
6–8: subject in tenor	32–34: subject in tenor, v
8–10: answer in bass	34–35: extension
	35–37: subject in soprano, ii
Extension of exposition	37–39: subject in bass, IV (–iv)
10–13: episode 1	39–41: extension
13–15: subject in bass	
15–16: extension to cadence in vi	**Final section**
16–18: answer in alto	41–43: subject in tenor
18–20: subject in tenor	42–44: answer in bass, I (–iv)
20–22: extension	44–46: extension
22–24: subject in soprano	46–50: coda
	48–50: subject in first tenor

This fugue is an enlargement of an early fughetta in F.[8] The original fughetta ended at bar 24 with a perfect cadence, and all its entries were in I or V. It now serves as an exposition and a slightly irregular counterexposition to the complete fugue in its final form.

The subject starts on the dominant and is therefore given a tonal answer. The answer appears to be harmonized in the dominant key from the beginning, but the effect of the following chromatic steps is to retain the tonic key until the end of bar 4, when it modulates to the dominant. The chromatic steps, with or without their continuation as in bar 4, form the first countersubject.

Bar 5 is a codetta, formed from the first seven notes of an illusory reentry of a real answer,[9] with an important semiquaver run above it. Besides providing material for episodes, it serves to show us that we may expect semiquaver runs with future entries.

In bar 6 the subject in the tenor has the first countersubject in full in the soprano, while the alto develops the semiquavers of bar 5 into a second countersubject. [10] From now on, the ear accepts other variants of the semiquaver run as equivalent to the second countersubject, which is certainly recognizable—again in the alto voice—with the bass entry of bar 8, where the tenor has the first countersubject.[11]

Bars 10–13 are the first episode, which is discussed later. The episode leads to the first entry of what we may now regard as a counterexposition (with a chromatic alteration in the subject at bar 14). At bar 15 the entry group is extended toward a cadence in vi [f] by free interchange of voices. By contrast with previous entries, the alto in bar 16 now has the answer accompanied by falling scales instead of by the countersubjects. [12] The tenor entry of the subject in bar 18 has the first countersubject above it, while the bass evolves a new version of the second countersubject.[13] At bar 20 the end of the entry group is extended as in bar 15, but now by interchanging only the upper voices, while the bass repeats a cadential figure. All four voices are heard together for the first time in the climactic passage of bars 22–24, where the soprano repeats the subject, accompanied by both countersubjects and an inconspicuous free part.

The original final cadence at bar 24 is adorned by a suspended seventh, and modulation immediately begins with the alto entry in vi [f]. The end of the entry group is extended by a falling sequence to a cadence in iii [c]. The second half of bar 27 is the beginning of the second episode, which modulates from iii to v [c→eb], in which distant key the tenor enters with the subject in bar 32.

The end of the entry group is extended differently this time, first as if beginning a falling sequence,[14] then (with small alteration) forming a rising sequence, above which the soprano alludes to the beginning of the answer in order to lead into its entry of the subject in ii [bb] at bar 35. A short extension of the phrase, avoiding exact sequence, acts as introduction to one of the masterstrokes of the fugue, the bass entry in bar 37. This entry has its normal accents reversed. Many a subject, if treated in this way, would lose all meaning; in the present case a new meaning is brought out for a particular subject in which the possibility of reversed accents was always latent. This entry begins in IV but ends in iv: its extension (bars 39–41) moves into i and v [ab→eb]. The imitation in the upper voices in bar 40 finally settles for a *tierce de Picardie* in v, as a dominant for the return of the main key in bar 41.

The tenor enters with the subject in bar 41, accompanied by an ornamented version of the first countersubject in the soprano. The bass arrives with the answer before the tenor entry is finished, and the soprano continues with its ornamental version of the first countersubject. The bass entry is harmonized with an avoidance of its expected ending in V, modulating instead to the key of bII (the "Neapolitan"). The bass run is continued in bars 45 and 46 with leaping figures that may recall the beginning of the subject, accompanied by chords, culminating in a dominant seventh. The coda, beginning at bar 46, adds a fifth part before the end and includes a final entry of the subject (starting like the answer)[15] and the first countersubject.[16]

Notes on the Episodes

Episode 1 (bars 10–13) is founded on the bass forming a continuous upward sequence out of the semiquavers in the first half of bar 5. The alto recalls the chromatic steps of the first countersubject and the downward run of bar 5 (with altered accentuation). The tenor alludes to the opening leaps of the subject. This material extends for 1½ bars; then at the middle of bar 11 the upper voices are interchanged. The real measure of this episode is $\frac{3}{2}$ time.

Episode 2 (bars 27–32) is a complete interchange and extension of episode 1. The original bass is in the soprano; the original soprano is in the bass, the original alto is again in the alto. After 1½ bars the voices are interchanged. Halfway through bar 30 they are again interchanged.

I.12: FUGUE IN F MINOR

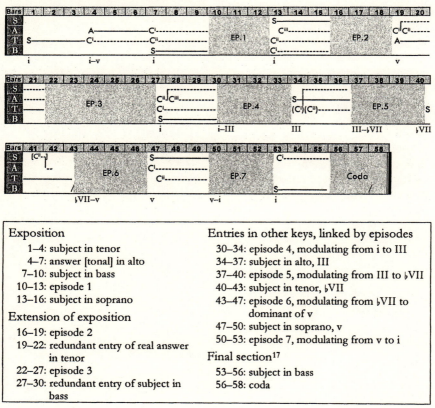

Exposition	Entries in other keys, linked by episodes
1–4: subject in tenor	30–34: episode 4, modulating from i to III
4–7: answer [tonal] in alto	34–37: subject in alto, III
7–10: subject in bass	37–40: episode 5, modulating from III to ♭VII
10–13: episode 1	40–43: subject in tenor, ♭VII
13–16: subject in soprano	43–47: episode 6, modulating from ♭VII to dominant of v
Extension of exposition	47–50: subject in soprano, v
16–19: episode 2	50–53: episode 7, modulating from v to i
19–22: redundant entry of real answer in tenor	Final section[17]
22–27: episode 3	53–56: subject in bass
27–30: redundant entry of subject in bass	56–58: coda

The subject has the dominant for its first and third notes, like that of **I.21**. In that fugue Bach answered both notes with the tonic. The same treatment would not work here, because of the chromatic downward step to the fourth note. The tonal answer, therefore, has the tonic only for its first note.

The tenor leads to a first countersubject in bars 4–7. This is suitably modified by the alto in order to fit the shape of the subject in the bass at bars 7–10. The tenor meanwhile adds a second countersubject, sounding above the alto for most of the entry because of the falling ninth, f'–$e\natural$, in the first countersubject in bar 7. After episode 1 (bars 10–13) the soprano also enters with the subject instead of the expected answer. The first countersubject is now in the bass, the second countersubject in the tenor. The alto adds a third countersubject,[18] making this fugue unique among the "48." The alto and tenor parts cross after the third beat of bar 13 and back a bar later.[19]

The exposition is extended by two redundant entries.[20] After episode 2 (bars 16–19) the tenor enters with a real answer,[21] accompanied by the first and second countersubjects. After episode 3 (bars 22–27) the bass again has the subject, accompanied by all three countersubjects; the first is in the tenor, the second in the soprano, and the third in the alto.

Modulation begins with episode 4 (bars 30–34), leading to a subject entry in the alto in III [A♭], with first countersubject in the soprano (lacking its first upward run) and second countersubject in the tenor (considerably altered). The bass is a free part, and the third countersubject never appears again.

Episode 5 (bars 37–40) modulates to the key of ♭VII [E♭], leading to an entry by the tenor in bar 40.[22] This entry is accompanied by figures from the countersubjects, continued from the previous episode, and by part of the second countersubject [in the soprano at bar 41, which is echoed] in the alto at bar 42.

Episode 6 (bars 43–47) modulates to the dominant of v, leading to an entry in the soprano,[23] with the first countersubject in the alto and the second countersubject in the tenor (starting above the alto). Episode 7 (bars 50–53) leads back to i.

The subject enters in the bass at bar 53. The first countersubject is in the soprano (again lacking its opening run). The other voices allude to figures from the other countersubjects. The entry is extended into a short coda.

Further Notes on Episodes

Episode 1 (bars 10–13) is made up by a falling sequence, with imitative treatment of the first figure of the first countersubject, using also the falling figure of the second countersubject.[24]

Episode 2 (bars 16–19) is a rising sequence, with imitative treatment of the first figure of the first countersubject, now falling as well as rising. The episode modulates from i to v.

Episode 3 (bars 22–27) is a falling sequence, made by adapting and developing the material of episode 2.

Episode 4 (bars 30–34) is a falling sequence, made by interchange and adornment of episode 1. (The bass of episode 4 is a combination of the soprano and alto parts of episode 1.) The episode modulates from i to III [f→A♭].

Episode 5 (bars 37–40): the last bar of the first countersubject (in the soprano of bar 36) is repeated in falling sequence (falling by thirds), with imitation in the alto, while the bass develops the figures of episode 2. The episode modulates from III to ♭VII [A♭→E♭].

Episode 6 (bars 43–47) is a falling sequence made by partial interchange and ornamentation of episode 1, extended to a cadence on the dominant of v.[25]

Episode 7 (bars 50–53) is a rising sequence, being a fuller version of episode 2.

I.14: FUGUE IN F♯ MINOR

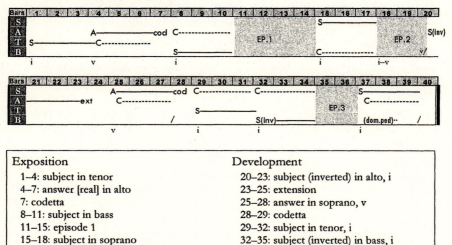

Exposition	Development
1–4: subject in tenor	20–23: subject (inverted) in alto, i
4–7: answer [real] in alto	23–25: extension
7: codetta	25–28: answer in soprano, v
8–11: subject in bass	28–29: codetta
11–15: episode 1	29–32: subject in tenor, i
15–18: subject in soprano	32–35: subject (inverted) in bass, i
18–20: episode 2, modulating from i to v	35–37: episode 3
	Final section[26]
	37–40: subject in soprano

The real answer is in the dominant key from its beginning. The countersubject at first follows the rising steps of the answer with similar falling steps, ornamented by anticipatory notes, with the effect of a new theme in falling sequence. Then it rises in canon a fourth below the answer, before leaping to its cadence formula. The two voices never exceed the interval of an octave and are therefore interchangeable at the octave.

Bar 7 is a codetta, continuing in rising sequence the canon of bars 5–6. At the bass entry of the subject in bar 8 the alto lengthens the beginning of the countersubject by inserting a group of notes similar to its main figure but now including decorated suspensions as well as anticipations. The tenor in bars 8–11 is a free part.[27]

Episode 1 (bars 11–15) is a three-part development of the codetta of bar 7.[28]

At bar 15 the soprano enters with the subject, instead of the expected answer.[29] The countersubject is in the bass, its beginning lengthened by a variant of the alto of bar 8. The leaps at the end of the countersubject now produce slightly unorthodox harmony in bar 17, where there are apparently three $\frac{6}{4}$ chords in succession with a leaping bass. (The only real $\frac{6}{4}$ is the chord on C♯.)

Episode 2 (bars 18–20) may be regarded, in view of what happens afterward, as finishing the exposition.[30] It starts by repeating the codetta with an added voice, then treats the main countersubject figure in two-part imitation, with added thirds or sixths, finishing with a cadence in v.

In bar 20 the alto presents the inverted subject,[31] starting on c♯″ as the keynote in v but harmonized almost immediately with an effect of iv, modulating to i. The bass alludes to the countersubject, also inverting its main figure. The end of the entry group is extended by falling sequence (bars 23–25),[32] leading to the answer in the soprano at bar 25, with quavers taking the place of its first two crotchets. The soprano is accompanied by the countersubject in the alto, exactly as in bars 4–7, with an independent bass in continuous quavers.

Bar 28 is a repeat of the codetta of bar 7. The tenor entry of the subject in bar 29 is accompanied by the countersubject in the soprano and a free part in the alto, almost exactly repeating bars 8–11. (To sum up, bars 25–32 are an almost exact repetition of bars 4–11 an octave higher, with the addition of the bass in bars 25–28.) The tenor entry of the subject is followed immediately by a bass entry of the inverted subject, starting on the keynote and harmonized with the general effect of i. The countersubject is there in essence in the soprano, though its shape is drastically altered.[33]

Episode 3 (bars 35–37): the main figure of the countersubject is treated by two-part imitation in falling sequence.[34]

At bar 37 the soprano has the final entry of the subject, extending to the very end of the fugue, accompanied by an altered version of the countersubject with added sixths and recalling its main figure just before the cadence. Most of the final entry is on a dominant pedal.

I.18: FUGUE IN G♯ MINOR

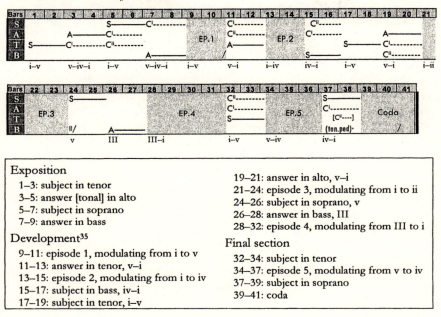

<table>
<tr><td colspan="2">

Exposition

1–3: subject in tenor

3–5: answer [tonal] in alto

5–7: subject in soprano

7–9: answer in bass

Development[35]

9–11: episode 1, modulating from i to v

11–13: answer in tenor, v–i

13–15: episode 2, modulating from i to iv

15–17: subject in bass, iv–i

17–19: subject in tenor, i–v

</td></tr>
</table>

Exposition	Final section
1–3: subject in tenor	19–21: answer in alto, v–i
3–5: answer [tonal] in alto	21–24: episode 3, modulating from i to ii
5–7: subject in soprano	24–26: subject in soprano, v
7–9: answer in bass	26–28: answer in bass, III
Development[35]	28–32: episode 4, modulating from III to i
9–11: episode 1, modulating from i to v	**Final section**
11–13: answer in tenor, v–i	32–34: subject in tenor
13–15: episode 2, modulating from i to iv	34–37: episode 5, modulating from v to iv
15–17: subject in bass, iv–i	37–39: subject in soprano
17–19: subject in tenor, i–v	39–41: coda

This fugue offers unusual problems of decision about tonality. Not only is it founded on a modulating subject, half in g♯ and half in d♯, but in its forty-one bars it has no less than fourteen apparent perfect cadences, on i, ii (with *tierce de Picardie*), III, iv, v, and VI.

The first seven notes of the subject are in i. The rest of it is unmistakably in v. An answer that simply reverses this key change would join its two keys by a major third, d♯' to f×', which is a poor substitute for the augmented fourth, g♯ to c×', in the subject. Experiment will show that Bach has chosen the only possible answer that makes musical sense, by dropping down a tone after the first note.[36] From the second note onward the answer therefore has the same intervals as the subject. But the change of pitch after the first note has meant that the answer is in the key of iv [c♯] for the next six notes, before modulating back to i.

The tenor in bars 3–5 has the first countersubject, which is unchanged when it reappears with the alto in bars 5–7. With the third note of the subject in bar 5 the tenor adds a second countersubject.[37] With the bass entry of the answer in bar 7 the soprano has the first countersubject; the second countersubject is missing.[38]

Episode 1 (bars 9–11) provides a simple modulation to the dominant by repeating the second half of bar 8 in an upward sequence, rising by thirds with apparent cadences on i, III, and v [g♯→B→d♯]. The last of these is endorsed as a true perfect cadence by the detail added by the soprano in bar 10 and the subsequent silence of the bass.

The tenor entry of the answer in bar 11 is as in bar 3, now accompanied by both countersubjects.

Episode 2 (bars 13–15) balances episode 1 with a downward sequence, falling by thirds, with apparent cadences on i, VI and iv [g#→E→c#]. By analogy with episode 1, we can regard the last of these as a true perfect cadence. The episode is formed by repetition of the end of the answer and of an altered version of the end of the first countersubject, while the falling steps of the second countersubject are continued by a chain of suspensions.

The bass entry of bar 15 is identical with the original answer except for its first note. Because of this note and the fact that the entry is in the context of iv [c#], this is the subject rather than the answer.[39] The first countersubject in the alto endorses this view, as does the second countersubject in the soprano (which melodically is in iv). The entry is immediately followed by an entry in the tenor at bar 17, whose first note would suggest that this is an answer to the previous subject entry. But it goes on exactly like the opening subject, modulating from i to v. Both countersubjects are missing[40]; they return with the entry of the answer in the alto at bar 19.

Episode 3 (bars 21–24) is announced in the bass by a new theme, which proves to be a variant of part of the subject (from its fifth to its ninth notes), followed in canon at the twelfth by the alto, in rising sequence. The tenor alludes to the final figure of the subject. The episode is clearly modulating with suggestions of keys v and VI [d# and E#] and ends with a more convincing perfect cadence than previous ones. The modulation is from i to an eventual ii, but the *tierce de Picardie* on the third beat of bar 24 makes it the dominant of v.

The entry in the soprano at bar 24 overlaps the end of the previous sequence and is in the form of the subject. In itself it goes from v to ii [d#→a#]; but for the first time the implied harmony of its cadence is now changed, so that it ends on a first inversion of v, with an apparent uncertainty of key.[41] The uncertainty is resolved by the sudden modulation to III [B] for the bass entry in bar 26.[42] (The first chord of bar 26 is approached as i in D# minor but left as III in B major.) The entry is the only major key entry in the fugue, and, unlike every previous entry of the answer, it is harmonized in one key throughout.

Episode 4 (bars 28–32) starts as an interchange of episode 3, the imitation being now between alto and soprano. Then at bar 30 it changes from a rising to a falling sequence, with a repeat of episode 2, modulating back to i.

The final section begins at bar 32 with a tenor entry of the subject, along with both countersubjects, and including in its bass an echo of the tenor run of bar 25 (but starting it two beats earlier this time). This subject entry has a remarkable sharpening of the third note of the scale, b#,[43] but ends without a cadential effect. It is followed by an apparent cadence on III, a third lower.

Episode 5 (bars 34–37) is a subtle variant of episode 2. If the pattern of falling thirds had been continued, as in episode 2, we would expect the next apparent or real cadence to be on i. Bach by a bold stroke changes the pattern here, moving instead to a cadence on VI [E], followed by a cadence (but not a full close) on iv [c♯]. The episode is held together by the continuation and subsequent doubling in tenths of the falling steps of the second countersubject and its eventual transference to the bass. Added tenths or sixths enrich the subject figure.

The final entry in the soprano at bar 37 starts with a shortening (or a repetition) of its first note.[44] Most of the entry is on a pedal, which starts as a dominant pedal in iv but ends as a tonic pedal in i. The avoidance of cadence at the end of the entry and the repeated reference to iv lead to one of the most effective of all short codas; it includes an allusion to the beginning of episode 1 and a final reinforcement of the tonic key.

I.24: FUGUE IN B MINOR

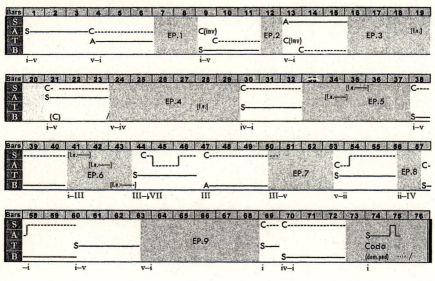

Exposition	Development[45]
1–4: subject in alto, i–v	16–21: episode 3
4–7: answer [tonal] in tenor, v–i	21–24: subject in alto, i–v
7–9: episode 1	24–30: episode 4, modulating from v to iv
9–12: subject in bass, i–v	30–33: subject in tenor, iv–i
12–13: episode 2	33–38: episode 5, incorporating two "false entries"
13–16: answer in soprano, v–i	38–41: subject in bass, i–v

cont.

41–44: episode 6, with three "false
    entries," modulating from i to III
44–47: subject in tenor, III–♭VII
47–50: answer in bass, III
50–53: episode 7, modulating from III to
    v
53–56: subject in tenor, v–ii
56–57: episode 8, modulating from ii to
    dominant of IV

57–60: subject in bass, IV to i
60–63: subject in tenor, i–v
63–69: episode 9, modulating from v to i

Final section[46]
69–70: subject in tenor, i
70–73: subject in bass, iv–i
73–76: coda (including subject in alto and
    soprano)

This is a fugue on a modulating subject that uses every note of the
chromatic scale. Most of the fugue is in three parts, four parts being reserved
for climactic passages, which occupy about one-fifth of the total length.

The subject begins on the dominant; the answer, therefore, begins on the
tonic. Since the subject is a modulating one, Bach could have treated it as he
did that of **I.18**, by dropping down to *g* for the second note of the answer and
then continuing with the intervals of the subject. But the subject of the B
minor fugue is like that of the G♯ minor fugue in only one respect, that it
modulates to the dominant key. In all other respects it is completely different.
There is already a passing reference to the key of E minor at bar 2; to have
made the answer *b–g–e–c′–b–e′–d♯′* would have overloaded the subdominant
return to B minor. Also it would have minimized the chromatic sense of *e′* to
d♯′ in the context in which Bach has placed these notes. Bach, in fact, has
treated the first five notes of his subject as if it were a nonmodulating one,
answering the *f♯′* in the first and fifth notes (dominant) by *b* (tonic) and then
proceeding from this lowered pitch through all the intervals of the subject, in
order to finish the answer in the tonic key.

The countersubject contains three ideas: the opening run of semiquavers,[47]
the falling crotchet steps, and the final run of semiquavers.

Episode 1 (bars 7–9) is initiated by the tenor, which imitates the end of the
countersubject.[48] The alto then adds a quaver figure (a variant of the semitone
steps in bar 1), which is followed by the tenor in canon at the fourth.

Because the first five notes of the answer differ from those of the subject,
the semiquaver run of the countersubject will not fit the subject entry of bar
9; Bach ingeniously inverts the opening run, giving it to the alto,[49] while the
tenor adds the falling crotchets and the final semiquavers.

Episode 2 (bars 12–13) is introduced by the bass, which imitates the final
run of the countersubject and repeats in a quasi sequence.[50]

The tenor in bar 13 also inverts the beginning of the countersubject; the
falling crotchets are transferred to the bass, along with the final run. There are
variant readings of the fifth note of the answer in this passage; it is either *b* as
in bar 4 (with *d♯′* in the alto) or *c♯′* (with *f♯′* in the alto).[51]

Episode 3 (bars 16–21) starts with the soprano, which imitates the final
run of the countersubject in the bass of bar 15. (The tenor has an allusion to
the opening figure of the subject in the tenor.) The pattern is extended for
one more bar. Then the soprano announces a new figure [♫♫ ♪ ♫♫] (which

has been foreshadowed in bars 23–24 of the prelude), followed by the tenor in canon at the fifth. The new figure is repeated in falling sequence, touching on the keys of ♭VII, v, III, and back to i [A→f♯→D→b]. The sequence is briefly interrupted in bar 19 by a "false entry" of the first three notes of the subject in the alto, anticipating the entry of bar 21.[52]

The alto entry of the subject in bar 21 is accompanied by the countersubject in a fragmented form; its opening run of semiquavers starts in the soprano and then moves to the bass; the soprano then resumes the countersubject with the falling crotchets. The entry ends with a perfect cadence in v [f♯].

Episode 4 (bars 24–30) is opened by the bass, which imitates the final run of the countersubject. The soprano and alto in thirds then allude to the quaver figure of episode 1. This pattern is repeated for one more bar, after which the episode reverts to the material of the previous episode. The canonic sequence now touches on the keys of III, i, VI, ending in iv [D→b→G→e]. Another "false entry" occurs in the tenor at bar 28.

In bar 30 the tenor enters with the subject in iv. (From its fifth note onward it is identical with the original answer.) The countersubject, slightly altered in its first run, is in the soprano (and momentarily in the alto in bar 32).

Episode 5 (bars 33–38) starts with the by now familiar imitation of the final figure of the countersubject. The episode incorporates two longer "false entries" of the subject, consisting of its first nine notes, in the alto (bar 34) in v and in the soprano (bar 35) in i.[53]

The bass entry at bar 38 starts as if it were the answer to the subdominant entry of bar 30. From its second note onward it reverts to the intervals of the subject. The soprano extends the opening run of the countersubject for an extra beat, so that the first note of the falling crotchet group is missing.

Episode 6 (bars 41–44) is an interchange and extension of bars 34 and 35 in the previous episode. It incorporates three "false entries" similar to those of the previous episode: in the soprano (bar 41) in i [b], in the alto (bar 42) in iv [e], and in the bass (bar 43) in ♭VII [A].[54]

The tenor entry of bar 44 times its arrival like the three previous "false entries" and continues with the circle of fifths (i–iv–♭VII–III). It proves to be a complete version of the subject. The countersubject in the soprano varies the pattern of bar 38 and is then transferred to the alto for the falling steps (starting with a quaver). Its final run, slightly altered, is in the soprano, with a sequential extension toward the following entry.

The bass entry of the answer in bar 47 is so harmonized that it begins and ends in III. The soprano varies still further the opening run of the countersubject and begins the falling steps with a minim.

Episode 7 (bars 50–53) develops the final figure of the countersubject more rigorously than ever before in four-part imitative treatment, modulating from III to v [D→f♯].

In bar 53 the tenor enters with the subject in v modulating to ii. The countersubject is shared between alto and soprano.

Episode 8 (bars 56–57)[55]: the last note of the tenor entry (c♯) is delayed by the suspended d♯, so that its resolution comes as part of an imitation of the final figure of the countersubject in the soprano. The soprano continues with the imitative figure, leading to the dominant of IV [i.e., B].

The bass enters in bar 57 with the subject in IV [E], modulating to i. The countersubject starts in the alto with a new variant of the opening run and is then transferred to the soprano. It is missing, however, with the tenor entry of bar 60, apart from its final figure in the soprano at bar 63.

Episode 9 (bars 63–69) returns to the canonic sequence of episodes 3 and 4. The canon is once again interrupted (in bar 67), this time not by a "false entry" but by an interpolation of the final figure of the countersubject.

The second tenor note of bar 69 is the beginning of an entry of the subject in i, so that the final section may be presumed to begin here, even though it is only a partial entry (similar to the "false entries" of episodes 5 and 6).[56] The soprano repeats the first figure of the countersubject.

From bar 53 all the texture has been three-part. With the bass entry of the subject in bar 70 (starting in iv) four-part texture is resumed, to become five-part before the end of the fugue. The countersubject in the soprano starts with a downward run (as in bar 44) before restoring its original shape in the third beat of bar 70.

The **coda** is marked by the final countersubject figure being repeated by the soprano. On a dominant pedal the alto and soprano allude to the first part of the subject, with echoes of the final figure of the countersubject in the bass and tenor.

II.8: FUGUE IN D♯ MINOR

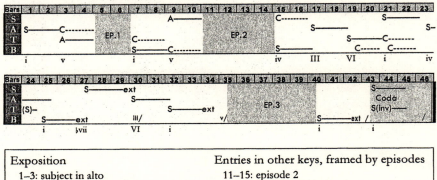

Exposition	Entries in other keys, framed by episodes
1–3: subject in alto	11–15: episode 2
3–5: answer [real] in tenor	15–17: subject in bass, iv
5–7: episode 1	17–19: subject in alto, III
7–9: subject in bass	19–21: subject in tenor, VI
9–11: answer in soprano	21–23: subject in soprano, i

23–25: subject in alto, iv
24: subject (incomplete) in tenor
25–27: subject in bass, i
27–29: subject in soprano, ♭vii
30–32: subject in alto, VI
32–34: subject in tenor, i
35–40: episode 3

Final section
  40–42: subject in bass, i
  43–46: coda (including subject in soprano,
    subject (inverted) in tenor

The real answer in bar 3 is accompanied by a countersubject; after its first falling steps this becomes a fourfold repetition of a three-note figure (♪♪ ♩.) in rising sequence.[57]

Episode 1 (bars 5–7) is led by the alto, which alludes to the upward steps and leaps of the subject, while the tenor extends the final figure of the answer (as in bars 2–3) and repeats the passage a step higher in augmentation.[58]

With the bass entry of the subject in bar 7, the tenor varies the beginning of the countersubject. The alto adds a counterpoint in semiquavers, which, while it is not a second countersubject, has importance for future development. The exposition completes with the soprano entry of the answer in bar 9; the countersubject is in the bass, beginning as in bar 3.

Episode 2 (bars 11–15) is an adaptation and development of the material of the first episode. The bass of bars 11–12 grows out of the end of the countersubject like the alto of bars 5–6 and is partially imitated by the tenor in bars 13–14.

Between episodes 2 and 3 there are nine entries of the subject (ten, if we count the partial one in bar 24) with little or no connecting matter:

15: the subject enters in the bass (with a drop of a third to its fourth note) in iv [g♯],[59] accompanied by the countersubject in the soprano (now beginning with chromatic steps) and with an allusion in the tenor to the counterpoint of bars 7–8.

17: the subject enters in the alto (as in bar 15) in III [F♯], without countersubject.[60]

19: the subject enters in the tenor (as in bars 15 and 17) in VI [B]; the countersubject in partial form is in the bass.[61]

21: the subject enters in its original form in the soprano in i [d♯]. The countersubject in the tenor now starts with rising chromatic steps, matching the falling steps of bar 15, closely imitated by the bass.

23: a short extension of the previous phrase leads to the subject in the alto in iv [g♯], followed closely by a partial entry in the tenor and a complete entry in the bass in i [d♯]. During all this group the countersubject is absent and does not reappear.[62]

27: a similar short extension of the previous phrase leads to the subject in the soprano in ♭VII minor [c♯]. The phrase is extended toward a cadence in III [F♯], overlapped by an alto entry (bar 30) in VI [B].

32: an entry in the tenor, starting on *d♯'*, is at first harmonized in iv [g♯] but ends in i [d♯]. The phrase is extended toward a perfect cadence in v [a♯] at bar 35.

Episode 3 (bars 35–40) is a development of the material of episodes 1 and 2, with allusions to the counterpoint of bar 8.

The bass entry of the subject in bar 40 is accompanied by detached chords, and the phrase is extended toward a cadence in bar 43. The following coda includes simultaneous entries of the direct subject in the soprano and the inverted subject in the tenor.

II.16: FUGUE IN G MINOR

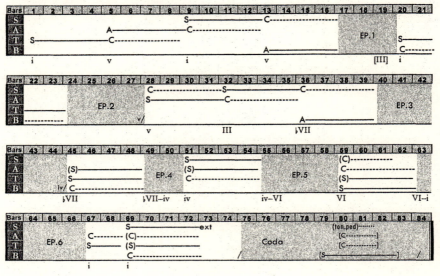

Exposition	45–49: subject in tenor (with added thirds in alto) ♭VII
1–5: subject in tenor	
5–9: answer [tonal] in alto	49–51: episode 4, modulating from ♭VII to iv
9–13: subject in soprano	51–55: subject in soprano (with added sixths in alto), iv
13–17: answer in bass	
Extension of exposition	55–59: episode 5, modulating from iv to dominant of VI
17–20: episode 1	
20–24: redundant entry of subject in tenor	59–63: subject in bass (with added thirds in tenor) VI
24–28: episode 2	63–67: episode 6, modulating from VI to dominant of i
28–32: redundant entry of answer [real] in alto	
Development[63]	**Final section**
32–36: subject in soprano, III	67–69: subject in tenor
36–40: answer in bass, ♭VII	69–73: subject in soprano (with added tenths in tenor)
40–45: episode 3	73–75: extension
	75–84: coda
	[79–83: subject (transformed) in bass]

The subject begins on the dominant; the answer, therefore, begins on the tonic. The countersubject is designed in such a way that it is interchangeable with the subject or answer at any of three intervals: tenth, twelfth, fifteenth.[64] Because of this fact it is possible to double either the subject or the countersubject (or both) in thirds or sixths.[65]

With the soprano entry of the subject in bar 9, the first figure of the countersubject in the alto is slightly altered. The tenor proceeds with a free part, incorporating figures from both subject and countersubject[66]; and also included in bar 9 is a leaping figure that will be used in the episodes. With the bass entry of the answer in bar 13, the countersubject is in the soprano, bars 5–9 being interchanged at the fifteenth [i.e., octave].

Episode 1 (bars 17–20) is mainly a falling sequence, first two bars with two-part imitative treatment of the leaping figure of bar 9, with the main countersubject figure in the bass, and the remaining bars leading sequentially into the entry of bar 20.[67]

Bar 20 is a redundant entry of the subject in the tenor, with the countersubject in its original relationship in the bass.[68]

Episode 2 (bars 24–28): the bass repeats in an irregular sequence the leaping figure of bar 9, while the tenor and soprano treat the main countersubject figure by imitation.

Bar 28 is a redundant entry of the answer (now a real answer) in the alto. The soprano has the countersubject, interchanging bars 5–9 at the twelfth. The tenor develops the opening figure of the countersubject into a continuous run of semiquavers.

At bar 32 the soprano has the subject in the relative major. The countersubject in the alto is not in the same relationship as in bars 5–9, being in fact a third higher up the scale. The two themes happen to fit in this way (so long as there is another voice beneath them to make the harmony clear). If one is mathematically inclined, it can be discovered that the themes of bars 5–9 have been interchanged at the tenth and then interchanged again at the octave. Besides adding important harmony notes, the tenor binds the passage together by continuing its semiquaver movement, which now incorporates the first figure of bars 10 and 11.

At bar 36 the answer in the bass is accompanied by the countersubject in the soprano, interchanging bars 5–9 at the tenth.

Episode 3 (bars 40–45) is made up by a free rising sequence, repeating figures from the countersubject, extended toward a perfect cadence in iv [c] at bar 45.

At bar 45 the tenor enters with the subject in ♭VII [F], while the bass has the countersubject in its original relationship. The tenor entry is enriched by added thirds in the alto.

Episode 4 (bars 49–51) is a free rising sequence, using figures from the countersubject.

At bar 51 the entry of the soprano after two bars' silence marks it as the chief voice, enriched by added sixths in the alto.[69] The countersubject in the tenor is related to the soprano as in the upper voices of bars 32–36. (While this is a true description of the music as we hear it, it could also be argued that the alto is the leading part (presenting the subject in iv [c]) while the soprano adds sixths above it. The alto and tenor are then in the same relationship as in bars 5–9.)

Episode 5 (bars 55–59): the end of the subject in the soprano is altered, to produce an imitation of the falling passage in the countersubject. The episode continues with a falling sequence based on figures from the countersubject.

At bar 59 the subject is in the bass in VI [Eb], doubled by the tenor in thirds. The countersubject is in the alto, doubled by the soprano in thirds, with an alteration as in bar 62.

Episode 6 (bars 63–67): the ending of the subject is again altered in the bass and tenor to allow the tenor to imitate the falling passage of the countersubject in the alto of bar 62. The imitation is continued through bars 64–65 and led toward a cadence on the dominant of i at bar 67.

At bar 67, the tenor (in a solitary note after so much four-part writing) announces the subject in the tonic key, while the alto adds the countersubject, interchanging bars 5–6 at the twelfth. At bar 69 the soprano also enters with the subject (as if in stretto), while the continuation of the tenor produces added tenths with the soprano. The countersubject is in the bass, so that the continuation of the alto produces added tenths with it. The ending is considerably altered, to lead toward the perfect cadence in bar 75.

The **coda** makes further references to the main figure of the countersubject; it recalls the detached chords that led to the cadence of bar 75 and includes a final transformed entry of the subject in the bass.[70]

I.5: FUGUE IN D MAJOR

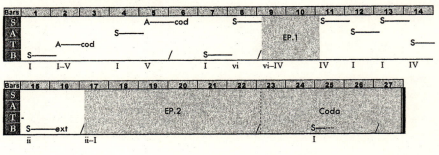

Exposition[71]	Extension of exposition
1–2: subject in bass	6–7: codetta
2–3: answer [real] in tenor	7–8: redundant entry of subject in bass
3–4: codetta	**Entries in other keys**
4–5: subject in alto	8–9: subject in soprano, vi
5–6: answer in soprano	

9–11: episode 1, modulating from vi to IV   Final section: coda
11–12: subject in soprano, IV
12–13: subject in alto, I   23–24: sequential introduction to subject
13–14: subject in soprano, I   24–25: subject in bass (altered)
14–15: subject in tenor, IV   25–27: extension of subject to cadence
15–16: subject in bass, ii
17–23: episode 2, modulating from ii to I

The continuation of the opening bass entry under the answer is not a countersubject but a free counterpoint.[72] The beginning of the answer is harmonized as if still in I, with an implied modulation to V at the last beat of bar 2. Bar 3 is a codetta with several interesting features: there is partial imitation between bass and tenor (the quick rising steps); tenor outlines the pattern of falling fifths (*f♯'* to *b*, *e'* to *a*); the last beat of bar 3 [♪♫♫] is an augmentation of part of the first figure of the subject [i.e., 5th–8th demisemiquavers ♫♫♫].[73] All these features will affect the character of the whole fugue.

After the alto entry of bars 4–5 the soprano entry is preceded by *g♯'* in the alto, so that the answer in bars 5–6 is now explicitly in V. Bar 6 is a codetta, developed from a free interchange of the codetta of bar 3, leading to the redundant entry of the subject in the bass at bar 7.

The extended exposition proceeds immediately to a soprano entry of the subject in the relative minor at bar 8.

Episode 1 (bars 9–11) is made up by a falling sequence, modulating from vi to IV [b→G]. The first nine notes of the subject are repeated in the bass at the beginning of each bar, leading in bars 9 and 10 to a sequential repetition of the last figure of bar 3 (a sequence within a sequence) and in bar 11 to a new entry.

Five entries now follow without any connecting episodes:

11:   subject in soprano in IV [G].
12:   subject in alto in I.[74]
13:   subject in soprano in I (coloured by harmony of IV).[75]
14:   subject in tenor in IV.
15:   subject in bass in ii [e],[76] extended to a perfect cadence at bar 17.

Episode 2 (bars 17–23) begins with a free interchange and extension of the first episode for three bars. After this, bar 20 treats the first figure of the subject by imitation in falling fifths; bar 21 is a brief reference to the material of the first episode, extended to the cadence at bar 23.

Bar 23 is a free interchange and development of the codetta of bar 6. In bar 24 the subject figure now ascends by fourths instead of falling by fifths. The movement in tenths from the second beat of bar 24 has a climactic effect and acts as a sequential introduction to a final entry at the last beat of bar 24. (Compare the extended final entry of the subject in the fugue in F (**II.11**), bar

89.) The altered ending of the entry is extended through bars 25 and 26 to the final cadence.

I.17: FUGUE IN A♭ MAJOR

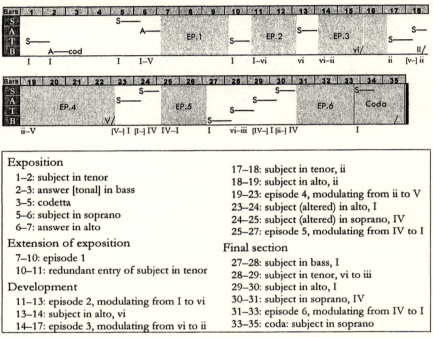

Exposition

1–2: subject in tenor
2–3: answer [tonal] in bass
3–5: codetta
5–6: subject in soprano
6–7: answer in alto

Extension of exposition

7–10: episode 1
10–11: redundant entry of subject in tenor

Development

11–13: episode 2, modulating from I to vi
13–14: subject in alto, vi
14–17: episode 3, modulating from vi to ii

17–18: subject in tenor, ii
18–19: subject in alto, ii
19–23: episode 4, modulating from ii to V
23–24: subject (altered) in alto, I
24–25: subject (altered) in soprano, IV
25–27: episode 5, modulating from IV to I

Final section

27–28: subject in bass, I
28–29: subject in tenor, vi to iii
29–30: subject in alto, I
30–31: subject in soprano, IV
31–33: episode 6, modulating from IV to I
33–35: coda: subject in soprano

Like the subject of the D-minor fugue (**I.6**), the subject of this fugue ends on the dominant but not in the dominant key.[77] Since the leading-note does not occur in the subject, the answer can be harmonized entirely in the tonic key. The tonal change at the second note of the answer makes the passage in bars 2–3 sound like a dominant pedal in A♭.

The continuation through bar 2 of the opening tenor entry need not be regarded as a countersubject, since it never recurs along with the subject or answer in anything like the same form.[78] The semiquaver run of bars 2–3 can be analyzed as consisting of two four-note figures, immediately followed by their inversions. All later entries are accompanied by varied combinations of some ten semiquaver figures (including one or other of the original figures of bar 2), six of these figures also being used in an inverted form.

The apparent countersubject of bars 2–3 has already run beyond the end of the answer, and bars 3–5 are a codetta that includes the "countersubject" in the bass. The process of varying the combinations of semiquaver figures has already begun with the soprano entry of bar 5 and goes further with the alto entry of bar 6.

Episode 1 (bars 7–10): the alto, beginning in imitation of the bass, repeats the bass run of bars 5–6. The soprano alludes to the falling steps of bars 3–4, while the bass recalls the range and the general character of the subject. The material is freely interchanged at each bar.

Bar 10 is a redundant entry of the subject in the tenor.

Episode 2 (bars 11–13) consists of triple interchangeable counterpoint built out of the beginning of the codetta (bar 3), together with varied "countersubject" figures, repeated in falling sequence, and modulating from the tonic to the relative minor.

Bar 13 is an entry of the subject in the alto, in vi [f].

Episode 3 (bars 14–17) begins as an interchange of episode 2. (Soprano and alto are in the some relationship as the tenor and bass of episode 2; the soprano of bars 11–12 has been displaced by a twelfth to form the new bass, or more accurately by three octaves and a twelfth.) The episode goes on to a cadence in vi at bar 16 and then refers to the material of episode 1.

The tenor enters with the subject in ii [b♭] at bar 17. The entry of the alto in bar 18 starts as if it were the answer but reverts to the subject shape, retaining the key of ii.

Episode 4 (bars 19–23) begins as another interchange of episode 2. (The soprano and bass are in the same relationship as the soprano and tenor of episode 2, but an octave closer together; the bass of episode 2 has been displaced by a fifteenth so that it can appear in the soprano above the other parts.) At bar 21 the immediate feeling is that there is further interchange[79]; in fact, the material is now different: the tenor continues the general pattern of the sequential run of semiquavers, while the alto alludes to the opening of the subject, imitated by the soprano, and led toward a cadence in V.

Before the cadence in bar 23, the alto had alluded to the "countersubject" figures of bars 2–3. Those are repeated in the bass (but out of phase by one beat) along with the alto entry of bar 23 and the soprano entry of bar 24. Both of these can be considered true entries of the subject,[80] but in each case Bach has enlarged the rising sixth to a seventh, with marvelous effect.

Episode 5 (bars 25–27): the tenor of bar 24 is repeated in falling sequence; the soprano and alto extend the last figure of the previous phrase, modulating to the dominant of I.

Starting with the bass in bar 27 (it has been silent for eight bars) there are four entries in close succession: the bass in I, the tenor in vi modulating to iii [f→c], the alto in I [(D♭→)A♭], the soprano in I modulating to IV [A♭→(b♭→)D♭]. All entries except the bass have the mixed shape of bar 18.[81]

Episode 6 (bars 31–33) is similar to episode 5, except that it has a harmonic sequence that rises to bar 32, which then falls toward an interrupted cadence in bar 33.[82]

Coda (bars 33–35): the subject in the soprano is extended toward a cadence, balancing that of bar 23.

Not the least remarkable feature of this fugue is the extraordinary variety of harmony that Bach has attached to his short, seven-note subject:

Key	bars	note 1	2	3	4	5	6	7
I	5–6	I	–	–	–	IV	–	$V^{7(\frac{4}{3})}$
	10–11	I^6	–	vi	–	IV^6	–	I
	23–24	V	–	–	–	–	–	I
	27–28	I	–	I^6	–	IV^6	–	V^7
	29–30	I^6	–	IV	–	$V^{7(\frac{4}{3})}$	–	I
	33–34	vi	V^6	I	–	IV	ii	V^6
V	6–7	IV^6	–	I	–	ii	–	$V^{7(\frac{4}{3})}$
ii	17–18	i^6	–	VI	–	iv^6	–	$V^{7(\frac{4}{3})}$
	18–19	i^6	–	iv	–	V^7	–	i
IV	24–25	V	–	–	–	–	–	I
	30–31	iii	–	ii	–	V^7	–	I
vi	13–14	♯vi	V^6	i	–	iv	–	i
vi and iii	28–29	(vi): $V^{7(\frac{4}{3})}$	–	i	–	(iii): dim7th	–	i

REVIEW OF THE FUGUES IN GROUP 4

The ten fugues of this group all follow the same general plan as those of Group 2, namely:

Exposition, etc.
Entries in related keys and episodes
Final section

The fugues of Group 4, however, show more clearly than those of Group 2 that a fugue may adhere to a general plan and yet display wide differences in the details of its form.

A certain stamp is given at the outset by adopting a particular order of voice entry. These fugues exploit this possibility not only by the order of pitch but also by varying even in the exposition the succession of subject–answer relationship.

Extensive use is made of countersubjects. Of these ten fugues,

four have one countersubject
three have two countersubjects
one has three countersubjects
two have no countersubject

They use generally a wider range of keys in the middle section (as many as five related keys in one of them). At the same time there is an increasing tendency in the four-voice fugues to use keys I and V for some of the middle entries. In several cases it is also harder to judge the exact point at which the middle section may be deemed to begin—though there is usually no doubt when we have arrived in it. Though major key fugues usually have at least one entry in the relative minor (and vice versa), the four-voice fugues do not always make this modulation their first one after the exposition, unlike most of the three-voice fugues.

THE KEY SCHEMES OF THE FUGUES IN GROUP 4

	Exposition	Counterexposition (or redundant entries)	Development	Final Section
With countersubject:				
Major: I.23	I I–V I I–V	EP I EP I–V	I V I ii	EP I V–I
II.17	I I–V I I–V	EP I I–V I I	vi EP v ii IV	I I I
Minor: I.12	i i–vi EP i	EP v EP i	EP III EP ♭VII EP v	EP i
I.14	i v i EP i EP		i v i i	EP i
I.18	i–v v–i i–v v–i		EP v–i EP iv–i i–v v–i EP v III	EP i–v EP iv–i
I.24	i–v v–i EP i–v EP v–i		EP i–v EP iv–v EP i–v EP III–♭VII III EP v–ii EP IV–i–v	EP iiv–i
II.8	iv EP iv		EP IV III VI I IV I–IV ♭vii VI	EP ii
II.16	iv iv	EP i EP v	III ♭VII EP♭VII EP iv EP VI	EP ii [I]
Without countersubject:				
Major: I.5	IV IV	I	vi EP IV I I IV ii	EP I
I.17	I I I–V	EP I	EP vi EP ii ii EP I IV	EP I vi–iii IV EP I

12

Group 5: Fugues for Four Voices,
with Stretto

With countersubject: **Without countersubject:**

(Major)   **II.7, 9**   **I.1; II.5**
(Minor)   **I.16, 20; II.2, 22**

II.7: FUGUE IN E♭ MAJOR

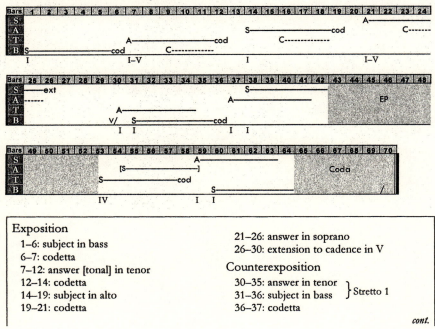

Exposition
  1–6: subject in bass
  6–7: codetta
  7–12: answer [tonal] in tenor
  12–14: codetta
  14–19: subject in alto
  19–21: codetta

  21–26: answer in soprano
  26–30: extension to cadence in V

Counterexposition
  30–35: answer in tenor   } Stretto 1
  31–36: subject in bass
  36–37: codetta

cont.

37–42: answer in alto } Stretto 2
38–43: subject in soprano }

Development

43–53: episode
53–58: subject in tenor, IV
58: codetta

Final section

59–64: answer in soprano }
60–65: subject in bass   } Stretto 3
65–70: coda

There can be differing opinions as to the length of the subject. The analysis is simpler if the subject is considered to end at the first note of bar 7, in which case there are only two passages of codetta in the whole fugue, namely, bars 13 and 20.[1] On the other hand, more than half the fugues in the "48" have subjects that end on the mediant. The cadence feeling in bars 5–6 would suggest that this subject ends at bar 6, with a bar of codetta before the entry of the answer.

The second note of the subject is the dominant, so that Bach has answered this note with the tonic in bar 8. The rest in bars 2 and 8 is all-important; without the rest Bach might well have preferred the real answer, which preserves the shape of the subject. Without the tonal answer, however, the three stretti would have been impossible.

The opening entry of the subject is led through the codetta of bar 6 to what appears to be the countersubject,[2] starting with an imitation of the codetta figure [♪) ♫ ♩ ♪ | ♩]. The countersubject proper begins with the second note of bar 9 and runs to the end of the answer at bar 12.[3] The two themes are interchangeable at the octave, but the countersubject, in fact, never appears above the subject or answer.

At the end of the answer the codetta is extended sequentially by an extra bar to lead to the alto entry of the subject, accompanied by the countersubject from bar 16. The codetta is extended in similar fashion in bars 19 and 20 (the sequence now being a second instead of a third lower). With the soprano entry of the answer, the countersubject starts halfway through bar 23. The exposition, ending at bar 26, is extended by the codetta figure toward a cadence in the dominant at bar 30.[4]

Since the exposition has occupied almost half the length of the fugue, one would expect at this point a modulating episode followed by entries in other keys. Instead, Bach goes on to a counterexposition in stretto. The necessity for the tonal answer now becomes clear, with the tenor entry in bar 30 followed one bar later by the subject in the bass, making one of the most natural-sounding and harmonious partnerships in all the many stretti of the "48." Stretti are often concealed by other voices, but here from bar 33 Bach has shown how two voices in stretto can be most effective without any supporting parts. All the more remarkable is the harmony that the lower voices add when the alto and soprano follow with an interchange of the first stretto in bars 37 and 38. (Bar 38 unfortunately cannot be played as written on one keyboard!)

Episode (bars 43–53)[5]: by way of compensation for the extended use of keys I and V, the single episode suggests keys vi, ii, V, I [c→f→Bb→Eb] before moving toward IV [Ab] for the following tenor entry. [6] Melodically, the episode is formed from the codetta figure, the octave leaps that accompanied the codetta in bars 12–13, and also figures from the first part of the subject.[7] For most of the time the soprano is followed by the alto in canon at the fifth.

The bass in bar 53 continues the sequential pattern of its previous runs, neatly dovetailing the episode into the tenor entry. In a way that we have found to be quite common, Bach starts the entry as if it were the answer but goes on with the intervals of the subject. The alto imitates the tenor,[8] and the bass develops the running passages of the episode.

The first stretto of bar 30 is now repeated with maximum effect, between the answer in the soprano and the subject in the bass, restoring the original length of the opening note. The alto and tenor by the use of imitative figures give the illusion that they also are taking part in the stretto. The **coda** alludes to figures from the subject and also echoes the soprano of bars 52–55.

II.9: FUGUE IN E MAJOR

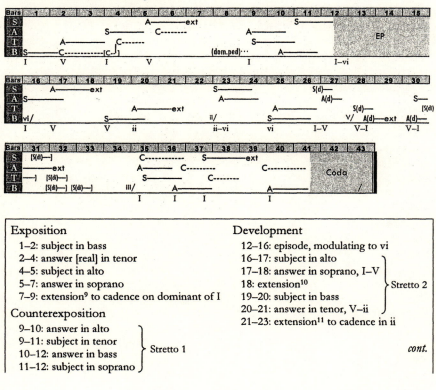

Exposition	Development
1–2: subject in bass	12–16: episode, modulating to vi
2–4: answer [real] in tenor	16–17: subject in alto
4–5: subject in alto	17–18: answer in soprano, I–V
5–7: answer in soprano	18: extension[10] ⎫ Stretto 2
7–9: extension[9] to cadence on dominant of I	19–20: subject in bass
Counterexposition	20–21: answer in tenor, V–ii
9–10: answer in alto	21–23: extension[11] to cadence in ii
9–11: subject in tenor ⎫ Stretto 1	
10–12: answer in bass	*cont.*
11–12: subject in soprano ⎭	

23–24: subject (ornamented) in soprano ⎫
    answer (ornamented) in alto, ii–vi ⎪ Stretto
25–26: subject (ornamented) in bass ⎬ 3
    answer (ornamented) in tenor, vi ⎭
26–27: subject (diminished) in soprano ⎫
27–28: answer (diminished) in alto, vi–V ⎪ Stretto
28–29: subject (diminished) in tenor ⎬ 4
    answer (diminished) in bass, V–I ⎭
29–30: extension[12] to interrupted cadence in I
30–31: answer (diminished) in bass, V
30–32: subject in alto, I
32–35: extension[13] to cadence in iii

Final section
35–36: answer in alto ⎫
35–37: subject in tenor ⎪ Stretto
36–38: answer in bass ⎬ 5
37–39: subject in soprano ⎭
39: extension
40–41: answer in bass
41–43: coda

Since the subject uses only four notes of the scale and does not include the leading-note, the answer can be harmonized as the lower tetrachord in V or the upper tetrachord in I. This fact has a bearing on the stretto entries in this fugue. The a♯ in bars 3 and 6 could be regarded as ornamenting the dominant of E rather than modulating to B, especially as in each case it is so soon contradicted by the a♮. The whole exposition (ending at bar 9) is more in E than in B and ends with a sense of a dominant pedal in E.

The countersubject (bars 2–3) is never again used in full, and after the exposition it does not reappear until the final section.[14] With most entries it is treated as starting from either the first or the second note of bar 3. Its beginning in bar 2 [♪♩♩], however, is very often used as an accompanying figure.[15]

Stretto 1 (bars 9–12): as in the E♭ major fugue (**II.7**), the counterexposition is in stretto. Here, too, the answer leads, followed after one note by the subject. The next entry of the answer (bar 10, bass) cannot arrive until the fourth note of the subject in the tenor. The soprano follows with the subject (bar 11), making a chromatic alteration of its final note.

Episode (bars 12–16) is firmly dovetailed into the end of the counterexposition, the bass extending the falling steps of the answer while the soprano begins an allusion to the countersubject. This is followed in canon at the fourth by the alto (bar 13), the bass (halfway through bar 13), and the tenor (bar 14) and extended toward a cadence in the relative minor.

Stretto 2 (bars 16–23) comprises two pairs of entries in subject–answer relationship. The subject in the alto (bar 16) is followed by the answer in the soprano (bar 17). Then, after a half-bar extension, the subject in the bass (bar 19) is followed by the answer in the tenor (bar 20). The whole passage is modulating, the tenor entry being in ii [f♯], with an extension toward a cadence in ii at bar 23. The entries of this stretto are accompanied by a pair of themes [♩ ♪ ♫♪ and ♩♩♩|♩.♩♩], which develop figures from the original countersubject. The rising steps of bar 3 are given a chromatic ornamentation, which rises from the bass (bars 16–17), through the tenor (bars 17–18), to the alto (bars 19–20).[16]

Stretto 3 (bars 23–26): the subject itself is now ornamented, by interpolating an extra step between its second and third notes and by lengthening its highest note. As in stretto 2 there are two pairs of entries, in subject–answer relationship. The subject in the soprano at bar 23 is followed one beat later by the answer in the alto. The subject in the bass at bar 25 is followed one beat later by the answer in the tenor. The passage is of great interest from the point of view of tonality. The soprano and alto entries start, respectively, on the tonic and dominant of key ii [f♯] but are harmonized so as to modulate to vi [c♯] before the end of the alto entry. The bass starts on the dominant of vi; the tenor, on the supertonic of vi.[17]

Stretto 4 (bars 26–30): overlapping by one note the end of the previous stretto, the soprano now begins a series of four entries by diminutions, again arranged in two pairs in subject–answer relationship. The tonality is again shifting throughout this passage. The soprano starts on the dominant of vi [i.e., *g♯*] but is then harmonized so as to end on the mediant in I on the third beat of bar 29. The alto starts on the leading-note of I on the second beat of bar 27 but is harmonized so that it ends on the mediant of V on the first beat of bar 28. The tenor starts on the tonic of V on the second beat of bar 28. The bass starts on the dominant of V on the fourth beat of bar 28 but ends on the supertonic of I on the third beat of bar 28. The passage is extended toward an interrupted cadence in I at bar 30.

The interrupted cadence almost conceals an extra entry of the diminished subject [answer] in the bass (with altered final note), whose importance is also minimized by the entry of the original subject in the alto. The entry is extended by a free rising sequence recalling bar 22 and also alluding to the rising steps of the episode, toward a cadence in iii at bar 35.[18]

Stretto 5 (bars 35–39) starts by recapitulating the first stretto (bar 9), but now including the countersubject in the soprano.[19] After the bass entry the countersubject is in the alto at bar 37. The soprano does not enter as in bar 11 but delays its entry till the bass has almost finished the answer. The countersubject is now in the tenor.[20] The end of the group is extended downward by sequential repetition of figures to meet the final entry of the answer in the bass at bar 40, with countersubject in the alto.

The **coda** is formed by extending the falling steps of the answer, imitated by the soprano, together with sequential repetition of the countersubject figure (interchanging the material of bars 38–39) and with further allusions to the rising steps of the countersubject.

Notes on the Stretti

In the stretti of this fugue Bach has obtained the maximum of variety by simple means. The stretti use the close relationship of answer–subject as well as the more distant relationship of subject–answer. In addition a closer relationship of subject–answer has been made possible by means of ornamentation. There is also an extraordinary variety shown by the order of entry of pairs of voices:

Exposition: bass, tenor: alto, soprano
Stretto 1:   alto, tenor: bass, soprano
Stretto 2:   alto, soprano: bass, tenor
Stretto 3:   soprano, alto: bass, tenor
Stretto 4:   soprano, alto: tenor, bass
Stretto 5:   alto, tenor: bass, soprano

I.16: FUGUE IN G MINOR

Exposition	19–20: codetta, modulating from VI to dominant of iv
1–2: subject in alto	20–21: subject in bass, iv
2–4: answer [tonal] in soprano	21–23: subject in soprano, iv
4–5: codetta	23–24: answer in alto, i
5–6: subject in bass	24–28: episode 2
6–8: answer in tenor	**Final section**
Development	28–29: subject in soprano, i ⎫
8–12: episode 1, modulating from v to III	28–29: subject in tenor, i ⎬ Stretto 2
12–13: subject in alto, III	29–30: subject in bass, i ⎭
13–15: answer in bass, ♭VII	30–31: codetta
15–16: answer [real] in soprano, ♭VII	31–33: subject in alto
17–18: subject in bass, III ⎫ Stretto 1	33–34: subject in tenor
17–19: answer in alto, ♭VII–VI ⎭	

The opening subject is overlapped by the answer. This occurs again in bar 6. Otherwise, the subject is treated as ending with the *b♭*.

The countersubject, entering after the fourth note of the answer, does not use any fresh material.[21] It begins by inverting the second half of the subject and ends by inverting the first half of the tonal answer.

Bar 4 is a codetta, formed by extending the latter part of the answer in rising sequence.

The exposition ends at bar 8. Its only claim to being a four-voice exposition (rather than three voices and a redundant entry of the answer) is the half-beat overlap in bar 6.[22]

Episode 1 (bars 8–12) develops from the end of the answer in the tenor by extending itself in rising sequence (as in the codetta of bar 4), which is further extended by the imitation in the bass and later in the soprano. The soprano also introduces an upward run of semiquavers, which will become important in the course of the fugue. The episode modulates to III [B♭]. The next five entries are all in major keys: subject in III in the alto (bar 12), with countersubject in the tenor; tonal answer in ♭VII [F] in the bass (bar 13), with countersubject again in the tenor; real answer in ♭VII in the soprano (bar 15),[23] with countersubject in the bass. The end of the soprano entry is extended by rising sequence to lead into the first stretto.

Stretto 1 (bars 17–19) begins at bar 17, where the subject in the bass in III is answered by the alto after four notes; the answer is altered at two points: e♭′ instead of the expected e♮′ and a repetition of f′ after the rest.[24] The countersubject in the soprano after the third beat of bar 17 accompanies the bass entry, starting as part of a sequential repetition.

The active figure of bar 2 [♩♪♫♩] or its inversion in bar 3 has been constantly present since bar 15. This figure alone is used to form the codetta of bars 19–20, in which the upper voices imitate the end of the subject in the bass. The codetta modulates to the dominant of iv [i.e., G].

Two entries of the subject in iv now follow: in the bass at bar 20, with countersubject in the alto, and in the soprano at bar 21, with countersubject in the bass (neatly joined by chromatic steps to the end of the previous subject entry). To these entries in iv the alto (bar 23) responds with the answer in iv modulating to i. The countersubject in the soprano marks the important cadence at bar 24.

Episode 2 (bars 24–28): the bass repeats the second half of the subject in an unusual type of sequence, with chords alternately falling a fourth and rising a second. The upper voices develop the semiquaver figure of episode 1, direct and inverted, in two-part imitation. The episode ends on the dominant of i at bar 28.

Stretto 2 (bars 28–30) differs from stretto 1, in which the entries were a twelfth apart. The three voices in bar 28 enter at the interval of an octave, the alto accompanying the soprano entry with the countersubject, altering its second half for the sake of euphony but preserving its rhythm. The tenor keeps the shape of the subject intact; the soprano alters its last note; the bass preserves only the first four notes of the subject and ends its entry by inverting the second half. (Alternatively, the alto of bar 30 can be thought of as completing the subject entry of the bass, albeit on the wrong step of the scale.)

The subject (or countersubject) figure is again used in imitation to provide the codetta of bars 30–31,[25] leading to the last two entries of the subject—in the alto of bar 31 and the tenor of bar 33, the latter being harmonized with an added fifth voice.

A remarkable feature of this fugue is that of its seventeen entries no less than eight have been entries of the subject in the tonic key.

I.20: FUGUE IN A MINOR

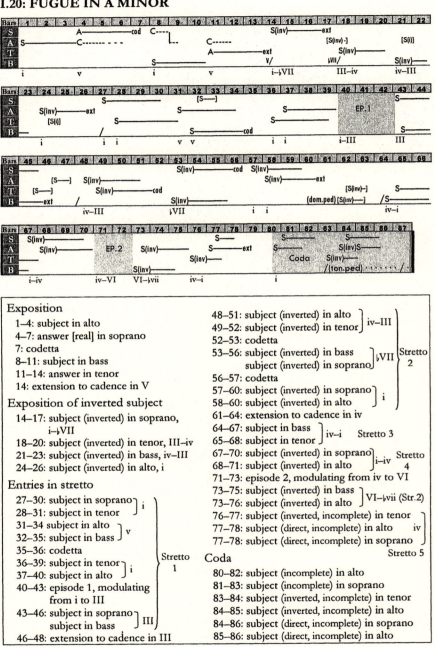

Exposition

1–4: subject in alto
4–7: answer [real] in soprano
7: codetta
8–11: subject in bass
11–14: answer in tenor
14: extension to cadence in V

Exposition of inverted subject

14–17: subject (inverted) in soprano,
    i–♭VII
18–20: subject (inverted) in tenor, III–iv
21–23: subject (inverted) in bass, iv–III
24–26: subject (inverted) in alto, i

Entries in stretto

27–30: subject in soprano ⎤ i
28–31: subject in tenor   ⎦
31–34 subject in alto   ⎤ v
32–35: subject in bass ⎦
35–36: codetta
36–39: subject in tenor ⎤ i   ⎫
37–40: subject in alto ⎦   ⎪ Stretto
40–43: episode 1, modulating   ⎬ 1
    from i to III   ⎪
43–46: subject in soprano ⎤   ⎪
    subject in bass   ⎦ III ⎭
46–48: extension to cadence in III

48–51: subject (inverted) in alto ⎤ iv–III
49–52: subject (inverted) in tenor ⎦
52–53: codetta
53–56: subject (inverted) in bass ⎤ ♭VII ⎫ Stretto
    subject (inverted) in soprano ⎦   ⎬ 2
56–57: codetta   ⎭
57–60: subject (inverted) in soprano ⎤ i
58–60: subject (inverted) in alto   ⎦
61–64: extension to cadence in iv
64–67: subject in bass ⎤ iv–i Stretto 3
65–68: subject in tenor ⎦
67–70: subject (inverted) in soprano ⎤ i–iv Stretto
68–71: subject (inverted) in alto   ⎦   4
71–73: episode 2, modulating from iv to VI
73–75: subject (inverted) in bass ⎤ VI–♭vii (Str.2)
73–76: subject (inverted) in alto ⎦
76–77: subject (inverted, incomplete) in tenor ⎤
77–78: subject (direct, incomplete) in alto   iv ⎬
77–78: subject (direct, incomplete) in soprano ⎦
                                      Stretto 5

Coda

80–82: subject (incomplete) in alto
81–83: subject (incomplete) in soprano
83–84: subject (inverted, incomplete) in tenor
84–85: subject (inverted, incomplete) in alto
84–86: subject (direct, incomplete) in soprano
85–86: subject (direct, incomplete) in alto

The opening voice, ending the subject at the first note of bar 4, immediately adds the countersubject.[26] The answer, which is in the key of v from its beginning, ends not in v but on the dominant of i, so that only a short codetta (bar 7) is needed before the bass entry of the subject. The codetta repeats in sequence the last figure of the countersubject [♪♫ ♩], adding rising and falling scales.

The bass entry of bar 8 is accompanied by the countersubject in the soprano, transferred to the alto at the beginning of bar 9, and finishing on the third beat of bar 9. The later figures of the countersubject are missing, but their influence is felt in the tied notes and suspensions of both soprano and alto in bar 10. Somewhat strangely, Bach has interchanged the material of bars 4–5 at the twelfth, so that the countersubject, apart from necessary accidentals, is now an octave higher than at its first appearance. With the tenor entry of bar 11 the interchange of bars 4–5 is now at the fifteenth, so that the countersubject in the alto is at the same pitch as it was with the previous entry. The countersubject is again abbreviated. It never appears again through the fugue, though its separate figures appear constantly. The end of the answer at the first note of bar 14 is extended by the soprano in imitation, to enable the exposition to end with a strong perfect cadence in V halfway through bar 14.

The exposition of inverted subject (bars 14–27) is a type of counterexposition, but since the keys are irregular, the term "subject" must now suffice for all entries.[27] The soprano entry in bar 14 is accompanied by allusions to the opening of the countersubject, both direct and inverted, in all three of the other voices. The entry, starting in i, soon modulates into ♭VII [G], and its ending is altered toward the cadence in bar 17.[28] Overlapping this cadence, the alto enters in bar 17 with the first bar of the subject, to be overlapped in its turn by a virtually complete entry in the tenor at bar 18. This starts in III but modulates to iv. The soprano imitates the beginning of the subject, an octave above the tenor entry, which itself was a fifth below the alto's false entry, thus anticipating the two intervals of stretto, which will be used later. The bass entry in bar 21 is in iv, modulating back to III, with an imitation at the octave by the alto. Finally, the alto in bar 24 has the subject, starting on the sixth degree of A minor, imitated a fifth lower by the tenor, with an extension toward the cadence in bar 27.

The entries in stretto are, in effect, the "development" section of the fugue where Bach makes use of various combinations of stretti.[29]

Stretto 1 (bars 27–48) comprises four pairs of entries of the direct subject, with stretto at half-bar distance, at the octave or fifteenth:

27–31: soprano, followed by tenor, in i;

31–35: alto, followed by bass in v (with imitation by the soprano). A codetta (bars 35–36) alludes to the beginning of the subject in two-part imitation between bass and soprano, with rising sequence that uses the scale figure of bar 7;

36–40: tenor, followed by alto, in i. The stretto is then interrupted by the first episode[30];

episode 1 (bars 40–43) extends the last figure of the soprano entry in a falling sequence, accompanied by the countersubject figure of bar 6. In bars 41–42 the scale passages in imitation between tenor, alto, and bass recall the codetta of bar 7[31];

43–46: soprano, followed by bass, receives the stretto in III, accompanied by figures from the countersubject and partial imitation and extended to a cadence at bar 48.[32]

Stretto 2 (bars 48–60) comprises three pairs of entries of the inverted subject, at the octave or fifteenth:

48–52: after a "false entry" of the first five notes of the inverted subject in the soprano, the alto begins the stretto followed by the tenor, starting in iv and modulating to III. Both alto and tenor finish by adding the cadence formula of bar 17 (soprano). A codetta alluding to that of bar 7 leads to the next pair of entries;

53–56: bass is followed by soprano in ♭VII, ending, as in the previous entries, with figures from the direct subject in the tenor. A half-bar codetta joins the passage to the next pair of entries;

57–60 the soprano states the subject inverted, followed by alto, in i. The passage is extended by a dominant pedal, on which the soprano and alto allude to figures from the direct and the inverted subject. The bass, imitated at the unison by the tenor, then recalls the first few figures of the inverted subject, starting in i and modulating to iv, with a cadence in the middle of bar 64.[33]

Stretto 3 (bars 64–68) comprises one pair of entries of the direct subject: the bass is followed by the tenor at the upper fifth, in iv modulating to i.

Stretto 4 (bars 67–71) comprises one pair of entries of the inverted subject: the soprano (beginning before the end of the previous tenor entry) is followed by the alto at the lower fifth, in i modulating to iv.

Episode 2 (bars 71–73): soprano and tenor, in canon at the ninth, develop in a rising sequence a free inversion of the falling figures of bar 40. The episode leads without cadence straight into the next pair of entries.

The **recapitulation of stretto 2** (bars 73–76) comprises one pair of entries similar to those in the stretto of bar 48. The bass in bar 73 is followed by the alto, beginning in VI and modulating to ♭VII minor [g]. Neither entry is complete.

Stretto 5 (bars 76–78): the tenor starts with the inverted subject on a pedal, which begins as the tonic in ♭VII minor and ends as the dominant seventh in iv. The tenor is followed a bar later and a ninth higher by the direct subject in the alto. After half a bar the soprano enters with the direct subject a fifth above the alto. None of these entries are completed. The stretto is in iv but is extended toward a cadence on the dominant seventh in i at bar 80.[34]

The **coda** (bars 80–87) includes more partial entries of the direct subject in the alto and soprano in stretto. Then in bar 83 on a tonic pedal the tenor and alto refer to the opening of the inverted subject, with final reference to the direct subject by soprano and alto.

II.2: FUGUE IN C MINOR

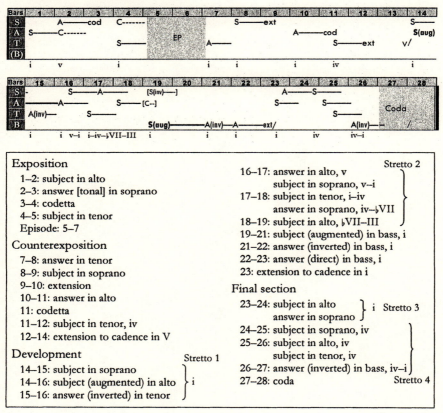

The present analysis follows Tovey in regarding this fugue as being in three voices until the entry of the bass in bar 19. Some editors have believed that the entry in bar 7 is that of the bass, the tenor resting at this point until bar 15.[35] Bach's manuscript is open to either interpretation, because of the lack of rests and the imprecise direction of the stems.[36]

The subject, starting on the dominant, is given a tonal answer. This is accompanied by the simplest of countersubjects, repeated in varied form in the codetta of bar 3 and recurring with the tenor entry of bar 4.[37]

Episode (bars 5–7) is marked by the tenor, which makes a new running theme by adding a scale to intervals from the subject in diminution. The scale is repeated a fifth higher, accompanied by the soprano in tenths. The soprano then imitates the theme by inversion.

Counterexposition: the running theme of the episode is used in varied form to accompany the tenor entry of the answer, which now has *b♮*, so that it is harmonized in i. At bar 8 the soprano shortens the first and third notes of the subject, accompanied in the tenor by the falling fifths and rising fourths of the subject. The phrase is extended by a falling sequence, modulating to iv. At bar 10 the answer in the alto and its running accompaniment in the tenor are a free interchange of bar 7. After a brief codetta the tenor (bar 11) has the subject in iv, accompanied by allusions to the figures of bar 8.[38] The phrase is extended by a quasi sequence to a cadence in v, preceded by an allusion to the countersubject in the alto [and the answer (displaced partially by an octave) in the tenor].[39]

The development consists of three subsections, consisting of two stretti and a chain of entries in the bass.[40]

Stretto 1 (bars 14–16) begins with the subject in the soprano in i, which is immediately followed by the augmented subject in the alto and later by the inverted answer in the tenor, altered at two points for the sake of euphony. (A rising sixth replaces the falling fifth, and the ending rises to *c′* instead of falling to *a*.) The running theme in the soprano of bar 15 satisfies the ear as being a new version of bars 7 and 10, which is founded on the material of the episode.

Stretto 2 (bars 16–19) comprises five entries, all overlapping by four notes[41]:

16–17: answer in the alto in v;
16–17: subject in the soprano, beginning on the tonic of v, ending on the mediant of I;
17–18: subject in the tenor, beginning on the tonic of i, ending on the mediant of iv with *tierce de Picardie*;
17–18: answer in the soprano, beginning on the flat 7th of iv [f], ending on the mediant of ♭VII [B♭];
18–19: subject in the alto, with decoration of its first intervals, in III [E♭] colored by ♭VII [B♭].

The long-delayed bass voice enters in bar 19 with the augmented subject (preceded by countersubject in the alto).[42] The bass immediately adds the inverted answer (bar 21), with its intervals as in bar 15, followed by the direct answer (bar 22). The phrase is extended to a cadence in i, balancing that of bars 13–14.

The final section is made up by two more stretti[43]:

Stretto 3 (bars 23–24) differs from stretto 2 in that the entries now overlap after two notes instead of four. The subject in the alto (bar 23) is followed by the answer in the soprano.

Stretto 4 (bars 24–27): reversing the previous order, the soprano now has the subject at the last note of bar 24, followed two notes later by the subject in the alto and four notes later by the subject in the tenor.[44] The repeated Cs, in the bass of bars 23–25 had implied a tonic pedal; the bass now emerges from this for a final entry of the inverted answer, altering its ending to lead into the brief coda.

II.22: FUGUE IN B♭ MINOR

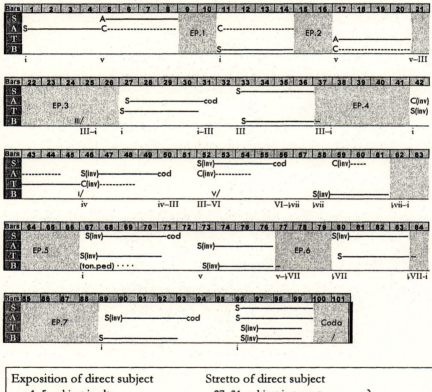

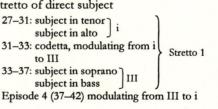

Exposition of direct subject	Stretto of direct subject
1–5: subject in alto	27–31: subject in tenor / subject in alto] i
5–9: answer [real] in soprano	
9–11: episode 1	31–33: codetta, modulating from i to III
11–15: subject in bass	
15–17: episode 2	33–37: subject in soprano / subject in bass] III
17–21: answer in tenor	
Episode 3 (21–27) modulating from v to III and i	Episode 4 (37–42) modulating from III to i

cont.

Exposition of inverted subject

42–46: subject (inverted) in tenor, i
46–50: subject (inverted) in alto, iv
50–51: codetta, modulating from iv to III
52–56: subject (inverted) in soprano, III–VI
56–57: codetta, modulating from VI to ♭vii
58–62: subject (inverted) in bass, ♭vii
Episode 5 (62–67) modulating from
    ♭vii to I

Stretto of inverted subject   Stretto 2

67–71: subject (inverted) in tenor ⎤
    subject (inverted) in soprano ⎦ i
71–72: codetta, modulating from i to v
73–77: subject (inverted) in alto ⎤ v
    subject (inverted) in bass ⎦
Episode 6 (77–80) modulating from
    v to ♭VII

Stretto of direct and inverted subject

80–84: subject (inverted) in soprano ⎤ ♭VII
    subject (direct) in tenor ⎦
84–89: episode 7, modulating from
    ♭VII to i   Stretto 3
89–93: subject (inverted) in bass
    subject (direct) in alto
93–95: codetta

Stretto of direct and inverted subject,
with added thirds and sixths

96–101: subject (direct) in soprano and alto ⎤
    subject (inverted) in tenor and bass ⎦
    Stretto 4

The d♭'s at the end of the subject are answered by a♮'s (*tierce de Picardie*). Of the ten fugues in minor keys whose subjects end on the mediant, in only one other does Bach use the *tierce de Picardie* for the first answer (**I.10**).

The countersubject at once introduces an important new idea: an almost complete rising chromatic scale.[45] Its quaver figure after the tied note [♩♫♩] anticipates by inversion the final figure of the answer [♫♩♪].

Episode 1 (bars 9–11) develops the final figure of answer and countersubject repeating in falling sequence.[46]

With the bass entry at bar 11 the alto again has the countersubject, while the soprano adds a significant counterpoint that will provide figures for later development.[47]

Episode 2 (bars 15–17) interchanges bass and alto of the first episode. The soprano continues its figures of bar 14 in a quasi sequence.[48]

With the tenor entry at bar 17 the bass has the countersubject. The alto alludes to the soprano of bars 11 and 13.

Episode 3 (bars 21–27) has two subsections; until bar 25 the tenor and alto treat the final figure of the answer in two-part imitation, while the bass develops a falling sequence out of the soprano figure of bar 15 and the chromatic steps of the countersubject; after the cadence in III at bar 25 the soprano and alto treat the final figure of the subject imitation, modulating to i.[49]

Stretto 1 (bars 27–37) features the stretto of direct subject.[50] The subject in the tenor (bar 27) is followed by the subject in the alto,[51] one beat later and a seventh higher. The soprano adds partial imitation. The end of the pair of entries is effectively lengthened by a codetta (bars 31–33), in which the canon at the upper seventh is subtly transformed into a canon at the lower fifth, with modulation to III.[52] This leads to the other pair of entries, the subject in the soprano (bar 33) being followed one beat later and a ninth lower by the subject in the bass. Tenor and alto in turn allude to the held note of the countersubject, thus turning most of this passage into entries above and below a dominant pedal in III.

Episode 4 (bars 37–42) develops the final figure of the subject in the bass, while the soprano alludes to the detached crotchets of bar 13, and the alto adds part of the countersubject. The combination is freely interchanged, with modulation from III to i.

The exposition of inverted subject starts with all four voices at bar 42 with the inverted subject in the tenor, with inverted countersubject (as far as the held note) in the alto, in i. Following the perfect cadence (bar 46), at which point the soprano disappears for a while, the inverted subject enters in the alto, with inverted countersubject in the tenor in iv [eb]. Bars 50–51 are a codetta, modulating from iv to III [eb→Db]. In it the continuation of the subject in the alto is imitated one bar later by the tenor.

At bar 52 the soprano reemerges as the inverted subject, with inverted countersubject in the alto, starting in III and modulating to VI [Db→Gb]. With the cadence in the dominant, the bass disappears until bar 58, restoring the three-part texture. The quaver run in the third bar of the subject is imitated a bar later by the tenor. Bars 56–57 are a codetta, in which soprano and bass treat the final figure of the inverted subject by imitation, modulating to bVII minor [ab].

At bar 58 the inverted subject is in the bass, with inverted countersubject (lacking its opening bar) in the soprano, reestablishing the four-part texture for four bars.

Episode 5 (bars 62–66) completes a new development of the final subject figure by the alto (recalling bars 49–50), imitated a bar later by the soprano and repeated in rising sequence, modulating from bVII minor to i [ab→(eb)→bb].[53]

Stretto 2 (bars 67–77) features the stretto of inverted subject.[54] The ornamental figure in the soprano at the first beat of bar 66—featured for the first time in episode 5—has already been imitated by the bass. The bass now uses this figure to decorate a tonic pedal on which the tenor enters with the inverted subject (bar 67), followed one beat later and a ninth higher by the inverted subject in the soprano.[55] In the codetta of bars 71 and 72 the soprano and tenor repeat in sequence the final figure of the inverted subject, while the bass recalls the chromatic steps of the countersubject. At bar 73 the alto enters with the inverted subject in v, followed one beat later and a seventh lower by the inverted subject in the bass.

Episode 6 (bars 77–80) is a rising sequence, based on the final figure of the inverted subject, treated mostly as in the tenor of bar 40. Soprano and bass, mainly in tenths, are imitated by alto and tenor, also in tenths. The episode modulates from v to bVII [f→Ab].[56]

Stretto 3 (bars 80–96) features stretto of direct and inverted subject.[57] The inverted subject in the soprano (bar 80) is followed one beat later and a sixth lower by the direct subject in the tenor. The alto uses part of the inverted countersubject in bar 82. The key is bVII.

Episode 7 (bars 84–89) unfolds from the end of the subject in the soprano, which is developed into a theme of four beats' length, which is repeated in rising sequence across the ordinary three-beat bar rhythm, with partial imitation in the tenor and bass. Having reached the peak of its sequence at bar 86, the episode restores the regular bar-rhythm, modulating to i [(A♭→e♭)→b♭].

The other pair of entries of stretto 3 is at bar 89; the direct subject in the bass is followed one beat later and a sixth higher by the inverted subject in the alto. The tenor alludes to the chromatic steps of the countersubject. A codetta (bars 93–95) has a dominant pedal in the tenor, transferred after one bar to the bass, with final allusions to the end of the subject.

Stretto 4 (bars 96–101) is effectively the final section.[58] The long-drawn-out cadence passage of bars 94–95 culminates in the simultaneous entry of soprano and alto with the direct subject in sixths (starting on chord VI), closely followed by the tenor and bass with the invented subject in thirds. The apparent *tierce de Picardie* in the alto of bar 97 is, in fact, a doubled leading-note to the subdominant chord. (Pedants might frown at the leap from d♮' to a♮' instead of the expected e♭'!) The sixths in the upper voices could have been continued after the rest, but hardly beyond the second beat of bar 98. The continuation in thirds sounds unexpected and leads magnificently to such a powerful climax that the ear can hardly be aware that the lower voices have omitted the final figures of the subject.

I.1: FUGUE IN C MAJOR

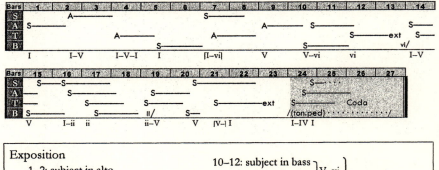

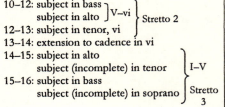

Exposition
  1–2: subject in alto
  2–4: answer [real] in soprano
  4–5: answer in tenor
  5–7: subject in bass

Development
  7–8: subject in soprano⎤ I Stretto 1
     answer in tenor ⎦
  9–10: answer in alto, V

10–12: subject in bass ⎤ V–vi
     subject in alto ⎦ V–vi ⎫ Stretto 2
12–13: subject in tenor, vi   ⎬
13–14: extension to cadence in vi ⎭
14–15: subject in alto   ⎤ I–V
     subject (incomplete) in tenor ⎥
15–16: subject in bass   ⎥ Stretto 3
     subject (incomplete) in soprano ⎦

```
16–17: subject in soprano ⎤ I                     Final section (coda)
16–18: subject in alto    ⎦    Stretto 4             24–25: subject in tenor ⎤          Stretto 6 ⎤
17–18: subject in tenor ⎤ ii                         24–26: subject in alto  ⎦ I–IV             ⎬
17–19: subject in bass  ⎦      Stretto 5             24–25: subject (incomplete) in soprano, I ⎦
19–20: subject in tenor                             26–27: coda on tonic pedal
        subject in alto         ⎤ ii–V
20–21: subject (incomplete) in bass ⎦
20–22: subject in soprano ⎤ V–I
21–23: subject in tenor   ⎦
23–24: extension to cadence in I
```

The normal cyclic order of voice-entry is disregarded in favor of A.S.T.B. The exposition is also unusual in that the first group of entries are in the order subject–answer–answer–subject.[59]

The fact that the subject uses only the first six notes of the scale, without the leading-note, makes its tonality flexible. Thus, while the soprano answer ends in V, the tenor answer begins and ends in I (because of the *f♮*'s in the alto). The tenor *b♭* in bar 5 so balances the previous F♯s that the whole exposition has the effect of being entirely in the tonic key.

The continuation of the opening voice in bars 2–4 is not a regular countersubject, though its figures are used constantly, throughout the fugue. The running semiquavers of bar 2 are inverted by the soprano in bar 4.[60]

Stretto 1 (bars 7–8) emerges from the end of the previous entry in the bass as in the first alto entry, so that it is now in a different harmonic relationship to the soprano entry in bar 7. The stretto is between the soprano and tenor.[61] The final figure of the subject in the soprano is repeated in rising sequence and partially imitated by the tenor, to lead to a single entry of the answer in the alto (bar 9), now harmonized more definitely in V.[62]

Up to this point entries have been distinguished as subject or answer by their starting on C or G. From now on, this distinction begins to disappear, so that all other entries will now be referred to as entries of the subject.[63]

Stretto 2 (bars 10–14) is an interchange of stretto 1, now between the bass and alto. The bass enters with the subject in V, while the alto enters on the dominant of V (i.e., in a new subject-answer relationship),[64] with alteration of its final figure so that it modulates into vi. The tenor in bar 12 barely overlaps the end of the alto entry starting on the dominant of vi. The phrase is extended to a cadence in vi.

Stretto 3 (bars 14–16) starts with the alto and tenor, which repeat the subject–answer pattern of bar 7 in closer position. They are joined by the bass in bar 15 and two beats later by an incomplete entry in the soprano. The key is I, modulating to V, with an implication of vi before the end of the group.

Stretto 4 (bars 16–19) commences on the fourth half-beat of bar 16 with the subject in the soprano immediately following the previous incomplete soprano entry, which is answered after one beat by the alto. In itself this pair of entries is repeating the subject–answer relationship of bar 14, and the main tonality of the passage as far as bar 18 is that of I. This tonality is, however, altered by the lower voices in bars 17–19 (entering in a new answer–subject relationship) to that of ii, rounded off by the cadence (with *tierce de Picardie*) in bar 19.

Stretto 5 (bars 19–24) overlaps the approach to the cadence in ii previously discussed and comprises five entries at various intervals of pitch. The tenor entry in bar 19 starts on *a*, harmonized as the dominant of D minor. The alto entry starts on *e′*, as the supertonic in D.[65] The held *d* in the bass changes its meaning to a dominant pedal in G, and the alto and tenor adjust their intervals to fit into the key of V. Barely overlapping the alto entry, the bass in bar 20 adds the first three notes of the subject, starting on *e* as the submediant of G. One beat later the soprano enters on *g′*, starting in V but ending its entry in I. The bass *g* in bars 22–23 becomes a dominant pedal in I, on which the tenor makes its entry from the leading-note.[66] The passage is extended in bar 23 to the final cadence in I.

Since there are no more cadences, the final section is all a coda on a tonic pedal, which includes one more stretto.

Stretto 6 (bar 24) begins with the subject in the tenor, starting on *c*, and is joined after two beats by the alto, starting on *f′*. One beat later the soprano adds the first four notes of the subject. The coda ends with allusions to the last figure of the subject and rising scales.

As with the E major fugue (**II.9**) and the E♭ major fugue (**II.7**) the basic pattern of the stretti in this fugue is that of subject–answer or answer–subject. The general flow of the music is so natural-sounding that the ear cannot take in all the other stretto intervals that also occur. But since they must make their contribution to the general effect, it is worthwhile analyzing them in detail. This analysis must include every pair of entries, not merely those in close conjunction. The analysis gives this result:

	Interval	Timing	Number of pairs
Subject–answer:	fifth higher or fourth lower	1 beat	6
Answer–subject:	fifth lower or fourth higher	4 beats	2
Other intervals:	octave lower	3 beats	1
	octave higher	2 beats	1
	octave higher	3 beats	1
	seventh lower	5 beats	2
	seventh lower	2 beats	1
	third lower	3 beats	1
	sixth lower	3 beats	1

II.5: FUGUE IN D MAJOR

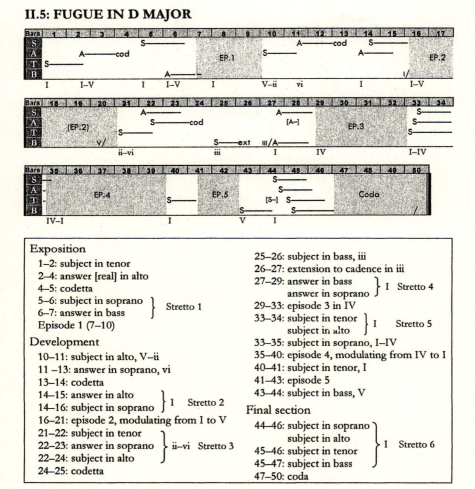

Exposition
  1–2: subject in tenor
  2–4: answer [real] in alto
  4–5: codetta
  5–6: subject in soprano } Stretto 1
  6–7: answer in bass
  Episode 1 (7–10)
Development
  10–11: subject in alto, V–ii
  11 –13: answer in soprano, vi
  13–14: codetta
  14–15: answer in alto
  14–16: subject in soprano } I   Stretto 2
  16–21: episode 2, modulating from I to V
  21–22: subject in tenor
  22–23: answer in soprano } ii–vi Stretto 3
  22–24: subject in alto
  24–25: codetta

25–26: subject in bass, iii
26–27: extension to cadence in iii
27–29: answer in bass
          answer in soprano } I Stretto 4
29–33: episode 3 in IV
33–34: subject in tenor } I   Stretto 5
          subject in alto
33–35: subject in soprano, I–IV
35–40: episode 4, modulating from IV to I
40–41: subject in tenor, I
41–43: episode 5
43–44: subject in bass, V
Final section
44–46: subject in soprano
          subject in alto
45–46: subject in tenor } I   Stretto 6
45–47: subject in bass
47–50: coda

This is without question the most close-knit fugue of the entire collection. The whole fugue is built out of the short subject, without any other thematic material. Besides the twenty-three entries of the complete subject, its second half provides a figure from which are derived all the five episodes and the three codettas. This figure [♫♫♪], which recurs over 100 times, is present in every bar except bars 3, 27, and 43.

There is no countersubject.[67] The figure of bar 2 is repeated a step higher to accompany the answer, so that the second half of the answer sounds like an imitation of the tenor a fourth higher. The codetta of bars 4–5 is made by continuing the imitation, first a fourth higher in the alto, then a fifth lower in the tenor.

Stretto 1 (bars 5–7): the soprano entry in bar 5 is at once accompanied by the same figure, first in the alto and then imitatively in the tenor. The bass entry of the answer in bar 6 is in stretto with the soprano.

Episode 1 (bars 7–10): the exposition ends, theoretically, at the second beat of bar 7. Effectively, it is extended by the first episode as far as the inverted cadence in V at bar 10.[68] The episode has already begun before the end of the bass entry, when the alto echoes the second half of the answer in a quasi canon at the octave.[69] Overlapping the alto figure, the tenor enters in imitation at the lower fifth, echoed by the soprano in a quasi canon at the octave. Most of the episode is in I, but the phrase ends with an inverted cadence in V.

The key of V is short-lived, for the subject in the alto at bar 10 is given new and unexpected harmony, first suggesting a return to I, then hinting at IV, and finally cadencing in ii (but on a $^6_4$). The answer in the alto (bar 11) is in vi [b]. The bass B started as a dominant pedal in ii [e] but became a tonic pedal in vi.

The codetta of bars 13–14 is formed in similar fashion to the first codetta (bar 4)[70]: the end of the answer is twice repeated by rising fourths, modulating from vi to V [b→A].

Stretto 2 (bars 14–16) starts with the answer in the alto, now harmonized in [the dominant of] I.[71] The soprano follows with the subject two crotchet-beats later, ending with a cadence in I.

Episode 2 (bars 16–21) is a development of episode 1. The subject figure is treated in quasi canon between various pairs of voices: alto and soprano, tenor and soprano, bass and soprano, bass and alto, leading to a cadence in V at bar 20.

Stretto 3 (bars 21–24): with allusion to the codetta from alto and soprano (i.e., with the subject figure imitated at the fourth but without overlap) the tenor enters with the subject, starting on the dominant of ii and ending on its leading-note.[72] One bar later the soprano adds the answer, starting on the dominant of vi and ending on its leading-note. Two crotchet-beats later the alto enters with the subject in vi, ending on the mediant.

The codetta in bar 24 uses the subject figure in the alto, imitated by the tenor at the lower seventh, modulating to iii [f#]. At bar 25 the bass makes a single entry starting on the tonic of iii,[73] and the phrase is extended toward a cadence in iii at bar 27. From this point onward the subject–answer relationship is discontinued, and all later entries will be regarded as entries of the subjects.

Stretto 4 (bars 27–29): after the emphatic cadence in iii, there is an immediate return to I with the bass entry of bar 27. The soprano enters two octaves higher after one crotchet-beat, and the alto, one crotchet-beat later, adds the first four notes of the answer before resting: its return with the subject figure in bar 29 can be accepted by the ear as a virtual completion of the answer.[74]

Episode 3 (bars 29–33) is a new presentation of the material of episodes 1 and 2, in IV, ending with an inverted cadence.

Stretto 5 (bars 33–35): the three upper voices enter at one crotchet-beat interval as in stretto 4, but at the upper sixth. The tenor is in I; the alto in itself is in vi; the soprano starts in I and modulates to IV. The total harmonic effect is that of a modulation from I to IV.

Episode 4 (bars 35–40): this is a new development of the quasi canons of earlier episodes. At first the tenor is imitated by the alto at the octave, with the soprano adding the imitation at the upper fourth; then in bar 36 the soprano figure is followed by the tenor at the octave, with the bass adding the imitation at the lower fifth, to be imitated in its turn first by the alto at the octave, then by the soprano. The episode is given special importance by the chromatic bass of bars 35–36 and by the two-octave descending scale with which it ends.

The single entry of the subject in the tenor at bar 40 emphasizes the return to I of the previous episode and is given such rich harmony that this might well serve as the final entry if Bach had not other plans for even more important events to follow.[75]

Episode 5 (bars 41–43): because of its extreme brevity this passage might be called a codetta. But its bass does overlap the end of the subject, as in the longer episodes, with quasi-canonic imitation by the alto. The soprano at the end of bar 41 is virtually adding the expected imitation at the fourth, but without the first note of the figure.

The short episode ends with a dominant pedal. The bass repeats the pedal as an entry (beginning with a $\frac{6}{4}$). The passage is remarkable in many ways; there are two chromatic alterations in the subject,[76] which combine to give the impression that the bass itself is in V minor, ending with *tierce de Picardie*; the alto also seems to be in V minor; the soprano in itself is in V major. The overall effect is that of I ending on its dominant rather than modulating to V. It is, in fact, an elaborate dominant preparation for the final section.

Stretto 6 (bars 44–47): all the previous stretti concerned either two or three voices. All four voices are now involved in an interchange and extension of the stretto of bar 33 (the upper sixth now appearing as a lower third).[77] The stretto itself is a tour de force; no less marvelous is the subtle control of tonality, apparently threatened by the cross-relations G♯–G♮ and C♯–C♮.

The **coda** (bars 47–50) provides a final variant of the material of the episodes, completing the unfinished pattern of the short episode 5 by lengthening the soprano of bars 41–43 into four bars and supplying the final perfect cadence, which was deflected in bar 43.

The basic pattern of the stretti in this fugue is that of answer–subject (as in the E major fugue, **II.9**) varied by the pattern subject–answer. In addition, other stretti are possible at various intervals of time and pitch. Analysis of the fourteen pairs of overlapping entries yields the following result:

Interval	Timing	Number of pairs
Fifth lower or fourth higher	2 crotchet-beats	5
Fifth higher or fourth lower	4 crotchet-beats	2
Octave higher	1 crotchet-beat	1
Sixth higher or third lower	1 crotchet-beat	5
Seventh lower	3 crotchet-beats	1

REVIEW OF THE FUGUES IN GROUP 5

In his stretti Bach frequently alters intervals in one or another voice for the sake of euphony. Wherever possible, the subject is completed by each voice's taking part in the stretto: at the same time the general effect of stretto can be preserved, even though not all voices are complete. While textbooks seem to agree in advising that the final entry of a stretto be always completed, Bach has no inhibitions about leaving the final voice incomplete—normally in order to lead toward a better climax.

The eight fugues of this group between them have shown the greatest possible variety in the use of stretto. While the subject–answer or answer–subject relationship pattern is the commonest, these fugues also have stretti at every other possible interval, as the following table shows:

	I.1	I.16	I.20	II.2	II.5	II.7	II.9	II.22
Up an octave (or down)	✓	✓	✓		✓			
Up a ninth (or down a seventh)	✓				✓			✓
Up a third (or down a sixth)	✓							✓
Up a fourth (or down a fifth)	✓			✓	✓	✓	✓	
Up a fifth (or down a fourth)	✓	✓	✓	✓	✓		✓	
Up a sixth (or down a third)	✓				✓			
Up a seventh (or down a ninth)			✓					✓

13

Group 6: Fugues with Countersubjects Introduced after the Exposition

Most of the fugues in the first five groups have a countersubject. Some have two. One (**I.12**) has three. A smaller number of fugues have no countersubject at all, and it has always become evident before the end of the exposition to which type a particular fugue belongs. From the examples so far studied it would seem reasonable to predict that other fugues would be likely to behave in a similar way. The four fugues grouped in this chapter show a different way of using countersubjects, and each one is a unique experiment in form.

1. There is no countersubject in the exposition; one countersubject is introduced later (**I.19**).
2. There is no countersubject in the exposition; two countersubjects are introduced later (**II.21**).
3. There is one countersubject in the exposition; later it is replaced by a new countersubject (**II.24**).
4. There is one countersubject in the exposition; one additional countersubject is introduced later (**I.13**).

I.19: FUGUE IN A MAJOR

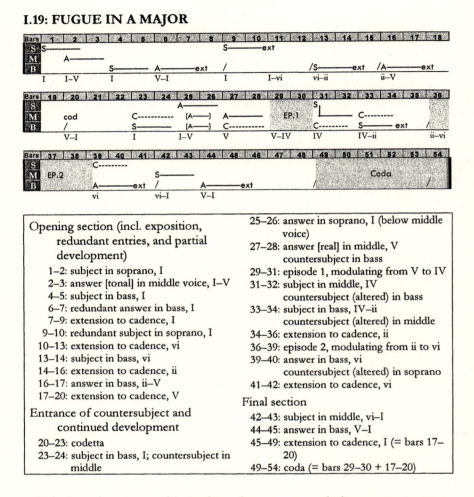

Opening section (incl. exposition, redundant entries, and partial development)

1–2: subject in soprano, I
2–3: answer [tonal] in middle voice, I–V
4–5: subject in bass, I
6–7: redundant answer in bass, I
7–9: extension to cadence, I
9–10: redundant subject in soprano, I
10–13: extension to cadence, vi
13–14: subject in bass, vi
14–16: extension to cadence, ii
16–17: answer in bass, ii–V
17–20: extension to cadence, V

Entrance of countersubject and continued development

20–23: codetta
23–24: subject in bass, I; countersubject in middle

25–26: answer in soprano, I (below middle voice)
27–28: answer [real] in middle, V countersubject in bass
29–31: episode 1, modulating from V to IV
31–32: subject in middle, IV countersubject (altered) in bass
33–34: subject in bass, IV–ii countersubject (altered) in middle
34–36: extension to cadence, ii
36–39: episode 2, modulating from ii to vi
39–40: answer in bass, vi countersubject (altered) in soprano
41–42: extension to cadence, vi

Final section

42–43: subject in middle, vi–I
44–45: answer in bass, V–I
45–49: extension to cadence, I (= bars 17–20)
49–54: coda (= bars 29–30 + 17–20)

This fugue is so unusual in its form that any one analysis cannot attempt to do more than point out some of its important features, without claiming to offer a complete explanation of all that happens in it. In listening to this fugue, one is conscious of four main divisions:

1. an opening section in continuous triplet rhythm, ending with a cadence in the dominant at bar 20;
2. after a three-bar introduction, a new beginning (similar to a counterexposition) where the subject is now accompanied by a running countersubject;
3. a return of the material of the opening section, reduced to one-third of its original length;
4. a return of the material of the second section, reduced to one-third of its original length.

There are differing opinions about the length of the opening subject. One commentator believed it to consist of only one note (in which case the bass of bars 39–40 is not an entry).[1] It can also be assumed to end at the first note of bar 2 (in which case it is like the subject of the A♭ major fugue (I.17), ending on the dominant but not in the dominant key). But its pattern of rising fourths and falling thirds continues into bar 2, so that the subject does seem to be more than one bar long and may, therefore, be regarded as ending with the c♯″ just before the end of bar 2.[2] Many fugue subjects end on the mediant, so that this may well be what Bach had in mind at the opening of this fugue. Seven of the fifteen entries support this view; the others are altered in one way or another. Already we have met several cases of a subject of uncertain length, notably in the fughetta, which ends the Prelude II.3, and the fugue II.3, in both of which the answer enters with the effect of stretto. The answer has already been discussed in Chapter 2. Here it may be pointed out that while there is no necessity for avoiding a real answer (since the dominant does not occur near the beginning of the subject), a real answer would have had the effect of a sudden move into the dominant key, which the present answer does not have. Furthermore, with a real answer the subject could not have continued its pattern of intervals into bar 2. Finally the present answer, unusual as it may be, does in fact sound perfectly natural.

The bass, having finished its first entry of the subject, goes on to add a redundant entry of the answer in bar 6. At bar 8 we meet the first of numerous instances of phrase extension in this fugue, usually toward a cadence as here.[3] The soprano in bar 9 follows with a redundant entry of the subject, extended by two bars toward a cadence in vi [f♯].[4]

In bar 13 the bass announces the subject in vi, with an alteration of its ending in order to lead into ii [b]. A one-bar extension ends with a cadence in ii. At bar 16 the ear accepts the bass as starting an entry, presumably in ii. Its continuation after the rests sounds natural enough, even though there are a large displacement of pitch and an uncertain ending. The phrase is extended toward the cadence in V at bar 20.[5]

The three bars 20–22 can be called a codetta, or an introduction to the chief event of the fugue—the arrival in bar 23 of a countersubject of completely unexpected nature, accompanying the subject entry in the bass.[6] Since the countersubject was in the middle voice, the entry of the answer in bar 25 is that of the soprano, though nothing can stop it from sounding like a middle voice until the first note of bar 27.[7] The answer is altered at the second beat of bar 26. At bar 27 the upper voices are back in their normal positions, the middle voice now having the real answers, starting an octave too high and altering its ending. The bass has the countersubject.

Episode 1 (bars 29–31): in bar 29 the bass develops the subject figure, soon turning the rising fourths into sixths and the falling thirds into fifths. The soprano run is derived from the countersubject. The two voices are interchanged in the following bar, providing modulation from V, through I, to IV [E→A→D].

Bar 31 is an entry of the subject in IV, starting with the high soprano *d″* and continuing in the middle voice from the *c♯′* onward. The entry is complete and is accompanied in the bass by a variant of the countersubject. In bar 33 the bass starts the subject in IV but makes chromatic alterations (already suggested by the altered countersubject in the middle voice) so as to bring it into vi. The phrase is extended toward a cadence at bar 36.[8]

Episode 2 (bars 36–39): while the upper voices refer to the subject figure in two-part imitation, the bass develops the countersubject.

Bars 39–40 may be regarded as an entry of the answer in the bass, lacking its first note and considerably lengthened, with phrase extension toward the cadence in bar 42. (Alternatively, bars 39–42 are part of the episode, the material of the previous bars being freely interchanged.)[9]

Perhaps the most striking feature of the fugue is the abrupt cessation of the running counterpoint figures and the resumption of the material of the opening section at bar 42. Because of this, the ear accepts without question a subject entry in the middle voice, which begins on *f♯′* and then goes on as if it had begun on *a*. The bass answer in bar 44 has an altered ending, which may pass unnoticed because the phrase extension soon moves in bars 45–49 into an almost exact recapitulation in the tonic of the passage in bars 17–20, which led to a cadence in the dominant. Even more sure is the sense of homecoming with the coda at bar 49,[10] which starts by repeating the first episode of bars 29–30. Having brought back the running semiquavers, it is natural to continue them to the end of the fugue. From bar 51 onward, as Tovey points out, the upper voices are an interchange of the upper voices of bars 46–48.

II.21: FUGUE IN B♭ MAJOR

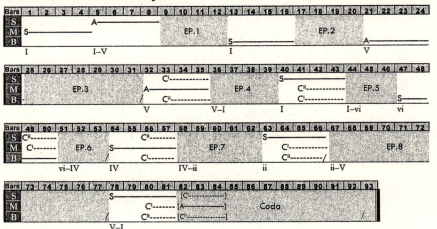

Opening section
  1–5: subject in middle voice
  5–9: answer [tonal] in soprano
  9–13: episode 1
  13–17: subject in bass
  17–21: episode 2
  21–25: redundant answer [real] in bass
  25–32: episode 3

Entrance of two countersubjects and
  development

  32–36: answer in middle, C^i in soprano,
    C^{ii} in bass, V
  36–40: episode 4, modulating from V to I
  40–44: subject in soprano, C^i in bass, C^{ii}
    in middle, I

  44–47: episode 5, modulating from I to vi
  47–51: subject in bass, C^i in middle, C^{ii} in
    soprano, vi
  51–54: episode 6, modulating from vi to IV
  54–58: subject in middle, C^i in bass, C^{ii} in
    soprano, IV
  58–63: episode 7, modulating from IV to ii
  63–67: subject in soprano, C^i in middle, C^{ii}
    in bass, ii
  67–78: episode 8, modulating from ii to V

Final section

  78–82: subject in soprano, C^i in middle, C^{ii}
    in bass, V–I
  82–93: coda (bars 90–93 = 29–32)

This fugue and the A major fugue (**I.19**) that we have just discussed are vastly different in style and musical effect. They have, however, three features in common: the first section comprises more than the exposition and ends with a strong cadence in the dominant; the second section introduces a countersubject (two in the present case); and the final section includes a recapitulation of the cadence passage of the first section.

The subject is unique among the "48" in starting on the supertonic. Its shape should be carefully noted, because its figures are the main ingredients of all the many episodes. It consists essentially of two figures, the second bar being almost the same shape as the first bar (i.e., mordent on *bb'* + descending arpeggio), while the fourth bar is a sequential repeat of the third bar (i.e., descending scale decorated with appoggiatura). The fifth note of the subject is the dominant, so that this note is answered by the tonic. Bach evidently regarded the third note of the subject as a decoration of the tonic by a lower diatonic auxiliary note; he therefore decorated the F of the answer with an *eb"* instead of an *e♮"*. The combination of this fact and the tonal change at the fifth note help to keep the first half of the answer in the tonic key.

The continuation of the middle voice at bar 5 is not a countersubject[11]: its most important feature is the otherwise conventional cadence formula in bar 8, which has an important bearing on later events in the fugue.

Episode 1 (bars 9–13) develops a variant of the first figure of the subject in two-part imitation.[12]

The bass entry at bar 13 is accompanied by the soprano in alternating sixths and thirds; this sets a pattern that will recur at intervals through the fugue.[13]

Episode 2 (bars 17–21) is led by the bass, which continues the rising sequence of the second figure of the subject, accompanied by the middle voice in sixths. The middle voice then adds its own version of the rising sequence (bar 18), and the episode continues with further allusion to both figures of the subject.

The episode leads without break into a redundant entry of the real answer in the bass at the second note of bar 21, again accompanied by thirds or sixths.[14]

Episode 3 (bars 25–32) is led by the soprano, which treats the first figure of the subject in falling sequence, imitated two bars later by the bass. After one reference to the second figure of the subject (bar 29) the soprano recalls the first figure (bar 30), to lead toward a cadence in the dominant at bar 32.

The second section—entrance of two countersubjects—is marked by the solo appearance in bar 32 in the middle voice with the real answer,[15] which is soon joined by two new themes, together forming triple counterpoint: a first countersubject in the soprano, consisting of a three-note figure in rising sequence [♩♩♩], and a second countersubject in the bass, consisting of long notes in rising steps.[16]

Episode 4 (bars 36–40) is led by the bass where the second figure of the subject is treated in two-part imitation between the middle voice and bass. The soprano adds the crotchet rhythm of bars 5–7.[17]

At bar 40 the soprano has the subject, still in the main key, accompanied by both countersubjects (which will be used in whole or in part with every entry). One is aware from the sound of this passage that it is an interchange of the material of the previous entry but hardly aware of the precise manner of the interchange. This simple-sounding passage, in fact, conceals one of the most complex pieces of counterpoint in the whole of the "48."

The simplest and most common type of interchange is at the octave or fifteenth. In the new pitch relationship between two voices, seconds become sevenths, thirds become sixths, and so on. That the combination after the entry of bar 40 is not a case of simple interchange can be easily proved by comparing the two upper voices of bar 34 with the two outer voices of bar 42. The tied seventh at the beginning of bar 34 with interchange at the octave or fifteenth would become a tied second or ninth. Allowing for the difference of key, this would appear as a tied *a♭* in the bass of bar 42, but the note here is *d*. The interchange between these two voices must, therefore, be at the twelfth. Further study will reveal that each pair of voices has been interchanged at a different interval. It is a time-consuming process to work out every detail of the changed relationships, but it would be advisable to check at least some of the explanations that are given in this commentary[18]:

- subject and first countersubject are interchanged at the twelfth;
- the two countersubjects are interchanged at the fourteenth;
- subject and second countersubject are interchanged at the fourteenth and interchanged again at the twelfth (i.e., they are a third closer in position than they were originally).

Episode 5 (bars 44–47) is introduced by two lower voices, the bass continuing the rising sequence of the first countersubject, combined with the first figure of the subject in the middle voice. The same figure is then used by soprano and bass in tenths in bar 45, and the second figure of the subject by the middle voice in bar 46. The episode modulates to vi [g].

At bar 47 (second note) the bass has the subject in vi, accompanied at first by the crotchet rhythm of bars 5–7, then from bar 49 by partial use of the two countersubjects. They are now organized in this way:

- subject and first countersubject are in their original relationship but an octave closer in pitch;
- the two countersubjects are interchanged at the twelfth;
- subject and second countersubject are also interchanged at the twelfth.

Episode 6 (bars 51–54) is led by the middle voice, which repeats the second half of the subject in ii, while the soprano alludes to the first countersubject, followed by the first figure of the subject in bar 53.

The middle voice in bar 54 enters with the subject in IV [E♭], in imitation of the soprano, with a semblance of stretto. As in the previous entry, the two countersubjects appear in partial form. Their pattern is now like this:

- subject and first countersubject are interchanged at the octave;
- the two countersubjects are interchanged at the twelfth;
- subject and second countersubject are also interchanged at the twelfth.

Episode 7 (bars 58–63) makes use of both subject figures treating in imitation between outer voices. The first countersubject figure also appears once in each voice (bars 58, 59, and 62), and where absent, the crotchet figure of bars 5–7 is used. The episode modulates to ii.

At bar 63 the soprano has the subject in ii, with the two countersubjects arranged like this:

- subject and first countersubject are interchanged at the octave;
- the two countersubjects are in their original relationship but an octave closer than before;
- subject and second countersubject are in their original relationship.

Episode 8 (bars 67–78) treats both figures of the subject in imitation and sequence. In addition, the soprano from bar 70 makes an extended falling sequence out of the simple cadence formula of bar 8. The episode modulates to V with a cadence at bar 78.

The soprano now has the final entry of the subject in bar 78, starting in V but soon harmonized in I.[19] (Its final note *a'* in bar 82 is the leading-note in I rather than the mediant in V.) The countersubjects are again used in the latter part of the entry, arranged in this pattern:

- subject and first countersubject are interchanged at the octave;

- the two countersubjects are a third closer than originally (i.e., they are interchanged at the fourteenth and again interchanged at the twelfth);
- subject and second countersubject are also interchanged at the fourteenth and again interchanged at the twelfth.

The final entry leads into a coda at bar 82. In the coda the partial entry of the subject is accompanied by both countersubjects:

- subject and first countersubject are in their original relationship;
- the two countersubjects are doubly interchanged, as in bar 80;
- subject and second countersubject also are doubly interchanged, as in bar 80.

The coda proceeds with further allusions to both figures of the subject and ends with a recapitulation in the tonic key of the final bars of episode 3 (bars 29–32).[20]

II.24: FUGUE IN B MINOR

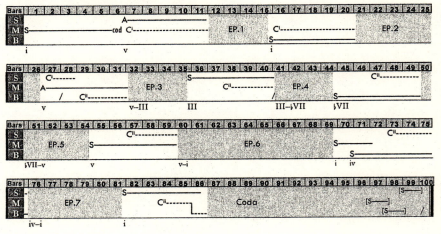

Exposition

1–6: subject in middle voice
    6: codetta
6–12: answer [tonal] in soprano, C^i in middle voice
12–15: episode 1
15–21: subject in bass, C^i in middle voice

Entrance of C^{ii}, and development

21–26: episode 2
26–32: answer [real] in middle voice, C^i in soprano, C^{ii} in bass, v

32–35: episode 3, modulating from v to III
35–41: subject in soprano, C^{ii} in middle voice, III
41–44: episode 4, modulating from III to ♭VII
44–50: subject in bass, C^{ii} in soprano, ♭VII
50–54: episode 5, modulating from ♭VII to v
54–60: subject in middle voice, C^{ii} in soprano v
60–69: episode 6, modulating from v to i

cont.

69–72: subject (partial) in middle voice, i	Final section[21]
70–76: subject in bass, C^{ii} in soprano, i–iv	81–87: subject in soprano, C^{ii} in middle
76–81: episode 7, modulating from iv to i	voice, transferred to bass, i
	87–100: coda

The subject starts on the dominant and is given a tonal answer. The subject ends on the first note of bar 6. A codetta leads without break into the first countersubject, which appears only twice in its complete form.[22]

Episode 1 (bars 12–15), which may at first sound as if it is a codetta,[23] repeats in falling sequence the final two figures of the answer in the soprano (as in bars 5–6). The middle voice has a figure of rising scale-steps, leading to a repetition of the countersubject figure of bar 11 at higher pitch. This apparent change from a falling to a rising sequence can be explained as a displacement of the sequence of falling thirds, bar 9 starting on *f♯*, bar 11 on *d♯*, and bar 13 on *b* instead of *B*.

At the bass entry of the subject in bar 15 the middle voice again has the countersubject, substituting an upward run for the figure of bar 7.[24]

Episode 2 (bars 21–26) is led by the bass, which adapts the countersubject figures of bars 10 and 11 to make a rising sequence, while the soprano follows in canon at the twelfth.

The entry of the real answer in bar 26 is at first accompanied by the beginning of the first countersubject in the soprano.[25] Then at bar 29 the bass introduces the second countersubject, which from now on is used to accompany every entry.

Episode 3 (bars 32–35): the rising steps of bar 12 are now developed by the middle voice into a rising and falling theme, imitated a fourth higher by the soprano. The bass combines the pattern of the second countersubject with the same rising steps, continuing them for a second bar, then repeating the same process a note lower. The episode modulates into III [D].

In bar 35 the soprano enters with the subject in III, overlapping the bass of the episode, accompanied by allusion to the codetta in the bass and by the second countersubject in the middle voice.

Episode 4 (bars 41–44) starts with the codetta figure, both direct (soprano) and inverted (middle). The soprano then repeats the rising and falling theme of the previous episode, while the middle voice alludes to the figure of the second countersubject. Rising semitones in the bass give a hint of chromatic development, to be used more fully in episode 5 and the coda. The episode modulates from III to ♭VII [D→A].

In bar 44 the bass entry of the subject in ♭VII overlaps the end of the previous episode. It is joined by the second countersubject in the soprano at bar 47.

Episode 5 (bars 50–54): a rising sequence develops the material of episode 3. The bass alternates between a variant of the second countersubject figure and the codetta figure; the falling steps of the middle voice are all chromatic;

the rising steps of the soprano are partly chromatic. The episode modulates from ♭VII to v [A → f♯].

In bar 54 the middle voice has the subject in v,[26] accompanied in the bass by the codetta figure, inverted and then direct; the soprano adds the second countersubject from bar 57.

Episode 6 (bars 60–69): all three voices treat the codetta figure by imitation in falling sequence, modulating from v to i.

In bar 69 the middle voice uses the last imitative figure of the episode as a decorated version of the beginning of the subject in i.[27] The bass, using the same figure by inversion, turns it into an entry of the subject in iv, which it completes.[28] The soprano adds the second countersubject from bar 73.

Episode 7 (bars 76–81) is again developed in a falling sequence, in which the bass repeats the end of the previous subject entry while the soprano develops the end of the second countersubject, modulating from iv to i.

The final section (bars 81–100) starts with the subject in the soprano. The second countersubject is added in the middle voice from bar 84, transferred to the bass in bar 86.

The **coda** (bar 87) arises out of the end of the subject, like the beginning of episode 3 (bar 32), to produce an extended version of the material of episode 3 with interchange of its upper voices. At bar 91 this pattern changes to a recapitulation of episode 5. Finally, all three voices allude to the first five notes of the subject: middle voice in bar 96, third beat; bass one bar later[29]; soprano one bar later, with an ornamentation of the opening of the subject that identifies it with the codetta figure.

I.13: FUGUE IN F♯ MAJOR

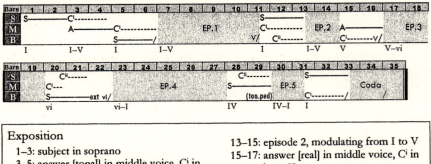

Exposition

1–3: subject in soprano
3–5: answer [tonal] in middle voice, Cⁱ in soprano
5–7: subject in bass, Cⁱ in middle voice

Entrance of second countersubject and development

7–11: episode 1, modulating from I to V
11–13: subject in soprano, Cⁱ in middle, Cⁱⁱ in bass, I

13–15: episode 2, modulating from I to V
15–17: answer [real] in middle voice, Cⁱ in bass, V
17–20: episode 3, modulating from V to vi
20–22: subject in bass, Cⁱ (partial) in middle, Cⁱⁱ in soprano, vi
22–23: extension to cadence in vi
23–28: episode 4, modulating from vi to I

cont.

28–30: subject in middle voice, C[ii] in soprano, IV 30–31: episode 5, modulating from IV to I	Final section 31–33: subject in soprano, C[i] in bass, I 33–35: coda

The subject, like so many in the "48," begins on the dominant and is answered by the tonic. The tonal answer is not used after the exposition.[30] [The first countersubject follows immediately the end of the subject, providing a characteristic smooth, flowing motion to the fugue.]

Episode 1 (bars 7–11): the bass entry alters its last note from $A\#$ to $F\#$, so that the episode begins without the more usual effect of overlap. The soprano introduces a new theme, formed by ornamentation of the last few notes of the subject [i.e., $a\#'-g\#'-c\#''-a\#'$]. This is treated imitatively by all three voices (the middle voice inverting it) and developed in a falling sequence by the bass, while the upper voices enlarge the falling steps of the subject into decorated suspensions. The episode, which began after a perfect cadence, also ends with a perfect cadence, in V [$C\#$].

In bar 11 the redundant entry of the subject in the soprano is accompanied by the first countersubject in the middle voice. The bass adds a second countersubject, formed by inverting and extending the main figure of episode 1 on a tonic pedal.

Episode 2 (bars 13–15) features the first four notes of the subject treated imitatively by the upper voices, while the bass develops the episodic figure of bar 7 in falling sequence.

The first countersubject returns in the bass to accompany the redundant entry of the real answer in the middle voice at bar 15.[31]

Episode 3 (bars 17–20) is a variant of the material of the first episode, modulating to the dominant of vi [$d\#$].

In bar 20 the bass has the subject in vi, accompanied by part of the first countersubject in the middle voice, while the soprano adds the second countersubject, with the somewhat unusual harmonies caused by the reiterated D$\#$. The entry is extended by one bar toward a cadence in vi at bar 23.

Episode 4 (bars 23–28) develops the material of episode 2 with imitation between the upper voices at the lower third instead of the unison and by repetition of the opening figure in falling sequence. At bar 26 there is a free interchange, the soprano inverting the previous bass figure, while the bass combines the previous soprano and alto, doubling the speed of chord changes.

The entry of the subject in the middle voice at bar 28 in IV has the effect of continuing the imitations of the episode. The bass, reverting to its figure of bar 23, also seems to be part of the episode. The second half of the entry is on a tonic pedal in IV, with the second countersubject in the soprano.

Episode 5 (bars 30–31) is a recapitulation of episode 2 with upper voices interchanged.

The final entry of the subject in the soprano at bar 31 is a recapitulation of bars 15–17 with upper voices interchanged.

The **coda** (bars 33–35) makes a final allusion to episode 1.

REVIEW OF THE FUGUES IN GROUP 6

The four fugues recently examined will have enlarged the concept of variable form within a fugal style. They illustrate, possibly more than those of any other group, the fact that within the fugal conventions two fugues may differ widely from each other in form, and yet both may be excellent fugues.

The following table shows their main outlines, S denoting an entry of subject or answer, C^i and C^ii the presence of countersubjects (but not their relationship of pitch to the entries).

```
                           C     C     C  C     C
I.19   S  S  S  S  S  S  S  S  S  S  Ep  S  S  Ep  S  S  S  Cod

                           C^i      C^i      C^i      C^i      C^i      C^i
II.21  S  S  Ep S  Ep S  Ep S  Ep S  Ep S  Ep S  Ep S  Ep S  Ep S  Cod
                           C^ii     C^ii     C^ii     C^ii     C^ii     C^ii

       C^i      C^i      C^i
II.24  S  S  Ep S  Ep S  Ep S  Ep S  Ep S  Ep S  Ep S  Cod
            C^ii     C^ii     C^ii     C^ii     C^ii     C^ii

       C^i C^i      C^i      C^i      C^i            C^i
I.13   S  S  S  Ep S  Ep S  Ep S  Ep S  Ep S  Cod
            C^ii          C^ii    C^ii
```

14

Group 7: Fugues with
Subsidiary Subjects

The four fugues in this group are sometimes described as having extra countersubjects. They are, however, somewhat different in form from those of Group 6 and therefore should be considered separately. In them the new themes assume a greater degree of importance, being given their own exposition as well as being combined with the original subject.

Fugues with one subsidiary subject: **II.4, 18,** and **23**.
Fugue with two subsidiary subjects: **II.14.**

(The fugue in C# minor, **I.4,** also has two subsidiary subjects. Since it is a five-voice fugue, it is considered in Chapter 15.)
   In addition, we should examine two preludes that are in fugal style:

Fugue on two subjects: (Prelude) **I.7**.
Fugue on three subjects: (Prelude) **I.19**.

II.4: FUGUE IN C♯ MINOR

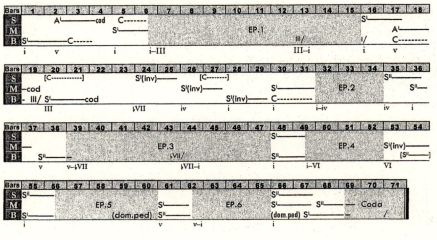

Exposition of first subject (Sⁱ)	Exposition of second subject (Sⁱⁱ)
1–2: subject in bass	35–36: Sⁱⁱ in soprano, iv
2–4: answer [real] in soprano	36–37: Sⁱⁱ in middle voice, i
5–6: subject in middle voice	37–39: Sⁱⁱ in bass, v
Episode 1 (6–16), modulating from i to III, then back to i	Episode 3 (39–47), modulating from v to ♭VII and i
Counterexposition	Combination of Sⁱ and Sⁱⁱ subjects
16–17: subject in soprano, i	48–49: Sⁱ in soprano, Sⁱⁱ in bass, i
17–19: answer in middle voice, v	49–52: episode 4, modulating from i to VI
19: codetta	53–54: Sⁱ (inverted) in middle voice, VI
20–21: subject in bass, III	55–56: Sⁱ in bass, Sⁱⁱ in soprano, i
Codetta (21–23)	56–61: episode 5
	61–62: Sⁱ in middle voice, Sⁱⁱ in bass, v
Exposition of inverted subject	62–65: episode 6
24–25: subject (inverted) in soprano, ♭VII	66–67: Sⁱ in middle voice, Sⁱⁱ in soprano, i
26–27: subject (inverted) in middle voice, iv	67–69: Sⁱ in bass, Sⁱⁱ in middle voice, i
28–29: subject (inverted) in bass, i	69–71: coda
30–31: subject (direct) in middle voice, i	
31–34: episode 2, modulating from i to iv	

The voices enter in an unusual order: bass–soprano–middle. This order is used in only one other fugue, **II.3**.

The subject may be presumed to end at the last note of bar 2 so that the answer overlaps its last four notes.[1] The bass accompanies the answer with a countersubject that is usually modified in its later appearances.[2] The final figures of the answer are repeated in sequence in the codetta of bar 4, giving the impression that the passage is modulating to III [E]. The entry in bar 5 at first seems to be part of an inverted, interrupted cadence in III.

Episode 1 (bars 6–16) starts as a three-part version of the codetta of bar 4 and proceeds with three-part imitation of the final figures of the subject, held together by the suspension figure of the countersubject. In bar 13 the soprano adds an important new figure [♫♩♫♩], which will provide material for later development. The episode modulates from i to III (with cadence in III at bar 13) and then back to i.

The **counterexposition** (bars 16–21) starts with the subject in the soprano, followed by the answer in the middle voice (with countersubject, modified, in the bass).[3] In bar 19 a three-part version of the codetta of bar 4 leads to the bass entry of the subject in bar 20, in III, instead of the expected i.[4] The passage is extended in sequence to form a codetta.[5]

The **inverted subject** is introduced in each voice as follows: bar 24 in soprano, ♭VII [B]; bar 26 in middle voice, iv [f♯]; bar 28 in bass, i [c♯]. At bar 30 the middle voice adds the direct subject in I, with the modified countersubject in the bass.

Episode 2 (bars 31–34) extends the end of the subject in sequence. Then in bar 33 the upper voices treat the new figure of bar 13 in imitation, modulating from i to iv [c♯→ f♯].

The **exposition of second subject** (bars 35–39) is marked by the soprano entry at bar 35 in iv (which has already been foreshadowed in the soprano of bar 20 [and again in smaller note-values in bar 27]).[6] The middle voice follows in stretto, in i.[7] The bass adds the second subject at the last note of bar 37, in v. In all this passage the accompanying voices have continued the figures of the previous episode.

Episode 3 (bars 39–47) develops the material of episode 1, modulating from v to ♭VII, with cadence at bar 44, and then to i [g♯→B→c♯].

The **combination of first and second subjects** is achieved at bar 48; the first subject is in the soprano, and the second subject in the bass.

Episode 4 (bars 49–52) treats the new figure of bar 13 in falling sequence. It goes on to combine figures from the first subject in the soprano, the chromatic steps of the second subject in the middle voice, and a repetition of its final figure in the bass modulating from i to VI [c♯→ A].

A return of the inverted first subject in the middle voice at bar 53, in VI [with an allusion to the beginning of the second subject in the bass] leads immediately to a new entry of both subjects in bar 55: first subject in the bass and second subject in the soprano. They are an interchange at the twelfth of the entries in bar 48.

Episode 5 (bars 56–61) is a development of the material of episode 2, with a dominant pedal in bars 59–60.

In bar 61 the middle voice has the first subject, and the bass has the second subject. They are related as in bar 48, but an octave closer.

Episode 6 (bars 62–65) uses canonic and imitative treatment of the final figures of the first subject in the upper voices, while the bass repeats in falling fifths the figure of the second and third beats of bar 1.

At bar 66 the middle voice has the first subject, and the soprano the second subject,[8] interchanging the entries of bar 48 at the octave. Through most of this entry, the bass holds a dominant pedal. The pedal is quitted from a $^6_4$, which becomes a final entry of the answer, but harmonized in i. The middle voice adds the second subject two beats later, imitated in its chromatic steps by the soprano, and extended into a short coda.

II.18: FUGUE IN G♯ MINOR

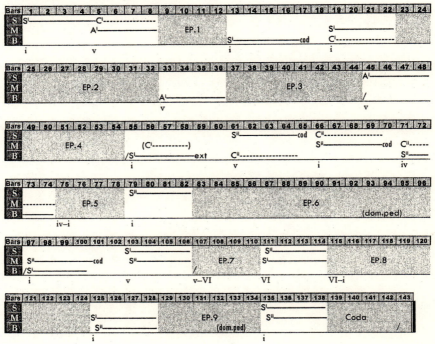

Exposition of first subject (S^i)	Exposition of second subject (S^ii)
1–5: subject in soprano	61–65: S^ii in soprano, v
5–9: answer [real] in middle voice	65–66: codetta
9–13: episode 1	66–70: S^ii in middle voice, i
13–17: subject in bass	70–71: codetta
17–19: codetta	71–75: S^ii in bass, iv
19–23: redundant entry of subject in middle voice	75–79: episode 5, modulating from iv to i
Episode 2 (23–33)	79–83: redundant entry of S^ii in soprano, i
	83–97: episode 6

Combination of S^i and S^ii

Counterexposition of first subject
33–37: answer in bass, v   97–101: S^i in bass, S^ii in middle voice, i
37–45: episode 3   101–102: codetta
45–49: answer in soprano, v   103–107: S^i in soprano, S^ii in middle voice, v
49–55: episode 4   107–111: episode 7, modulating from v to VI
55–59: subject in bass, i   111–115: S^i in middle voice, S^ii in soprano, VI
59–61: extension to cadence

cont.

115–125: episode 8, modulating from VI to i	135–139: S^i in soprano, S^{ii} in middle voice, i
125–129: S^i in middle voice, S^{ii} in bass, i	139–143: coda
129–135: episode 9	

Perhaps more than any other fugue, this fugue illustrates Bach's skill in developing a large structure out of small and apparently unimportant figures. The first subject itself is of deceptively simple nature, its second half being a replica of its first half one step higher (except for the last note of bar 3). The whole subject is a subtle ornamentation of the rising steps *g#′–a#′–b′*. The first countersubject reinforces the sequential nature of the subject, while adding its own chromatic version of the three-note rising steps in bars 5 and 7.[9]

Episode 1 (bars 9–13) is led by the rising chromatic steps of the countersubject in the middle voice, which are immediately echoed by rising diatonic steps in the soprano, and the pattern is repeated in falling sequence. It continues with reference to figures from the subject, with free interchange.[10]

At bar 13 the bass entry of the subject is accompanied by free counterpoint. The harmony of bars 16–17 is suggestive of the key of III [B], so that the exposition does not sound as if it is ending at this point. A codetta in bars 17 and 18 leads to a redundant entry of the subject; the soprano inverts and extends the main rising steps of the subject, the middle voice develops the soprano figures of the first episode [♩♩♪ ♪♩♪ ♩], and the bass uses the complete rhythm and some of the melodic figure of the middle voice in the first episode [♩ ♪ ♩ ♪], joining smoothly into the countersubject at bar 19 to accompany the redundant entry in the middle voice. The five-note rising steps of bars 18–19 have an important bearing on the second subject of bar 61.[11]

Episode 2 (bars 23–33) develops the material of the codetta bars 17–19, with the five-note scale steps now in the bass and with three-part imitation of the suspension figure of the middle voice of that codetta. It also uses figures from the first subject and countersubject.

The **counterexposition** begins with the answer in the bass in bar 33, accompanied by figures from the previous episode.

Episode 3 (bars 37–45): the middle voice alludes to the countersubject, which was absent from the previous entry. It goes on to develop figures from episode 2.[12]

The answer in the soprano at bar 45 is accompanied by free counterpoint, which includes in the bass of bars 47–48 a chromatic version of the five-note falling steps of bars 17–19. (This chromatic scale passage, like the ascending bass of bars 18–19, is a foreshadowing of the second subject.)

Episode 4 (bars 49–55) starts by interchanging the voices of episode 1, then goes on to further development of material from episode 2.[13]

The final entry of the counterexposition is the subject in the bass of bar 55, with an altered version of the countersubject in the middle voices. The entry is extended in bars 59–61 toward an imperfect cadence in the tonic key.[14]

With an abrupt move from the imperfect cadence at bar 61, the soprano announces a **second subject** in v [d♯].[15] In its context the new subject as a whole has the air of a completely fresh theme, even though its separate figures have all been heard before (the falling chromatic steps in the bass of bars 47–48, the rising partly chromatic steps in the bass of bars 18–19, and the cadential suspension in the counterpoint of bars 7–9.) The second subject has its own new countersubject based on figures from the first subject and also including an important ornamental version of the suspension figure of bars 17 and 18 [♩♪ ♫♪].

The middle voice now enters (bar 66) with the second subject in i. The soprano has the **second countersubject**, somewhat disguised at its opening but clearly recognizable toward the end of the entry. After a short codetta (bars 70–71), the second subject enters in the bass in iv [c♯]. The middle voice has the second countersubject, with additional ornamentation.

Episode 5 (bars 75–79) is closely linked with the previous entry, developing the ornamented suspension figure imitatively in all voices.[16] (It had already found its way up to the soprano before the end of the entry.) It also uses the falling steps of bars 17–19 both in their original rhythm and also in that of the second subject.

In bar 79 the soprano has the second subject in i, accompanied by the suspension figure in the middle voice and with an imitation of its latter half in the bass.

Episode 6 (bars 83–97) develops the second half of the second subject along with the suspension figure and includes a dominant pedal.

The **combination of two subjects**—third main section of the fugue—begins at bar 97 with the first subject in the bass and the second subject in the middle voice. After a short codetta (using the ornamental suspension figure) the soprano enters with the first subject in v in bar 103.[17] The second subject is in the middle voice.

Episode 7 (bars 107–111)[18]: the bass develops the codetta of bar 17, the middle voice repeats the decorated suspension figure in falling sequence, and the soprano presents the falling chromatic steps of the second subject in a new rhythm. After two bars the upper voices are interchanged.

Bar 111 is the only major key entry of the entire fugue; the middle voice has the first subject in VI [E], with the second subject in the soprano.

Episode 8 (bars 115–125) is a free interchange of episode 7, followed by further development of figures in episode 6.

At bar 125 both subjects return in i.

Episode 9 (bars 129–135): the final figures of the first subject in the middle voice of bars 128–129 are imitated first by the bass, then by the middle voice, then in bar 130 by the soprano. The episode includes a dominant pedal.

The two subjects finally are heard in close position at bar 135. A **coda**, beginning at bar 139, alludes to the material of the previous episode.

II.23: FUGUE IN B MAJOR

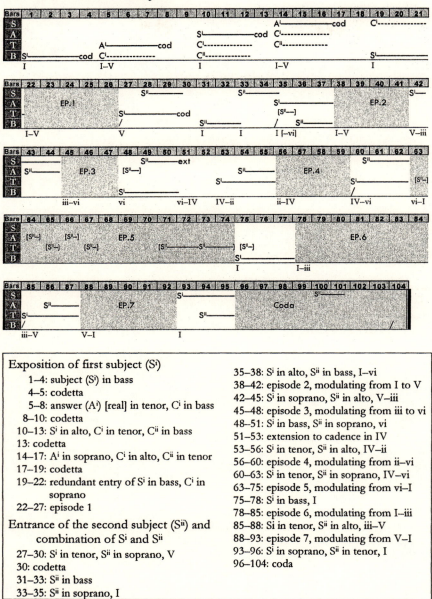

Exposition of first subject (S^i)

   1–4: subject (S^i) in bass
   4–5: codetta
   5–8: answer (A^i) [real] in tenor, C^i in bass
   8–10: codetta
   10–13: S^i in alto, C^i in tenor, C^{ii} in bass
   13: codetta
   14–17: A^i in soprano, C^i in alto, C^{ii} in tenor
   17–19: codetta
   19–22: redundant entry of S^i in bass, C^i in soprano
   22–27: episode 1

Entrance of the second subject (S^{ii}) and combination of S^i and S^{ii}

   27–30: S^i in tenor, S^{ii} in soprano, V
   30: codetta
   31–33: S^{ii} in bass
   33–35: S^{ii} in soprano, I

   35–38: S^i in alto, S^{ii} in bass, I–vi
   38–42: episode 2, modulating from I to V
   42–45: S^i in soprano, S^{ii} in alto, V–iii
   45–48: episode 3, modulating from iii to vi
   48–51: S^i in bass, S^{ii} in soprano, vi
   51–53: extension to cadence in IV
   53–56: S^i in tenor, S^{ii} in alto, IV–ii
   56–60: episode 4, modulating from ii–vi
   60–63: S^i in tenor, S^{ii} in soprano, IV–vi
   63–75: episode 5, modulating from vi–I
   75–78: S^i in bass, I
   78–85: episode 6, modulating from I–iii
   85–88: Si in tenor, S^{ii} in alto, iii–V
   88–93: episode 7, modulating from V–I
   93–96: S^i in soprano, S^{ii} in tenor, I
   96–104: coda

The subject ends at the first note of bar 4. A codetta joins it to the first countersubject. The answer, ending at bar 8, leads to a two-bar codetta that repeats the falling steps of bar 4 [♪♪♪] and then adds the countersubject figures of bar 5 [♩♩♩]. With the alto entry of the subject in bar 10 the tenor leads into the first countersubject in a quasi sequence. The bass in bar 10 adds a second countersubject.[19] After a one-bar codetta (a three-part version of bar 4), the soprano entry of the answer is accompanied by the first countersubject in the alto and the second countersubject in the tenor, the bass being silent. Bars 17–18 are a three-part version of the codetta of bars 8–10, leading to a redundant entry of the subject in the bass of bar 19, with the first countersubject in the soprano but without the second countersubject.

Episode 1 (bars 22–27): the exposition theoretically finishes at bar 22 but in effect is rounded off by the first episode. It uses figures from the codettas and both countersubjects, with a quasi sequence (bar 24 is similar to bar 22, a third lower) and with a strong perfect cadence in V. The episode introduces a new figure in the alto in the second half of bar 22 [♪♪♪♪|♩], with its inversion in bar 24 [♪♪♪♪|♪], which is not used again until the coda in bars 98 and 99.

The tenor entry of the first subject [answer] in V (bar 27) marks the beginning of a new section.[20] It is joined after its third note by a second subject in the soprano,[21] developed out of figures in the second countersubject (bar 11) and the codetta (bar 9). After a codetta (bar 30),[22] the bass repeats the second subject in I, immediately followed in bar 33 by the soprano.[23] At bar 35 the alto enters with the first subject in I, followed after its third note by the second subject in the bass.[24] The two voices interchange the combination of bars 27–30 at the twelfth. Before the end of the entry the passage has modulated to vi [g♯].

Episode 2 (bars 38–42) develops the soprano figure of the codetta bar 30, modulating to V [(g♯→B)→F♯].

At bar 42 the first subject [answer] in the soprano and the second subject in the alto are in the same relationship as in bars 35–38 but an octave closer.[25] The entry starts in V and modulates to iii [i.e., F♯→d♯].

Episode 3 (bars 45–48) is a two-part version of episode 1, modulating to vi [(d♯)→g♯].

In bar 48 the first subject in the bass and the second subject in the soprano are in the same relationship as in bars 27–30 in vi. The entry is extended to a cadence in IV by a two-bar codetta, with a falling sequence based on the rhythm of the first countersubject.

The tenor enters with the first subject in bar 53, beginning in IV and modulating to ii [i.e., E→c♯]. The alto adds the second subject in bar 54 a fifth closer than in its original setting (i.e., the two voices of bar 27 are interchanged at the twelfth and interchanged again at the octave).

Episode 4 (bars 56–60): before the end of the previous entry the bass has already begun a pattern that is developed into the episode, formed out of an irregular sequence based on the main figure of the second subject. The episode modulates back to IV.

At bar 60 the tenor starts the first subject on *g♯*, the mediant of IV, modulating to vi [i.e., E→g♯]. The soprano adds the second subject, but half a bar earlier than in previous combinations.

Episode 5 (bars 63–75) is mostly based on the main figure of the second subject. It also alludes to the material of bar 51. Bars 63 and 64 are repeated in sequence a third lower; then at bar 68 a new sequence begins, rising a third at each bar. The episode reverts to its original sequence of falling thirds in bars 71–74. The episode has included in its rising sequence a new figure of semiquavers [♩ ♫♫ ♪], which is not used again after this episode.[26]

At bar 75 the bass, which has been silent since the cadence at bar 60, enters with the first subject in I, accompanied by a brief allusion to the second subject in the tenor.

Episode 6 (bars 78–85) grows naturally out of the counterpoint of the previous entry, with four-part treatment of the material of episode 2, ending with a cadence in iii [(B→g♯)→d♯].

At bar 85 the tenor enters with the first subject [answer] on f♯, the mediant of iii (in similar fashion to its entry in bar 60), modulating to V.[27] The alto adds the second subject at bar 86, an octave closer than in the original combination of bar 27.

Episode 7 (bars 88–93) treats the second subject figure in falling sequence in the bass, while the upper voices add rich harmony, alluding to the material of the codetta of bars 8–9.

At bar 93 the soprano has the climactic entry of the first subject, accompanied at first by the continuing thirds of the previous episode. The tenor adds the second subject in the following bar. The interchange is at the twelfth, as in bars 35–38.

The **coda** (bars 96–104) arises without break from the previous entry. It asserts strongly the mordentlike figure of the first episode (bar 22) and also includes an allusion to the second subject in the soprano at bar 100.

II.14: FUGUE IN F♯ MINOR

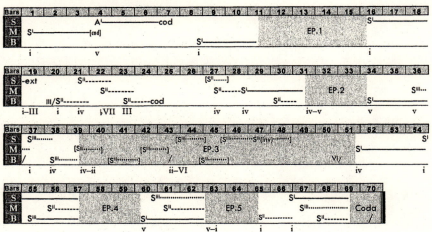

Exposition of first subject (S^i)	Exposition of third subject (S^{iii})
1–4: subject in middle voice	36–37: S^{iii} in middle voice, v
4–7: answer [tonal] in soprano	37–38: S^{iii} in soprano, i
7–8: codetta	38–39: S^{iii} in bass, iv
8–11: subject in bass	39–51: episode 3, modulating from iv to ii,
11–16: episode 1	and then to VI
16–19: redundant entry of subject in	51–54: S^i in middle voice, iv
soprano	**Combination of S^i, S^{ii}, and S^{iii}**
19–20: extension to cadence in III	54–57: S^i in soprano, S^{ii} in middle, S^{iii} in
Exposition of second subject (S^{ii})	bass, i
20–21: S^{ii} in bass, i	57–60: episode 4, modulating from i to v
21–22: S^{ii} in soprano, iv	60–63: S^i in bass, S^{ii} in middle, S^{iii} in
22–23: S^{ii} in middle voice, ♭VII	soprano, v
23–24: redundant entry of S^{ii} in bass, III	63–65: episode 5, modulating from v to i
24–27: codetta	65–67: S^{ii} in bass, i
27–28: redundant entry of S^{ii} in middle	65–69: S^i in soprano, S^{ii} in bass, S^{iii} in
voice, iv	middle, i
Combination of S^i and S^{ii}	69–70: coda
28–31: S^i in middle voice, S^{ii} in bass, iv	
31–34: episode 2, modulating from iv to v	
34–37: S^i in bass, v	

The accompaniment to the tonal answer in bar 4 appears to be designed as a countersubject.[28] It does not, however, recur as such, though its separate figures are used for later development. Bars 7–8 are a codetta, formed from the falling fifth of the subject (imitated as a rising fourth by the middle voice) and the falling steps of the subject, now treated as plain instead of decorated suspensions. The bass entry of bar 8 is accompanied by the first figure of the subject [♪ ♩] and the first figure of the tonal answer by inversion [♪ ♩]. The rests in the upper voices also seem to add something of the spirit of bars 5–6, though the melodic outline is different.

Episode 1 (bars 11–16) grows directly out of the bass entry and is a subtly constructed sequence, rising by thirds: the bass steps *d–c♯–B* are followed by an allusion to the subject, leading to the steps *f♯–e–d♯*; then, after another allusion to the subject, the steps *a–g♯–f♯*.[29] The sequential pattern forms groups of six beats within the framework of common time. The upper voices use the figures of the last entry, with interchange.

The soprano at bar 16 adds a redundant entry of the subject,[30] extended toward a perfect cadence in III at bar 20.

The **exposition of the second subject** (S^{ii}) starts at bar 20, where the bass announces S^{ii} in i,[31] consisting of seven notes.[32] (Only in the final section does it become complete with eight notes.) From bar 20 onward the ear hears what appear to be a large number of entries in stretto, at almost every half-bar. Most of these on analysis prove to be imitations of the first four notes of S^{ii}. The actual entries are bar 20, bass in i; bar 21, soprano in iv [b]; bar 22, middle voice in ♭VII [E].

The exposition of S^{ii} is extended by redundant entries: bar 23, bass in III [A], accompanied by figures from S^i in the middle voice; then after a codetta (bar 24) using the rising fourths of the first codetta (bar 7), another redundant entry in the middle voice at bar 27 in iv, preceded by an allusion to S^{ii} in the soprano.

The middle voice immediately goes on to announce S^i in iv (bar 28), preceded by allusions to its first figure in soprano and bass. The soprano accompanies the entry with the first four notes of S^{ii} and the falling fifths of the codetta of bar 7. The bass adds a real entry of S^{ii} in bar 30, combining two subjects.

Episode 2 (bars 31–34) uses imitative treatment of figures from both S^i and S^{ii}, modulating from iv to v [b→c♯].

At bar 34 the bass has S^i [real answer] in v, accompanied by the first figure of S^{ii} in soprano and middle voice.

Before the bass entry has finished, the middle voice introduces the **third subject** (S^{iii}) in v (bar 36), marking the beginning of the exposition of S^{iii}.[33] This is followed by S^{iii} in the soprano, in i. In bar 38 the bass adds S^{iii} in iv.

Episode 3 (bars 39–51) extends and develops the figures of the third subject by imitation in all voices, combining with it figures from the first subject and its tonal answer and leading to a perfect cadence in ii at bar 43. After this, the figures of S^{iii} are developed separately, direct and inverted. The episode also alludes to the codetta of bar 7 (in bar 46) and to the rising steps of bars 5–6 (in the bass and middle voice of bars 47–48), modulating to VI [D] at bar 51.

At bar 51 the middle voice has S^i in iv, accompanied by continuous use of the figures of S^{iii} in the bass and the falling fifths of the codetta of bar 7 in the soprano.

The **combination of all three subjects** (S^i, S^{ii}, and S^{iii}) appears for the first time at bar 54, where the soprano glides unobtrusively into an ornamented version of the opening of S^i in i,[34] with S^{ii} in the bass. At bar 56 the middle voice adds S^{iii}, now in its complete form of eight notes.[35]

Episode 4 (bars 57–60): the bass continues the running rhythm of S^{iii}, while the upper voices treat in free imitation the opening figure of S^i by inversion, also referring to the opening of S^{ii} but without its jerky rhythm. The episode modulates from i to v.

At bar 60 the bass begins another permutation of the three subjects in v, decorating the opening of S^i [answer] as in the previous soprano entry. The soprano now has S^{iii}, and the middle voice adds S^{ii} in bar 61.

Episode 5 (bars 63–65) recalls the material of episode 4, now treated in a regular falling sequence, modulating from v to i.

The running bass of the episode merges at the last three notes of bar 65 into an entry of S^{ii}. The soprano in bar 66 introduces the final permutation of the three subjects with an entry of S^i, followed by S^{iii} a bar later in the middle voice. The entry of S^{ii} in the bass at bar 68 is followed by the briefest of codas.

I.PR.7: PRELUDE IN E♭ MAJOR (BARS 25–70)

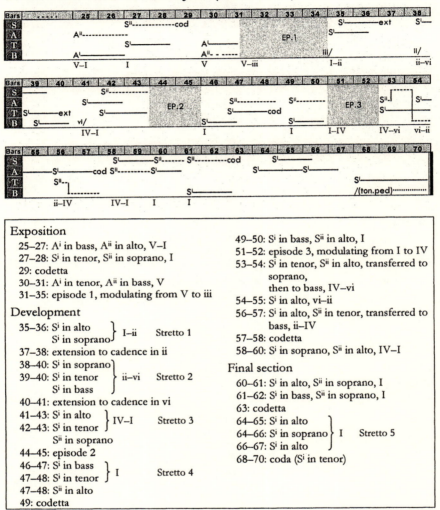

Exposition

25–27: Aⁱ in bass, Aⁱⁱ in alto, V–I
27–28: Sⁱ in tenor, Sⁱⁱ in soprano, I
29: codetta
30–31: Aⁱ in tenor, Aⁱⁱ in bass, V
31–35: episode 1, modulating from V to iii

Development

35–36: Sⁱ in alto ⎫ I–ii　Stretto 1
Sⁱ in soprano ⎭
37–38: extension to cadence in ii
38–40: Sⁱ in soprano ⎫
39–40: Sⁱ in tenor ⎬ ii–vi　Stretto 2
Sⁱ in bass ⎭
40–41: extension to cadence in vi
41–43: Sⁱ in alto ⎫ IV–I　Stretto 3
42–43: Sⁱ in tenor ⎬
Sⁱⁱ in soprano ⎭
44–45: episode 2
46–47: Sⁱ in bass ⎫ I　Stretto 4
47–48: Sⁱ in tenor ⎭
47–48: Sⁱⁱ in alto
49: codetta

49–50: Sⁱ in bass, Sⁱⁱ in alto, I
51–52: episode 3, modulating from I to IV
53–54: Sⁱ in tenor, Sⁱⁱ in alto, transferred to
　　　　soprano,
　　　　then to bass, IV–vi
54–55: Sⁱ in alto, vi–ii
56–57: Sⁱ in alto, Sⁱⁱ in tenor, transferred to
　　　　bass, ii–IV
57–58: codetta
58–60: Sⁱ in soprano, Sⁱⁱ in alto, IV–I

Final section

60–61: Sⁱ in alto, Sⁱⁱ in soprano, I
61–62: Sⁱ in bass, Sⁱⁱ in soprano, I
63: codetta
64–65: Sⁱ in alto ⎫
64–66: Sⁱ in soprano ⎬ I　Stretto 5
66–67: Sⁱ in alto ⎭
68–70: coda (Sⁱ in tenor)

The final section of this prelude, starting at bar 25, consists of a double fugue (i.e., a fugue on two subjects, combined from the beginning). The main subject [♩ ♪♪|♪♪|♪] is derived from the fugato section of the prelude (bars 10–25), while the second subject is a development of the toccata theme of bar 1 [♪♫♪ ♫♫].[36] The fugato section ends at bar 25 with a B♭ major chord, which in its context is V in the key of E♭. This explains the fact that the two "subjects" at bar 25 are in B♭, while the two "answers" are in E♭ rather than F. Understood in relation to the earlier part of the prelude, it sounds perfectly natural, even though, technically speaking, the fugue starts with its two answers before announcing its two subjects. In this analysis every entry after the exposition will be referred to simply as an entry of the subject.

The exposition (bar 25–31) starts with A^i in the bass, A^{ii} in the alto, in V modulating to I. These are immediately followed by the pair of subjects, S^i in the tenor, S^{ii} in the soprano in I.[37] Bar 29 is a codetta, leading to a third pair of entries at bar 30; A^i is again in the tenor, A^{ii} [beginning altered] in the bass, in V. The exposition is extended, without cadence, into the first episode.

Episode 1 (bars 31–35): beginning in the alto before the end of the previous entry, the first figure of S^{ii} is treated imitatively in a falling sequence, changing in bar 33 to a rising sequence, modulating from V to iii [B♭→g].

The development (bars 35–61) begins with pairs of entries of S^i in stretto accompanied by almost continuous reference to the first figure of S^{ii}:

35: S^i in alto is followed two beats later by S^i in soprano, related as subject–answer, harmonized in I modulating to ii, extended toward a cadence in ii at bar 38;

38: S^i in soprano is followed two beats later by S^i in tenor, followed two beats later by S^i in bass,[38] in ii modulating to vi [f→c], extended to a cadence in vi at bar 41;

41: S^i in alto is followed after two beats by S^i in tenor, now with S^{ii} in the soprano (leaping up an eleventh instead of a fourth to its repeated notes), in IV modulating to I.

Episode 2 (bars 44–45): the end of the previous entry was deflected from I to the dominant of ii. The episode has a transitory modulation to vi before returning to ii [c→f]. It is formed from the same continuous imitation of the first figure of S^{ii}, with a strong rising scale passage in bar 45, developed out of the rising fourth of S^i and the scale steps bounded by a fourth in S^{ii}.

The main key is restored by the bass entry of S^i in bar 46, followed by S^i in the tenor a bar later. The alto adds S^{ii} to the tenor entry, but in a different relationship from the original combination of the two subjects in bar 25; they have been interchanged at the fifteenth and interchanged again at the twelfth.

Stretto is discontinued for the rest of the development section, the interest once again being on the combination of the two subjects. In bar 49 the bass has S^i in I, while the alto has S^{ii} in the same relationship as in bar 47.

Episode 3 (bars 51–52): the opening figure of S^{ii} is now fragmented, in two-part imitation between alto and soprano. With the return of the complete figure in the bass of bar 52, the alto and soprano now divide the rising scale of bar 45 into two four-note groups. The episode modulates from I to IV [E♭→A♭].[39]

At bar 53 the tenor has S^i, starting in IV and modulating to vi [A♭→c]. S^{ii} at this point is divided between the other three voices, starting in the alto, moving into the soprano, and then into the bass. Its relationship with S^i is a fresh one, interchanging the original combination of bar 25 at the fifteenth and interchanging it again at the tenth.

S^i appears in the alto at bar 54, starting in vi and modulating to ii [c→f], accompanied by the first figure of S^{ii}. The entry of bar 54 is overlapped by another entry of S^i also in the alto (bar 56), starting in ii and modulating to IV [f→A♭], with S^{ii} in the tenor transferred to the bass. A codetta, still using the first figure of S^{ii}, leads to an unexpected high entry of S^i in the soprano before the end of bar 58. S^{ii} in an altered form is in the alto. The entries start in IV and modulate to I [A♭→E♭].

In the closely woven texture of this double fugue there is no clear demarcation between development and final section, which may be assumed to begin at bar 60, since from now onward the main key is fully restored.[40] The alto disguises the beginning of its entry of S^i by alluding to the four-note rising figures of episode 3 (bar 51). S^{ii} appears in altered form in the soprano.[41] With the bass entry of bar 61 we are more clearly in the final section, repeating S^i at the original pitch of bar 25 with S^{ii} in the soprano, at first in an altered form but settling into its original shape during bar 62.

A codetta in bar 63 leads to a final stretto of S^i between alto (at the first note of bar 64) and soprano (at the lost note of bar 64). The soprano extends its entry with an extra leaping fourth (now a diminished fourth), while the alto adds another entry of S^i at the first note of bar 66.

The **coda** (bar 68) on a tonic pedal includes one more entry of S^i in the tenor, with allusion to S^{ii} in alto and soprano.

I.PR.19: PRELUDE IN A MAJOR

	Exposition	Entries in related key
	1–3: S^i in soprano S^{ii} in bass } I S^{iii} in middle voice	12–14: S^i in soprano S^{ii} in bass } vi S^{iii} in middle voice
	3: codetta.	14–17: episode 2, modulating from vi to I.
	4–6: A^i in bass A^{ii} in middle voice } V A^{iii} in soprano	Final section
	6–8: episode 1	17–20: S^i in bass S^{ii} in middle voice } I S^{iii} in soprano
	8–11: S^i in middle voice S^{ii} in soprano } I S^{iii} in bass	20–22: S^i in soprano S^{ii} in middle voice } I S^{iii} in bass
	11–12: extension to cadence in vi	22–24: coda

The three subjects end at the third beat of bar 3. The second half of this bar is a codetta that modulates to V for the three answers in bar 4. At bar 4 the soprano at first accompanies A^i in the bass by repeating in sequence the first figure of S^i leading into A^{iii} on the last quaver of the bar. A^{ii} and A^{iii} are slightly altered toward their ending in bar 6.

Episode 1 (bars 6–8) starts with the codetta figure in the bass, and continuing with a falling sequence, combining the first figure and the suspension figure of S^i [♫ ♩ ♫ , which is modified to ♪♫ , in the upper voices].

The third group of entries begins halfway through bar 8, with S^i in the middle voice completed at bar 11. S^{ii} and S^{iii} are once more altered in bar 10. The phrase is extended toward a cadence in vi [f#] at bar 12.

In the middle section (bars 12–14), the three subjects in vi are related as at the opening, S^i now falling a third instead of rising a sixth after its fourth note. All three subjects are altered toward their ending.[42]

Episode 2 (bars 14–17) uses a combination of the codetta figure (inverted) in the lower voices and the suspension figure of S^{ii} in the soprano. It modulates from vi to I [f#→A].

The final section (bars 17–24) is marked by the return of the three subjects in I. S^{ii} and S^{iii} are slightly altered in bar 19. The entries are immediately followed by more entries in I at bar 20. S^{ii} is slightly altered toward its ending.

The **coda** (bars 22–24) is based on the first figure of S^i and the codetta figure, both of them direct and also inverted.

It is noteworthy that Bach used only four out of the six possible permutations of his three subjects:

(1)	S^i (twice)	(2)	S^{iii} (twice)	(3)	S^{ii}	(4)	S^i
	S^{iii}		S^{ii}		S^i		S^{ii}
	S^{ii}		S^i		S^{iii}		S^{iii}

PLAN OF THE FUGUES IN GROUP 7: THE USE OF SUBJECTS 1, 2, AND 3

II.4	II.18	II.23	II.14	I.Pr.7	I.Pr.19
1	1	1	1	1+2	1+2+3
1	1	1	1	1+2	1+2+3
1	EP	1	1	1+2	EP
EP	1	1	EP	EP	1+2+3
1	1	1	1	1 ⎫ Stretto	1+2+3
1	EP	EP	2	1 ⎭	Ep
1	1	1+2	2	1	1+2+3
1 (inv)	EP	2	2	1 ⎫ Stretto	1+2+3
1 (inv)	1	2	2	1 ⎬	Coda
1 (inv)	EP	1+2	2	1 ⎭	
1	1	EP	1+2	1 ⎫ Stretto	
EP	2	1+2	EP	1+2 ⎭	
2	2	EP	1	Ep	
2	2	1+2	3	1 ⎫ Stretto	
2	EP	1+2	3	1+2 ⎭	
EP	2	EP	3	1+2	
1+2	EP	1+2	EP	EP	
EP	1+2	EP	1	1+2	
1 (inv)	1+2	1	1+2+3	1	
1+2	EP	EP	EP	1+2	
EP	1+2	1+2	1+2+3	1+2	
1+2	EP	EP	EP	1+2	
EP	1+2	1+2	2	1+2	
1+2	EP	Coda	1+2+3	1 ⎫	
1+2	1+2		Coda	1 ⎬ Stretto	
Coda	Coda			1 ⎭	
				Coda	

15

Group 8: Fugues
for Five Voices

I.4, 22

Our final group consists of two fugues whose only point of similarity is that they are both for five voices. Otherwise, they are different in almost all respects. The C♯ minor fugue (**I.4**) has its first group of entries in ascending order. Its main subject is later joined by two subsidiary subjects, as in the three voices fugue **II.14**. The chief events of the fugue are the various permutations of the three subjects, and the stretto passages made out of two of them. The B♭ minor fugue (**I.22**) has its first group of entries in descending order and its single subject dominates the fugue almost to the exclusion of any other material. Its chief events are two passages of stretto involving all five voices.

I.4: FUGUE IN C♯ MINOR

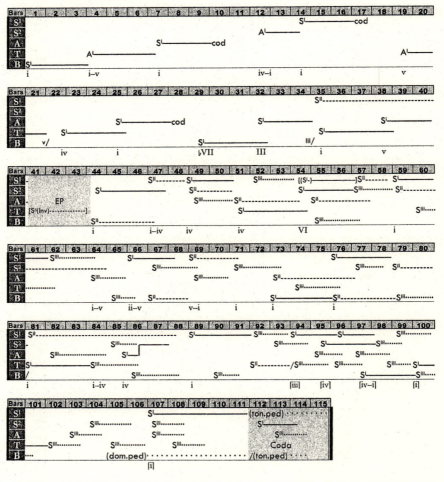

Exposition of first subject (Sⁱ)

1–4: Sⁱ in bass, i
4–7: Aⁱ [real] in tenor, v
7–10: Sⁱ in alto, i
10–12: codetta
12–14: Aⁱ in soprano 2, iv–i
14–17: Sⁱ in soprano 1, i
17–19: codetta

Counterexposition of Sⁱ

19–22: Aⁱ in tenor, v
22–25: Sⁱ in tenor, iv
25–28: Sⁱ in alto, i

28–29: codetta
29–32: Sⁱ in bass, ♭VII
32–35: Sⁱ in alto, III

Entrance of second subject (Sⁱⁱ) and combination of Sⁱ and Sⁱⁱ

35–38: Sⁱ in tenor, Sⁱⁱ in soprano 1, i
38–41: Sⁱ in alto, Sⁱⁱ in soprano 1, v
41–44: episode
44–47: Sⁱ in soprano 2, Sⁱⁱ in bass, i
47–49: Sⁱⁱ in soprano 1, i–iv

cont.

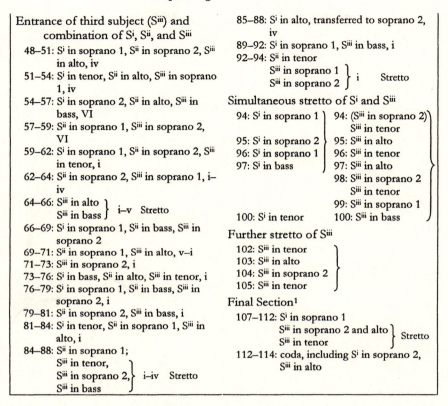

Entrance of third subject (S^iii) and combination of S^i, S^ii, and S^iii

48–51: S^i in soprano 1, S^ii in soprano 2, S^iii in alto, iv

51–54: S^i in tenor, S^ii in alto, S^iii in soprano 1, iv

54–57: S^i in soprano 2, S^ii in alto, S^iii in bass, VI

57–59: S^ii in soprano 1, S^iii in soprano 2, VI

59–62: S^i in soprano 1, S^ii in soprano 2, S^iii in tenor, i

62–64: S^ii in soprano 2, S^iii in soprano 1, i–iv

64–66: S^iii in alto / S^iii in bass } i–v Stretto

66–69: S^i in soprano 1, S^ii in bass, S^iii in soprano 2

69–71: S^ii in soprano 1, S^iii in alto, v–i

71–73: S^iii in soprano 2, i

73–76: S^i in bass, S^ii in alto, S^iii in tenor, i

76–79: S^i in soprano 1, S^ii in bass, S^iii in soprano 2, i

79–81: S^ii in soprano 2, S^iii in bass, i

81–84: S^i in tenor, S^ii in soprano 1, S^iii in alto, i

84–88: S^ii in soprano 1; S^iii in tenor, / S^iii in soprano 2, / S^iii in bass } i–iv Stretto

85–88: S^i in alto, transferred to soprano 2, iv

89–92: S^i in soprano 1, S^iii in bass, i

92–94: S^ii in tenor / S^iii in soprano 1 / S^iii in soprano 2 } i Stretto

Simultaneous stretto of S^i and S^iii

94: S^i in soprano 1 / 94: (S^iii in soprano 2) S^iii in tenor

95: S^i in soprano 2 / 95: S^iii in alto

96: S^i in soprano 1 / 96: S^iii in tenor

97: S^i in bass / 97: S^iii in alto

98: S^iii in soprano 2 / S^iii in tenor

99: S^iii in soprano 1

100: S^i in tenor / 100: S^iii in bass

Further stretto of S^iii

102: S^iii in tenor

103: S^iii in alto

104: S^iii in soprano 2

105: S^iii in tenor

Final Section[1]

107–112: S^i in soprano 1 / S^iii in soprano 2 and alto / S^iii in tenor } Stretto

112–114: coda, including S^i in soprano 2, S^iii in alto

This very short subject, using only four notes of the scale, is unmistakably in the key of C♯ minor. It demands a real answer, which in itself is just as clearly in the key of G♯ minor. The unsatisfactory implication that the tonality is likely to shift suddenly every three bars or so is very carefully avoided by various means. In the first place the answer overlaps the subject by one note, so that the tonality of i is maintained through bar 4. Second, the answer is so harmonized that its ending in bars 6–7 is already less strongly in the dominant key. The overall tonality of C♯ minor is further strengthened by the codetta of bars 10–12. This leads to an unexpected and unconventional alteration of the answer in bar 12, where the drop of a minor third to e♯′ briefly suggests the subdominant key, thus balancing the dominant of the first answer and reinforcing the sense of the tonic key.

There is no countersubject, but the rich texture is unified by frequent use of the falling scale figure of bar 7 [♩♩♩♩].[2] This figure is inverted by the bass in the codetta of bars 17–19.

The counterexposition of S^i (bars 19–35) is irregular in several respects. Starting with the answer in the tenor, it proceeds to another entry in the tenor, but in the key of iv [f♯], so that the distinction between subject and answer now ceases to have any validity.[3] The alto has the subject in bar 25 in i; from now on there are rapid changes of key. The bass enters at bar 29 in ♭VII [B], and the alto in bar 32 in III [E]. The counterexposition is punctuated by a perfect cadence in v [g♯] after its first entry at bar 22 and by a perfect cadence in III at bar 35.

The tenor entry of S^i of bar 35 is immediately joined by S^{ii} in the first soprano. The rhythm of S^{ii} has already been suggested by bar 26.[4] Its melodic outline is that of a continuously falling scale passage, with one main note in each bar. Each scale step is ornamented by two distinct figures [♩♪♪♩ and ♪♪♪♩], the effect being that of an unbroken falling sequence.[5] Because of its shape (or lack of shape), the same sequence can cover two successive entries of S^i: the tenor of bar 35 and the alto of bar 38.

The single episode starts at bar 41. The soprano alludes to the general shape of S^i, the alto uses the figures of bars 5 and 6, and the tenor inverts the two figures of S^{ii}, dividing its main scale steps into semitones in a rising sequence.

The episode leads to an entry of S^i in the second soprano at bar 44, with S^{ii} in the bass and again in the first soprano at bar 47.

The entrance of S^{iii} in the alto of bar 49 marks the first of nine entries of all the three subjects[6]; S^i is in the first soprano, starting on the last note of bar 48 (its first note now reduced to one-eighth of its original length), and S^{ii} is in the second soprano. In all, five out of the six possible permutations are used in this section of the fugue:

$\left.\begin{array}{l} S^i \\ S^{ii} \\ S^{iii} \end{array}\right\}$ in bars 48–51, 54–57,[7] 59–62.

$\left.\begin{array}{l} S^{ii} \\ S^{iii} \\ S^i \end{array}\right\}$ in bars 73–76, 81–84.

$\left.\begin{array}{l} S^{iii} \\ S^{ii} \\ S^i \end{array}\right\}$ in bars 51–54.

$\left.\begin{array}{l} S^{ii} \\ S^i \\ S^{iii} \end{array}\right\}$ in bars 85–88.[8]

$\left.\begin{array}{l} S^i \\ S^{iii} \\ S^{ii} \end{array}\right\}$ in bars 66–69, 76–79.

$\left[\begin{array}{l} S^{iii} \\ S^i \\ S^{ii} \end{array}\right\}$ not used. $\Big]$

The complete groups of entries are varied by partial combinations: S^{ii} and S^{iii} in bars 57–59,[9] 62–64,[10] 69–71,[11] and 79–81; S^i and S^{iii} in bars 89–92. The third subject is also treated in stretto in bars 64–66,[12] 84–88,[13] and 92–94.

The whole of this section of the fugue is unified by constant use of the figures of S^{ii} and also by the frequent return to the tonic key for certain entries (bars 59, 73, and 89). Between those entries there is a fairly wide range of keys: iv [f♯] in bars 49 and 85, VI [A] in bar 54, and ii [d♯] in bar 66.

From bar 94 onward, S^{ii} disappears from the scene, and the main interest is centered on the simultaneous stretto of S^i and S^{iii}. The two interwoven stretti produce a contrapuntal texture of such complexity that the absence of S^{ii} is hardly noticed. Nor does it seem to matter that of the four entries of S^i in this passage, only the final one (the bass in bar 97) is complete; all the others lack the final note of the subject. The tenor entry in bar 100 is hardly part of the stretto, since it overlaps only the last note of the bass entry and uses only the first three notes of S^i (though its continuation can be traced in the alto part of bar 102). The entries of S^{iii} are all at one-bar intervals until bar 98, where the tenor enters half a bar after the alto (leaping up a fifth instead of a fourth), followed by the first soprano after half a bar (leaping up a diminished fifth).

A new series of four entries of S^{iii} in stretto begins at bar 102.[14] The last of these, in the tenor at bar 105, is extended sequentially to lead into the final section (bars 107–12).[15] A dominant pedal had begun in bar 105, and on this pedal the first soprano brings back S^i, extending the entry to the cadence at bar 112. S^i is joined in bar 107 by a simultaneous entry of S^{iii} in the second soprano and alto, followed by S^{iii} in stretto in the tenor a bar later. This fugue has lacked many perfect cadences, and even the final one at bar 112 is decorated with a suspension in the second soprano and an appoggiatura in the tenor. The **coda** (bars 112–5) that follows is on a tonic pedal with another tonic pedal in the first soprano.[16] Between them the second soprano recalls S^i, and the alto in bar 113 adds a final entry of S^{iii}, with augmentation of its last notes.

I.22: FUGUE IN B♭ MINOR

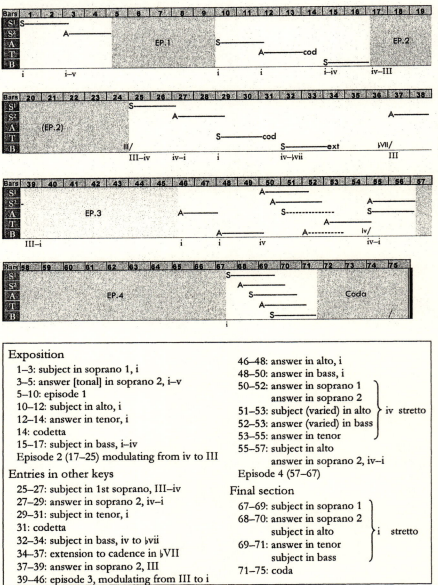

Exposition	
1–3: subject in soprano 1, i	46–48: answer in alto, i
3–5: answer [tonal] in soprano 2, i–v	48–50: answer in bass, i
5–10: episode 1	50–52: answer in soprano 1
10–12: subject in alto, i	answer in soprano 2
12–14: answer in tenor, i	51–53: subject (varied) in alto } iv stretto
14: codetta	52–53: answer (varied) in bass
15–17: subject in bass, i–iv	53–55: answer in tenor
Episode 2 (17–25) modulating from iv to III	55–57: subject in alto
	answer in soprano 2, iv–i
Entries in other keys	Episode 4 (57–67)
25–27: subject in 1st soprano, III–iv	**Final section**
27–29: answer in soprano 2, iv–i	67–69: subject in soprano 1
29–31: subject in tenor, i	68–70: answer in soprano 2
31: codetta	subject in alto } i stretto
32–34: subject in bass, iv to ♭vii	69–71: answer in tenor
34–37: extension to cadence in ♭VII	subject in bass
37–39: answer in soprano 2, III	71–75: coda
39–46: episode 3, modulating from III to i	

There is no countersubject. The tonal answer is accompanied by an inversion of the second half of the subject [♩ ♩ ♩ ♩] and by a new figure of quavers [♪♪ ♩] in bar 4.[17]

Episode 1 (bars 5–10) starts by inverting each of the voices of bar 4 and then changes the direction of the new figure in order to introduce a canon at the lower fourth.[18]

The other entries of the exposition are accompanied by the second half of the subject, direct or inverted, and by new versions of the quaver figure of bar 4 [♩♩ ♩].

Episode 2 (bars 17–25) develops the material of the first episode, modulating to III [D♭].

At bar 25 the first soprano begins the subject in III but leaps up a tenth as in the tonal answer, thus producing a modulation to iv [e♭]. The bass entry of the subject in bar 32 has a similar effect, starting in iv and ending on the dominant of ♭VII [i.e. E♭].[19] The codetta at bar 34 extends the phrase toward a cadence in ♭VII minor [a♭] at bar 37. Another *tierce de Picardie* at this point turns the ♭VII into the dominant of III, for the entry of the answer in the second soprano.[20]

Episode 3 (bars 39–46) starts by using the second bar of the subject, both direct and inverted, and goes on to a three-part version of the canon in the first episode. (The two canonic voices are the bass and the second soprano, interchanging the voices of episode 1.)

At bar 46 the alto has a syncopated entry of the answer in i, followed two bars later by the bass.

At bar 50 we hear the first of two stretti. The first soprano, second soprano, and alto enter at half-bar intervals; the entries of bass and tenor are separated by a whole bar. While the general effect is that of a complete stretto, it should be noticed that the entries of alto and bass are irregular.[21] The key is iv [e♭].

The stretto is followed by a simultaneous entry of tonal answer and subject in the second soprano and alto; with the upward leap they reverse their roles.

Episode 4 (bars 57–67) develops the material of episode 2.

The final section starts at bar 67, where the second stretto begins with the first soprano. From the beginning of bar 68 every minim does double duty, as the second note of one entry and the first note of the following entry. The short coda (bar 72) alludes to both figures of the subject.

16

Episodes (2)

Now that all the fugues of the "48" have been examined, we are able to review the episodes in fuller detail than was possible in Chapter 8. A knowledge of all the episodes throws new light on many aspects of Bach's craftsmanship, without invalidating any of the main principles that were established in the earlier chapter.

In the analyses of the fugues the term "codetta" or "extension" was used to describe certain passages where the subject as such was absent.[1] The term "episode" was reserved for those passages, generally longer, of definite character in which there was significant development of thematic material.

In the entire "48" there are well over 200 passages long enough and important enough to rank as episodes.

A fugue may have no episode at all (**I.1**) or may have any number from one to nine. A long fugue does not necessarily have more episodes than a short fugue; **II.19** is twenty-nine bars long and has seven episodes, while **II.17** is fifty bars long and has only two. Nor does the prevalence of stretto in a fugue mean that episodes are unimportant; they are still treated with the same care as in a purely episodic fugue.

An episode can fulfill several purposes. At its simplest it is a passage that gives relief to an otherwise continuous series of entries of the subject. It also serves as the chief means of obtaining modulation to other keys. In addition, the episodes of a fugue can have an effect similar to that of the development section of a movement in sonata form. This is especially noticeable in the longer episodes, such as **I.3** (bars 28–42), and **II.11** (bar 25–52), but no less true in other cases, where a process of development is often begun in one episode and continued in another. Bach's fugues always display a sensitive balance between the opposite principles of unity and diversity. A fugue with few episodes might seem to be most easily unified; diversity is gained by change of pitch or key for the entries and by treatment of the subject through augmentation, diminution, inversion, or stretto. We might expect a fugue with many episodes to show more diversity than unity; but the diversity is always kept within bounds. Bach achieves this most often by using his episodes to develop melodic figures that have first been heard in the exposition (i.e., figures derived from the subject or answer, the countersubject, a "free part," or a codetta). Occasionally (notably in **I.24**), he introduces completely new melodic material into an episode, but when he does this, he is careful to repeat this material in later episodes. Even when melodic figures seem to be new ones, they can often be found to have some connection, however slight, with what has gone before. Or completely new figures are supported by an accompaniment that uses earlier figures. The main patterns of all the episodes of the "48" are shown in outline form in Appendix A on page 185.

SEQUENCE

Almost all episodes make use of sequence. From the melodic point of view the commonest type of sequence is the simple falling sequence, where a melodic figure is repeated a step lower down the scale. A far smaller number of episodes use the simple rising sequence, where a figure is repeated a step higher up the scale. In a few episodes a melodic figure is repeated a third or fourth higher or lower, usually the latter.

A melodic sequence is nearly always supported by a harmonic sequence (i.e., a repeated pattern of chord progressions). Thus, a simple rising sequence is harmonized by chords whose roots alternately rise a fourth and fall a third. A simple falling sequence is harmonized by chords whose roots all fall a fifth or rise a fourth.

An episode is sometimes described as a "continuation" of a previous episode. By this is meant not a literal continuation, as if one might cut out all the passage of entry between two episodes, but a return in one episode to the sort of development process that had been started in a previous episode. The material of an episode is sometimes "extended" in a later episode (e.g., a sequence is repeated but lengthened the second time).

IMITATION AND CANON

Imitation, in one form or another, is used in almost all episodes. A melodic figure is presented by one voice and then repeated by another voice. When the figures are of the same general shape, we call it imitation; when the melodic intervals are the same (though not necessarily of the same quality), we call it canon. Two or more voices may start in canon and go on in imitation, or they may start in imitation and go on in canon. There is no clear dividing line, since Bach himself frequently made alterations for the sake of euphony in pieces that he called canons. Textbooks on fugue often state that one of the episodes (the final one?) should be in canon, but this is not a rule with Bach, who uses canon or quasi canon as and when he feels inclined or avoids it altogether. The following list includes a number of effective passages of canon in the episodes:

I.2 (bars 9–11)   II.1 (bars 33–39)
  13 (bars 23–24)   5 (bars 7–10, etc.)
  18 (bars 21–24)   7 (bars 45–53)
  20 (bars 71–73)   9 (bars 12–16)
  22 (bars 5–10)   10 (bars 37–41)
  24 (bars 7–9; 16–21)   11 (bars 9–14)
                                         14 (bars 47–49)
                                         20 (bars 11–13; 19–21)
                                         22 (bars 62–66)
                                         24 (bars 21–26)

Most of the passages in canon are of the type known as "2 in 1" or more often "2 in 1 with a free part." The interval of canon can vary greatly. The short canons in the "48" use the intervals of the lower ninth, the octave, the lower seventh, the lower fifth or upper fourth, the lower fourth or upper fifth, the lower third or upper sixth.

INTERCHANGE

The frequent use of this term in the analyses points to the importance of this device. At least thirty of the fugues use interchange in one or more episodes. In some fugues it is the main principle of all the episodes.

Interchange (also known as "harmonic inversion") is evident in many fugues before the end of the exposition, since an effective countersubject is designed in such a way that it sounds equally well above or below the answer (or subject), which is another way of saying that either tune can make a good bass to the other. In fugues that have two countersubjects the harmonic intervals between the subject and the two countersubjects are so organized that any one of the three voices can be used as bass below the other two, without causing harmonic confusion. With any one voice in the bass the other two voices can be used in either of two positions, so that there are theoretically six possible permutations of such passages of triple counterpoint. The principle of interchange operates in a similar way in many of the episodes, with some special features that are peculiar to episodes.

Simple Interchange of Two Voices

This is most clearly illustrated by the first and third episode of **I.10**. The third episode, starting at bar 24, is a complete interchange of the voices of the first episode, starting at bar 5 (there is one small difference, noted in the commentary on this fugue, which does not invalidate the principle).

Simple Interchange of Two Voices, with Addition of a Third Voice

This can be found in the second episode of **I.21**, beginning at bar 33, where there is a reversal of the voices of the first episode (bar 17), together with a third part. Another example is the fourth episode of **I.2**, beginning at bar 17, which uses the two voices of the first episode (bar 5) in reversed position, with the addition of the first subject figure in tenths. The interchange in this example is at the twelfth, instead of the more common octave or fifteenth.

Simple Interchange within an Episode

I.10 uses this plan in the second episode, beginning at bar 15. Each bar is an interchange (at different pitch) of the previous bar. The fourth episode, beginning at bar 34, uses the same idea and is also a complete interchange of the second episode.

Interchange of Upper Voices

This is extremely common as a means of linking two episodes. In **II.12** the third episode, beginning at bar 33, uses the same material as the second episode, beginning at bar 17: the bass is identical, but the two upper voices have reversed their positions. Interchange of upper voices can also occur during a single episode as in **II.17**, bar 10, where the upper voices are interchanged after a bar and a half, above an unchanging bass.

Triple Counterpoint

The same fugue (**II.17**) has a splendid example of this in the second episode, beginning halfway through bar 27. After a bar and a half all three voices change their position. After another bar and a half they once more change their positions. The pattern is like this:

$$3\ 1\ 2$$
$$2\ 3\ 1$$
$$1\ 2\ 3$$

That is, the voices are interchanged in cyclic order.

Even more remarkable is the fact that the whole of the second episode is a development and extension of the first episode of bar 10.

The same principle of interchange of three voices can be found in short and very clear examples in three of the episodes of **I.17** (bars 11, 14, and 19). In these episodes different pairs of voices are interchanged at different intervals, resulting in fascinating changes of harmony.

A more complex example of interchange occurs in **II.13**.[2] In the first episode (bars 12–20) every alternate bar is written in triple interchangeable counterpoint (i.e., bars 13, 15, 17, and 19). The same material is used in similar fashion in the third episode, beginning at bar 44.

THE CONTEXT OF EPISODES

While we can examine episodes in isolation or in relation to each other, they have no real meaning outside their context. An episode sometimes seems to start abruptly (after some sort of cadence) or to end abruptly (with a cadence before an entry), but it is more common to find that an episode grows naturally out of the end of an entry and/or leads naturally into the following entry. We can examine some examples of how this is done.

The Beginning of an Episode

During the exposition we have become accustomed (in many of the fugues) to the sound of a voice leading straight from the subject or answer into the countersubject. The exposition is finished when the last voice has completed the subject (or answer). The most natural way to lead into the following episode is to use the countersubject after the last entry of the exposition, accompanying it with figures from the subject or with new figures. This plan seems to work especially well when the bass is the last voice to enter during the exposition.

This is the plan used in **I.11**:

```
Exposition        Episode
     A——C        (figure development)
S——C      Free
          S——C
```

While it is quite common to use the whole countersubject in this way, Bach sometimes uses only the first figure of a countersubject in order to start an episode, and it is not necessarily in the same voice as that which has just completed the subject or answer. The exposition of **I.12** is punctuated by an episode after the entry of the bass (this is a four-part fugue, in which the soprano has not yet made its first appearance) and starts this episode with the first figure of the countersubject in the alto:

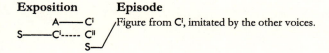

```
Exposition        Episode
     A——C^i      /Figure from C^i, imitated by the other voices.
S——C^i----- C^ii /
          S——/
```

A very smooth join into the beginning of an episode can be made by repeating in sequence the final figure of a subject entry, when the shape of the figure lends itself to the use of sequence. In **II.19** every one of the seven episodes is started in this way. In **I.18** not only the final figure of the subject but also its three accompanying voices are repeated in rising sequence to lead into episode 1 (bar 9) and again in falling sequence to lead into episode 2 (bar 13).

The End of an Episode

Just as important is the smooth joining of an episode into the following entry. When a voice enters with the subject after rests, the other voices often continue their episodic figures until after the beginning of the entry. If there is a cadence, it is made not before the entry but just after its beginning. This can be noticed in **I.18** at the end of episode 3: the episode clearly ends with the cadence of bar 24, thus overlapping the soprano entry. A similar example occurs in **I.9**, where the second episode ends with the cadence of bar 17, overlapping the entry in the middle voice at bar 16.

Very often an episode can use the opening figure of the subject, repeating it in sequence to lead into the following entry. Two outstanding examples can be found in **I.2**. The second episode, beginning at bar 9, treats the opening figure of the subject in two-part canon and in falling sequence. The second soprano note in bar 11 is the beginning of an entry, which is also part of the episodic sequence. Just as effective is the rising sequence of episode 4, beginning at bar 17, where the opening figure of the subject in the soprano is led in sequence into the actual entry at bar 20.

The foregoing examples have been chosen because of their clarity; they can be matched by countless examples of similar plans in other fugues.

17

Tonality in the "48"

Tonality is concerned with the establishment of a key, the modulation to other keys, and the final sense of return to the main key. The control of tonality can present a problem in the composition of any piece of music; in writing a fugue, the problem can be a very great one. Any attempt at fugal composition that ignores the problem of tonality may produce fugues of a sort, but they will be unsatisfying, even though they may be packed full of all the scholarly devices of counterpoint. In this, as in all aspects of fugal composition, we can learn from Bach whatever we need to know. His principles may sometimes be hard to follow, and they do not always seem to correspond in every respect with rules laid down in textbooks.

FUGUES ON NONMODULATING SUBJECTS: ESTABLISHING THE MAIN KEY

A sonata movement starts by establishing its main key before modulating into any other key (e.g., the dominant). In the exposition of a fugue the main key must be just as firmly established before radical departure is made from it. This is not necessarily as easy as it sounds, since the fugal convention does seem to suggest a swinging from tonic key to dominant key and back. In spite of this apparent vacillation Bach does manage to make the tonic key sound as if it really *is* the main key.

In a three-voice fugue the very fact that up to two-thirds of the exposition involves the subject in the main key ought in itself to establish that key firmly enough, even if the answer has been harmonized in the key of the dominant. But it is normally only in a fugue on a long subject (forming a complete phrase) that Bach uses the dominant key from the very beginning of the answer (viz., **I.15; II.10, 12,** and **13**).[1] With a shorter subject he is usually most careful to avoid the sense of sudden change to the dominant key at the beginning of the answer. Even a real answer, whenever possible, is harmonized in the tonic key for its first few notes (viz., **I.5, 9; II.4, 6, 18, 19**). A tonal answer frequently gives the sense of remaining in the tonic key for much of its length, even for the whole of its length, if the subject did not use the leading-note (viz., **I.2, 3, 8, 11, 13, 17, 19, 21, 23; II.1, 2, 11, 14, 15, 21, and 24**).

In a four-voice exposition the control of tonality may appear to present a greater problem if we use the conventional order of entry "subject–answer–subject–answer." Even when tonic harmony has been retained for the beginning of the answer (thus keeping most of the exposition in the tonic key), Bach is often reluctant to end the exposition with the dominant key. More often he prefers to end the exposition with the tonic key still firmly established before moving into other keys. This he manages in various ways. After the fourth voice has completed its entry of the answer, he either adds at least one redundant entry of the subject (viz., **I.17, 23; II.7, 9, 16, 22, and 23**)[2] or he restores the sense of the main key during an episode, only then modulating into a related key (viz., **I.16; II.5, and 8**). Alternatively, he establishes the main key more firmly by adapting an unconventional order of entries within the exposition. Thus, **I.1** has the order "subject–answer–answer–subject," and **I.12** and **I.14** have the order "subject–answer–subject–subject." Either of these allows immediate modulation to a related key, since the main key is maintained up to the end of the exposition.

MODULATION INTO OTHER KEYS

The exposition has asserted the main key, varied by reference to the dominant key. At the end of the exposition the main key is still unchallenged. From this point onward real modulation can take place. Writers of textbooks, no doubt with the best of intentions, have suggested a small number of keys that ought to be used in the middle section of a fugue; for example, a fugue in a major key ought to modulate to vi and then to IV; a fugue in a minor key ought to modulate to III and then to iv. Within the limited time of an examination a simple scheme may have to suffice, but in learning the craft of fugal composition, it is surely wise to try some of the many patterns of modulation that Bach himself used. The list is impressive!

Modulation from a major tonic:	**Modulation from a minor tonic:**
vi	III iv (i) iv III (i) iv
vi (I) ii	III iv VI ♭vii (i) ♭VII
vi (I, V) ii (V) IV	III (v, i) iv
vi ii (I, V) IV ii vi	III (v) IV III (i) iv VI (i) iv III VI III VI iv
vi ii (I) IV (I) iii (I) IV	III ♭vii iv (i) ♭vii iv
vi iii	iv
vi iii (I) IV	

vi iii v ii IV   iv (i) III (v) IV (i) iv
vi IV   iv (i, v, i) iv ♭vii III (i) iv
vi IV ii   iv (i, v) VI
vi IV (I) IV ii   iv III VI (i) iv (i) ♭vii VI
ii   iv ♭VII III iv (v, i) iv
ii (I) vi   ♭VII III (i, v) iv VI
ii vi (I) vi iii (I) IV   ♭VII III iv (i, v, i) III iv ♭VII (i) iv (i) VI

The thought of following Bach in some of these complex patterns of modulation may be somewhat daunting; in spite of all the evidence for his delight in modulation, it is also a fact that some of the most expressive fugues use no modulation at all or hardly any (e.g., **I.14** and **II.6**).

THE RETURN TO THE MAIN KEY

Tonality is a matter of relationships; the listener is not expected to possess absolute pitch. Therefore, the final section must be so planned as to give clear indication of having finished with modulation. The main key must be once more established. This is done in a variety of ways.

If there is only one entry of the subject in the final section, it must be immediately recognizable as the last important event in the fugue. The episode leading to the final entry can be a recapitulation of an earlier episode (which in itself may give a sense of returning home to the tonic) or noticeably climactic in character, culminating in the entry of the subject (which may be in any voice). The entry is almost always followed by a coda, however short. Bach also uses other devices in order to underline the importance of the single final entry; it is often preceded by a dominant pedal, or it enters on a dominant pedal. It may be enriched by added thirds or by chromatic ornamentation, or it may be harmonized in a new way. The coda will frequently include a tonic pedal, on which extra voices are introduced in a more harmonic than contrapuntal style, sometimes with further allusion to the subject. Irrespective of the number of keys used in the middle section, a single final entry of the subject can be fully sufficient to restore the main key (viz., **I.12, 13, 17, 21; II.10, 12, 15, 16, 19, 20, 23,** and **24**).[3]

Bach also ends certain fugues with two entries of the subject in the main key (viz., **I.4, 9; II.8,** and **11**) or even with three (viz., **I.2** and **II.1**). When this can be done without producing a feeling of repetitiveness, it is obviously one of the surest ways of asserting the main tonality of the fugue.

In writing a fugue on a nonmodulating subject, there is sometimes doubt as to the advisability of using the answer in the final section. Bach sometimes brings in the answer toward the end of a fugue, following it with the subject. More interesting is the use of subject and answer in a manner recalling the exposition so that the final section sounds like a recapitulation of the opening (viz., **I.3; II.13,** and **17**). In **I.3** he follows the recapitulation with an extra entry of the subject, and in **II.17** he adds an extra entry of the subject during the coda. In the fugue on three subjects (**II.14**) the effect of an enhanced recapitulation is produced by the combination of all three subjects in the tonic, the dominant, and finally the tonic key.

Bach occasionally ends a fugue with the answer rather then the subject. In **I.19** the final entry is that of the answer. It is, however, immediately followed by a coda that recapitulates episode 2 in the tonic key. In **II.21** the final entry is that of the answer; it is modified in shape and so harmonized that it sounds as if it is in the tonic key.[4] A similar device is used in **I.23**, where the last two entries are those of subject and answer, in that order, but the answer is harmonized in the tonic key and is followed by a coda, which leaves no doubt of the main tonality.

FUGUES ON MODULATING SUBJECTS

The term "modulating subject" is an unfortunate one, but it is likely to remain in use. It is unfortunate because it gives a wrong impression, suggesting that there is a real change of key during an unaccompanied melody a few bars long. The term, in fact, has a special meaning in the jargon of fugalists, rather different from its usual meaning. A real modulation in music occurs when a key has first been firmly established, and it normally involves the use of a pivot chord. The key to which modulation is made must be defined by a cadence. When any of these conditions are missing, we ought properly to speak of a transition rather than a modulation. With these facts in mind we can now examine the four examples in the "48" from the point of view of their tonality.

Example 1: I.7

The first half of the subject (as far as the rest) is assumed to be in the key of E♭. The a♮′ immediately suggests the key of B♭, and this impression is strengthened by the stepwise descent to b♭′. From the fugal point of view it therefore ranks as a modulating subject. But it is altogether too short a passage for the key of B♭ to displace the key of E♭, which is restored (if indeed it was ever in doubt) by the A♭ in the codetta. When we arrive at bar 3, the feeling is that we have never left the key of E♭ at all. If that impression can be made by a single melodic line, it is made even more clearly by the two-part harmony of bars 3–4, where the answer is entirely in the main key. With the bass entry of the subject in bar 6 Bach carefully avoids the effect of a real move into the dominant key by the d♭″ in the countersubject and by the inverted cadence in bar 7. The main key is still supreme in the following episode and in the redundant entry of the answer in bar 11.

Real modulation begins in the third episode (bar 12), and it is fairly obvious by bar 15 that its direction is toward the key of C minor. This modulation is made explicit by the first perfect cadence of the fugue, in bar 17. The choice of answer rather than subject for the following entry means that harmony in the key of C minor can be retained. In bar 20 the bass has the subject, beginning in C minor, and "modulating" to its dominant, G minor, but without a perfect cadence.

The fifth episode, bar 22, certainly starts as if it were in G minor, but by its sequential pattern and the fact that its main chords are all in the key of E♭ (decorated by local dominants), we are once more, by implication, in the main key.

The impression of the main key is strengthened by another entry of the answer in the bass at the last note of bar 25, reproducing in three-part counterpoint the original passage of answer in bar 3. From now on there is no sense of any other key than E♭. Even the perfect cadence at the end of the subject entry beginning on the last soprano note of bar 28 sounds in its context like the dominant chord in E♭ rather than the tonic chord in B♭. All the accidentals from now to the end of the fugue (D♭, E♮, A♮, G♭, B♮, C♭) are purely ornamental in their effect. The whole fugue, in fact, is in the key of E♭ major, with one real modulation to its relative minor.

Example 2: I.10

The first impression of this fugue is that it is constantly modulating. The subject begins in E minor and ends in B minor, and the answer begins in B minor and—without any modification of shape—apparently goes on into F♯ minor (with *tierce de Picardie*). The other entries are in G major, D major, A minor, E minor, D minor, A minor, and finally E minor, and yet somehow the final impression is that the main key definitely is E minor. How is the tonality controlled?

While the subject certainly seems to glide almost imperceptibly from E minor into B minor and is therefore to be classed as a "modulating subject," its move into B minor is not begun until the second beat of bar 2 and is made only by the implied chords of dominant and tonic in B minor. If it is a real change of key, it is even less convincing than the modulation at the end of the subject of I.7. In that fugue a codetta immediately reasserted the main key, and the answer was harmonized entirely in the main key. The case here is different; there is no codetta, and the answer at its beginning is harmonized in B minor. Provisionally, we have to accept that there has been a modulation to B minor. Instead of an answer with altered intervals, to lead us back to E minor, there is a real answer, faithfully copying the shape of the subject until the first note of bar 5. If the subject modulated from E minor to B minor, then presumably the real answer modulates from B minor to F♯ minor. But the *A♯* in the bass at bar 5 is more than a *tierce de Picardie*, in the light of the two *a♯*'s in the treble of bar 4. This answer does not modulate away from B minor but ends on the dominant chord in B minor.

The exposition of this two-part fugue is now complete, and it has used two keys, E minor and B minor. In the first episode beginning at bar 5 Bach assumes a control of tonality that at first seemed threatened. This episode is not only found on chords whose roots fall a fifth or rise a fourth, but each of the three main chords (B minor in bar 6, A minor in bar 8, G major in bar 10) is preceded by its own local dominant. From bar 10 to bar 11 there is an implied cadence in G major. What we have, therefore, during the first episode is a modulation to the key of G major, which is the key most likely to be used at the beginning of the middle section of a fugue in E minor. In spite of the passage of B minor in bars 2–4 the overall effect is now that of a conventional modulation from a minor key to its relative major.

From now on, other modulations in this fugue can be understood in the light of the foregoing passage. It is interesting to find that the first perfect cadence, a brief one at bar 13, is to the key of D major (bVII). No other cadences occur until the final one in E minor.

The earlier commentary on this fugue pointed out that it is held together formally by its four episodes, the third being an almost exact interchange of the first, while the fourth is an exact interchange of the second. The episodes also help to control the tonality, since episode 3 repeats episode 1 a fifth lower, and episode 4 repeats episode 2 a fifth higher, thus producing an effect of balance.

If there were any doubt about the tonality of E minor, it would be dispelled by the two entries of the first half of the subject in bars 39 and 40 and the allusion to its second half, without modulation, in the treble of bar 41.

Example 3: I.18

The main key of G♯ minor is firmly set by the first seven notes of the subject. It now moves suddenly into the dominant key, through the distinctive interval of the tritone. The cadential shape of the ending seems to make this a truly modulating subject.

If we examine the answer by itself without the countersubject, we can say that it starts on the dominant; then by the drop of a third to b♯ it is in the subdominant key; it then repeats exactly all the intervals of the subject, so that it ends in the tonic key. A first impression is that this fugue is even more uncertain in its tonality than those that we have recently examined, since three keys are used in the first four bars.

The addition of the countersubject makes the tonality clearer. Even before the answer has finished its allusion to the subdominant key, the countersubject is already moving back into the tonic key. With the entry of the third voice in bar 5, Bach lessens the cadential effect of the subject ending by the tied G♯ in the tenor. The fourth voice has the same effect as the second voice, and the exposition finishes at bar 9 with a reasonably firm adherence to the main key of G sharp minor.

The first episode (bars 9–11) treats the end of the exposition in a sequence of rising thirds, with apparent cadences on III and also v. The redundant answer in bar 11 repeats the effect of the previous entry, ending in the tonic key. The second episode (bars 13–15) matches the first episode with a sequence of falling thirds, with apparent cadences on VI and also iv. The bass entry of bar 15 starts with the subject in iv and therefore ends in i. Thus three successive entries have ended in i, presumably to assert the main tonality without a shadow of doubt. Further modulation can now safely take place.

Example 4: I.24

In spite of using all the notes of the chromatic scale, the subject quite clearly establishes the main key of B minor in its first bar, alludes briefly to the key of E minor, and then modulates to the dominant, F♯ minor. The altered shape of the answer in the third beat of bar 4 already suggests the return to the main key, even though it is not at this moment supported by tonic harmony in the countersubject.

The main tonality of B minor is made even clearer during the first episode (bars 7–9), where the imitative, and later canonic, passage reaches bar 9 with a definite sense of the dominant in the main key. The second episode (bars 12–13) again emphasizes the main key, which is hardly disturbed by the beginning of the answer in the soprano. The exposition ends at bar 16 with a firm sense of B minor, even though there is no cadence at this point. It is surely significant that the semiquaver run at the end of the countersubject in the bass of bar 15 is now imitated in the soprano at the fifteenth. (In bar 7 the imitation was at the lower fifth, in bar 12 at the lower ninth.)

The longer third episode begins from bar 16 to suggest various keys, without establishing any of them (A major, F♯ minor, D major), before moving back into the main key. The "false entry" in the alto at bar 19 can now be regarded in a new light; it is a reminder of the main key, before further modulation is made away from it.

During the course of this long fugue there is a wide range of keys used, including E minor, D major, and E major. But none of these keys are endorsed by a perfect cadence. There are, in fact, only two perfect cadences in the entire fugue: in the dominant at bar 23 and in the tonic in the final bar.

STRETTO FUGUES

Since the exposition of a stretto fugue is not usually any different from that of a nonstretto fugue (with the odd exception of II.3), it presents no special problem in the control of tonality. During the middle section problems may begin to arise, especially when the overlapping entries are a fourth or fifth apart (i.e., in the relationship of subject–answer or answer–subject). Since this, in fact, is the commonest type of stretto, it should be carefully studied from the point of view of tonality in all those fugues where it occurs (viz., I.1, 6, 8, 16, 20, 22; II.2, 3, 5, 6, 7, and 9). In many of these fugues the subject avoids the leading-note and is therefore more flexible in its tonality. When a stretto is formed from the tonal answer closely followed by the subject (as in II.7), the first voice abandons its previous harmonization in the dominant key and adopts the tonality of the second voice. Each voice in a passage of stretto in itself may suggest a different key; the passage as a whole is, of course, harmonized in one key.

While the tonality of the stretto passages of **II.7** is not in doubt, the tonality of certain stretti in other fugues is more difficult to ascertain. This seems to be specially noticeable in **I.8**. Each voice may be striving to maintain its own tonality, and without definite cadences it is sometimes impossible to state categorically that any one key is supreme at certain moments. When there is a genuine doubt about the overall tonality of such a passage of stretto, it can best be regarded not as a specific modulation but rather as a passage of transition between more definite areas of tonality, like many a passage in the development section of a movement in sonata form.

KEYS DEFINED BY PERFECT CADENCES

It was observed early in this survey that perfect cadences are of rare occurrence in the fugues. Their very rarity gives them a special importance. An episode may end with a perfect cadence, synchronizing with the next entry of subject or answer, or an entry (or a group of entries) may end with a perfect cadence. While these are the points at which we would expect to find cadences, other moments are sometimes used instead; for example, a perfect cadence can occur in the middle of an episode or in the middle of an entry. Wherever they occur, it is certain that they serve to define the main tonal areas of a fugue, and that tonality is controlled by the cadences more than by the nominal keys of the entries.

While passages in the fugues may seem to range at times through distant keys, those keys are never rounded off with perfect cadences. Without exception, perfect cadences are reserved for the keys most clearly related to the main key.

KEYS OF PERFECT CADENCES

From a major tonic:

I IV I
I V I
I V iii I
I VI ii V ii vi I

V I (two fugues)
V I I
V I IV iii I
V ii I (two fugues)
V ii iii I V I
V ii V I
V iii I

From a minor tonic:

i i
i v i

III i i
III i III VI VI i
III i v i
III v i i
III v ii VI i
III ♭VII i iv i
III ♭VII iv i

v i (three fugues)

V IV vi V I   v i i
V V vi I   v i i v i
V vi I   v ii i
V vi iii I   v III i
V vi IV ii I I   v III i i (two fugues)
                               v iv i i
vi ii I   v v i
vi ii V I   v ♭VII i III iv i
vi ii V iii I
vi iii I I   ♭VII i (two fugues)
vi V I (two fugues)

Conclusion

The student who has worked his way through even a few of the fugues in each group, on the lines suggested by the analyses and commentaries, will have acquired some understanding of the almost unlimited possibilities of fugal composition. At every stage of study these wonderful examples can guide the student in his or her own efforts. Even if progress is slow, a legitimate pride can be taken in the gradual mastery of this specialized type of musical thought, with the intellectual challenge of solving more and more complex fugal problems.

The "48" represent only a small part of Bach's enormous output of compositions in fugal style, but in them can be found most things that a student needs to know about fugue. To make even a modest acquaintance with the "48" takes some time; to acquire an intimate knowledge of all that is in them may take a very long time.

A fugue of a sort—even a fugue good enough to pass an examination—can no doubt be written as a mere intellectual exercise. The value of Bach's examples is that they are not mere intellectual exercises but real pieces of music, each one conveying its own distinct variety of mood, all of them expressing a wide range of emotion. It was to this end that Bach directed all his consummate craftsmanship. The student who conscientiously tries to follow Bach's lines of thought may hope to catch something of his creative joy.

Appendix A: Episodes

NUMBER OF EPISODES IN EACH FUGUE

I.1	0	II.1	4
I.2	5	II.2	1
		II.Pr.3	1
I.3	6	II.3	2
I.4	1	II.4	6
I.5	2	II.5	5
I.6	4	II.6	3
I.Pr.7	3		
I.7	7	II.7	1
I.8	1	II.8	3
I.9	4	II.9	1
I.10	4	II.10	5
I.11	3	II.11	5
I.12	7	II.12	5
I.13	5	II.13	4
I.Pr.14	5		
I.14	3	II.14	5
I.15	6	II.15	2
I.16	2	II.16	6
I.17	6	II.17	2
I.18	5	II.18	9
I.Pr.19	2		
I.19	2	II.19	7
I.20	2	II.20	6
I.21	2	II.21	8
I.22	4	II.22	7
I.23	3	II.23	7
I.24	9	II.24	7

FUGUES WITH ONE EPISODE

I.4 (bars 41–44): S^{ii} figures in rising sequence
I.8 (bars 15–19):   development of figure from "free part"
II.2 (bars 5–7):   development of S figure
II.Pr.3 (bars 10–13): S figure in two-part imitation
II.7 (bars 43–53):   codetta and S figures, with two-part canon
II.9 (bars 12–16):   C figure in two-part canons

FUGUES WITH TWO EPISODES

I.5	EP.1 (bars 9–11):	S and codetta figures
	EP.2 (bars 17–23):	interchange of EP.1; development of S figure; allusion to EP.1
I.16	EP.1 (bars 8–12):	S figure in three-part imitation
	EP.2 (bars 24–28):	development of EP.1
I.Pr.19	EP.1 (bars 6–8):	S^i and S^{ii} figures
	EP.2 (bars 14–17):	S^{ii} and codetta figures
I.19	EP.1 (bars 29–31):	S and C figures, with interchange
	EP.2 (bars 36–39):	development of EP.1
I.20	EP.1 (bars 40–43):	S, C and codetta figures
	EP.1 (bars 71–73):	free inversion of alto of EP.1, in two-part canon
I.21	EP.1 (bars 17–22):	S figures
	EP.2 (bars 30–35):	interchange of EP.1, with further interchange
II.3	EP.1 (bars 12–14):	S figure and suspensions
	EP.2 (bars 19–24):	free interchange and development of EP.1
II.15	EP.1 (bars 23–33):	S and "C" figures in two-part imitation
	EP.2 (bars 45–62):	S and "C" figures in three-part imitation
II.17	EP.1 (bars 10–13):	S, C^i and C^{ii} figures, with interchange of upper voices
	EP.2 (bars 27–32):	interchange of EP.1

FUGUES WITH THREE EPISODES

I.Pr.7	EP.1 (bars 31–35):	S^i and S^{ii} figures in imitation
	EP.2 (bars 44–45):	S^{ii} figures in imitation
	EP.3 (bars 51–52):	S^{ii} figures in imitation
I.11	EP.1 (bars 13–17):	$\left(\begin{array}{l} \text{new figure in two-part imitation} \\ \text{C figure} \end{array} \right)$
	EP.2 (bars 31–36):	$\left(\begin{array}{l} \text{S figure (a) in two-part imitation} \\ \text{S figure (b)} \end{array} \right)$
	EP.3 (bars 56–64):	development of EP.2, with interchange
I.14	EP.1 (bars 11–15):	development of codetta
	EP.2 (bars 18–20):	codetta + added voice; C figure in three-part imitation
	EP.3 (bars 35–37):	C figure in tenths and sixths
I.23	EP.1 (bars 9–11):	S and C figures

	EP.2 (bars 13–16):	interchange of EP.1, with added voice
	EP.3 (bars 26–29):	repeat and extension of EP.1
II.6	EP.1 (bars 8–10):	end of entry repeated with interchange
	EP.2 (bars 12–14):	interchange of EP.1
	EP.3 (bars 18–25):	S figure in three-part imitation; allusion to EP.1
II.8	EP.1 (bars 5–7):	S figures
	EP.2 (bars 11–15):	development of EP.1
	EP.3 (bars 35–40):	development of EP.1

FUGUES WITH FOUR EPISODES

I.6	EP.1 (bars 10–13):	end of entry repeated in sequence
	EP.2 (bars 25–27):	S and C figures
	EP.3 (bars 31–34):	interchange of EP.1
	EP.4 (bars 36–39):	S and C figures
I.9	EP.1 (bars 5–6):	$\begin{pmatrix} \text{new figure in two - part imitation} \\ \text{S figure} \end{pmatrix}$
	EP.2 (bars 11–16):	development of EP.1, with interchange
	EP.3 (bars 17–19):	development of EP.1
	EP.4 (bars 22–25):	interchange of EP.2
I.10	EP.1 (bars 5–11):	S and C figures
	EP.2 (bars 15–19):	S and C figures with interchange
	EP.3 (bars 24–29):	interchange of EP.1
	EP.4 (bars 34–38):	interchange of EP.1
I.22	EP.1 (bars 5–10):	S and "C" figures in two-part canon
	EP.2 (bars 17–25):	S figures in imitation
	EP.3 (bars 39–46):	allusion to EP.2; interchange of EP.1
	EP.4 (bars 57–67):	allusion to EP.2
II.1	EP.1 (bars 13–22):	$\begin{pmatrix} \text{S figure in two - part imitation} \\ \text{"C" figure} \end{pmatrix}$
	EP.2 (bars 29–39):	$\begin{pmatrix} \text{S figure} \\ \text{"C" figure} \end{pmatrix}$ with interchange
	EP.3 (bars 43–47):	$\begin{pmatrix} \text{new figure in two - part imitation} \\ \text{"C" figure} \end{pmatrix}$
	EP.4 (bars 55–68):	repeat of EP.1; $\begin{pmatrix} \text{suspensions} \\ \text{"C" figure} \end{pmatrix}$
II.13	EP.1 (bars 12–20):	S and C figures, with interchange
	EP.2 (bars 24–32):	S figures
	EP.3 (bars 44–52):	interchange of EP.1
	EP.4 (bars 56–64):	interchange of EP.2

FUGUES WITH FIVE EPISODES

I. 2	EP.1 (bars 5–7):	$\begin{pmatrix} \text{S figure} \\ \text{C}^i \text{ figure} \end{pmatrix}$

	EP.2 (bars 9–11):	$\begin{pmatrix} \text{S figure in two - part canon} \\ \text{C}^i \text{ figure} \end{pmatrix}$
	EP.3 (bars 13–15):	$\begin{pmatrix} \text{C}^i \text{ figure } (= \text{bass of EP.2}) \\ \text{C}^{ii} \text{ figure} \end{pmatrix}$
	EP.4 (bars 17–20):	interchange of EP.1, with further interchange
	EP.5 (bars 22–26):	interchange of EP.2; allusion to EP.1
I.13:	EP.1 (bars 7–11):	new figure (a) in three-part imitation.
	EP.2 (bars 13–15):	$\begin{pmatrix} \text{S figure in two - part imitation} \\ \text{development of (a)} \end{pmatrix}$
	EP.3 (bars 17–20):	interchange of EP.1
	EP.4 (bars 23–28):	interchange of EP.1
	EP.5 (bars 30–31):	development of EP.2
I.Pr.14	EP.1 (bars 3–4):	$\begin{pmatrix} \text{C figure} \\ \text{S figure} \end{pmatrix}$ with interchange
	EP.2 (bars 5–6):	variant of EP.1
	EP.3 (bars 8–9):	development of EP.1
	EP.4 (bars 10–12):	development of EP.1
	EP.5 (bars 16–19):	development of EP.1
I.18	EP.1 (bars 9–11):	end of entry repeated in rising sequence
	EP.2 (bars 13–15):	end of entry repeated in falling sequence
	EP.3 (bars 21–24):	new figure in two-part canon, with free part
	EP.4 (bars 28–32):	interchange of EP.3
	EP.5 (bars 34–37):	allusion to Epp.1 and 2
II.5	EP.1 (bars 7–10):	S figure in canon and imitation
	EP.2 (bars 16–21):	development of EP.1
	EP.3 (bars 29–33):	development of EP.1
	EP.4 (bars 35–40):	development of EP.1
	EP.5 (bars 41–43):	development of EP.1
II.10	EP.1 (bars 18–23):	$\begin{pmatrix} \text{S figure (a) in two - part imitation} \\ \text{S figure (b)} \end{pmatrix}$
	EP.2 (bars 35–41):	figure (b) in three-part imitation
	EP.3 (bars 47–49):	as EP.1
	EP.4 (bars 55–59)	development of EP.1
	EP.5 (bars 65–70):	allusion to EP.1 and 2
II.11	EP.1 (bars 9–14):	S figure (a) in two-part canon
	EP.2 (bars 18–21):	S figure (b) in three-part imitation
	EP.3 (bars 25–52):	development of EP.2; allusion to EP.1
	EP.4 (bars 56–66):	variant of EP.1
	EP.5 (bars 70–85):	allusion to Epp.1 and 2
II.12	EP.1 (bars 8–11):	$\begin{pmatrix} \text{"C" figure} \\ \text{S figure (a)} \end{pmatrix}$
	EP.2 (bars 17–24):	$\begin{pmatrix} \text{S figure (b)} \\ \text{"C" figure} \end{pmatrix}$ with interchange
	EP.3 (bars 33–40):	interchange of EP.2
	EP.4 (bars 44–50):	variant of EP.1
	EP.5 (bars 54–71):	S figure (b); allusion to EP.2

II.14   EP.1 (bars 11–16):   S^{i} figure (a) in three-part imitation
         EP.2 (bars 31–34):   figure (a) + "C" figure + S^{ii} figure
         EP.3 (bars 39–51):   S^{iii} figure + figure (a); allusion to EP.1
         EP.4 (bars 57–60):   figure (a) in two-part imitation + S^{iii} figure
         EP.5 (bars 63–65):   variant of EP.4

Fugues with six episodes

I.3   EP.1 (bars 7–10): $\left(\begin{array}{c} \text{S figure (a)} \\ \text{C}^{i}\text{ figure} \end{array} \right)$ in two-part imitation

         EP.2 (bars 12–14):   interchange of EP.1
         EP.3 (bars 16–19):   development of EP.1
         EP.4 (bars 22–24):   S figure (b)
         EP.5 (bars 28–42):   development of Epp.1 and 4
         EP.6 (bars 48–51):   variant of EP.1

I.15   EP.1 (bars 17–19): $\left(\begin{array}{c} \text{C figure} \\ \text{Suspensions} \\ \text{codetta figure} \end{array} \right)$ in triple counterpoint

         EP.2 (bars 31–37):   interchange of EP.1
         EP.3 (bars 48–50):   interchange of EP.2
         EP.4 (bars 54–60):   development of codetta
         EP.5 (bars 65–69):   interchange of EP.3
         EP.6 (bars 73–76):   development of codetta

I.17   EP.1 (bars 7–10): $\left(\begin{array}{c} \text{codetta figure} \\ \text{C figure} \\ \text{S figure} \end{array} \right)$ with interchange

         EP.2 (bars 11–13):   development of EP.1 in triple counterpoint
         EP.3 (bars 14–17):   interchange of EP.2
         EP.4 (bars 19–23):   interchange of EP.3
         EP.5 (bars 25–27):   variant of EP.1
         EP.6 (bars 31–33):   end of entry repeated in sequence

II.4   EP.1 (bars 6–16): $\left(\begin{array}{c} \text{S figure} \\ \text{C figure} \end{array} \right)$ with interchange

         EP.2 (bars 31–34):   development of EP.1
         EP.3 (bars 39–47):   development of EP.1
         EP.4 (bars 49–52):   development of EP.1
         EP.5 (bars 56–61):   development of EP.1
         EP.6 (bars 62–65):   development of EP.1

II.16   EP.1 (bars 17–20): $\left(\begin{array}{l} \text{C}^{ii}\text{ figure in two - part imitation} \\ \text{C}^{i}\text{ figure} \end{array} \right)$

         EP.2 (bars 24–28):   interchange of EP.1
         EP.3 (bars 40–45): $\left(\begin{array}{c} \text{S figure} \\ \text{C}^{i}\text{ figure} \end{array} \right)$
         EP.4 (bars 49–51):   C^{i} figure
         EP.5 (bars 55–59):   C^{i} figure
         EP.6 (bars 63–67):   interchange of EP.5

II.20   EP.1 (bars 5–6): $\left(\begin{array}{l}\text{S figure (a)}\\ \text{C}^i\text{ figure (b)}\end{array}\right)$

        EP.2 (bars 8–9):   repeat of EP.1 with added voice; then C^i figure in two-part imitation

        EP.3 (bars 11–13): C^i figure (c) in three-part imitation
        EP.4 (bars 15–17): repeat half of EP.1, with interchange; then allusion to EP.2

        EP.5 (bars 19–21): $\left(\begin{array}{l}\text{C + S figures}\\ \text{development of C}^i\end{array}\right)$ in two-part imitation

        EP.6 (bars 23–25): end of entry repeated in sequence; repeat of EP.1; allusion to EP.4

FUGUES WITH SEVEN EPISODES

I.7   EP.1 (bars 4–5): $\left(\begin{array}{l}\text{suspensions}\\ \text{codetta figure}\end{array}\right)$

        EP.2 (bars 7–10):   codetta figure in three-part imitation
        EP.3 (bars 12–17): interchange of EP.2; development of codetta figure
        EP.4 (bars 19–20): interchange of EP.2

        EP.5 (bars 22–25): $\left(\begin{array}{l}\text{S figure}\\ \text{C figure}\end{array}\right)$; then development of codetta

        EP.6 (bars 27–28): continuation of EP.5
        EP.7 (bars 30–33): interchange of EP.2

I.12   EP.1 (bars 10–13): C figure in three-part imitation
        EP.2 (bars 16–19): C figure (inv) in three-part imitation
        EP.3 (bars 22–27): development of EP.2
        EP.4 (bars 30–34): development of EP.1
        EP.5 (bars 37–40): development of EP.2
        EP.6 (bars 43–47): continuation of EP.5
        EP.7 (bars 50–53): interchange of EP.3

II.19   EP.1 (bars 4–5): $\left(\begin{array}{l}\text{S figure}\\ \text{new figure}\end{array}\right)$

        EP.2 (bars 8–9):   interchange of EP.1
        EP.3 (bars 11–12): development of EP.1
        EP.4 (bars 13–16): development of EP.2
        EP.5 (bars 17–20): interchange of EP.3; development of S figure
        EP.6 (bars 21–23): development of S figure
        EP.7 (bars 25–27): development of S figure, with interchange

II.22   EP.1 (bars 9–11): $\left(\begin{array}{l}\text{S figure}\\ \text{C figure}\end{array}\right)$: end of entry repeated in sequence

        EP.2 (bars 15–17): interchange of EP.1, with added voice
        EP.3 (bars 21–27): S figure in two-part imitation, with bass of EP.2; then S figure in two-part imitation with free part

        EP.4 (bars 37–42): $\left(\begin{array}{l}\text{S figure}\\ \text{C figure}\end{array}\right)$ in three-part imitation, with interchange

        EP.5 (bars 62–67): S figure in two-part imitation, with free part

	EP.6 (bars 77–80):	S figure in two-part imitation
	EP.7 (bars 84–89):	S figure in three-part imitation
II.23	EP.1 (bars 22–27):	development of codetta and C figures
	EP.2 (bars 38–42):	codetta figure in imitation
	EP.3 (bars 45–48):	two-part version of EP.1
	EP.4 (bars 56–60):	S^{ii} figure
	EP.5 (bars 63–75):	S^{ii} figure
	EP.6 (bars 78–85):	development of EP.2
	EP.7 (bars 88–93):	S^{ii} and codetta figures
II.24	EP.1 (bars 12–15):	$\left(\begin{array}{l} \text{S figure + codetta figure} \\ C^{i}\ \text{figure} \end{array} \right)$
	EP.2 (bars 21–26):	C^{i} figure in two-part canon
	EP.3 (bars 32–35):	$\left(\begin{array}{l} \text{new figure (a)} \\ C^{ii}\ \text{figure} \end{array} \right)$
	EP.4 (bars 41–44):	figures from codetta, C^{ii}, (a)
	EP.5 (bars 50–54):	development of EP.3
	EP.6 (bars 60–69):	codetta figure in three-part imitation
	EP.7 (bars 76–81):	$\left(\begin{array}{l} C^{ii}\ \text{figure} \\ \text{S figure} \end{array} \right)$

FUGUES WITH EIGHT EPISODES

II.21	EP.1 (bars 9–13):	S figure (a) in two-part imitation; then S figure (b)
	EP.2 (bars 17–21):	figure (b) in two-part imitation, then (a)
	EP.3 (bars 25–32):	figure (a) followed by (b)
	EP.4 (bars 36–40):	figure (b)
	EP.5 (bars 44–47):	figure (a) followed by (b)
	EP.6 (bars 51–54):	figure (b) followed by (a)
	EP.7 (bars 58–63):	figures (a), (b), and C figure
	EP.8 (bars 67–78)	figures (a) and (b), with new figure (c)

FUGUES WITH NINE EPISODES

I.24	EP.1 (bars 7–9):	C figure (a) in two-part imitation, followed by new figure (b) in two-part canon
	EP.2 (bars 12–3):	$\left(\begin{array}{l} \text{C figure (a)} \\ \text{C figure (c)} \end{array} \right)$
	EP.3 (bars 16–21):	$\left(\begin{array}{l} \text{C figure (a)} \\ \text{S figure (d)} \end{array} \right)$ followed by new figure (e) in two-part canon
	EP.4 (bars 24–30):	$\left(\begin{array}{l} \text{figure (a)} \\ \text{figure (b)} \end{array} \right)$ followed by continuation of canon on (e)
	EP.5 (bars 33–8):	$\left(\begin{array}{l} \text{figure (a)} \\ \text{figure (d)} \end{array} \right)$

EP.6 (bars 41–4):	continuation of EP.5
EP.7 (bars 50–3):	figure (a)
EP.8 (bars 56–7):	figure (a)
EP.9 (bars 63–9):	figure (a), followed by continuation of canon on (e)

II.18

EP.1 (bars 9–13):	C figure followed by S figures, with interchange
EP.2 (bars 23–33):	codetta figure + S + C figures
EP.3 (bars 37–45):	C figure followed by development of EP.2
EP.4 (bars 49–55):	interchange of EP.1, followed by development of EP.2
EP.5 (bars 75–79):	codetta figures
EP.6 (bars 83–97):	Sⁱⁱ figures
EP.7 (bars 107–11):	codetta and Cⁱⁱ figures, with interchange
EP.8 (bars 115–25):	interchange of EP.7, followed by development of EP.6
EP.9 (bars 129–35):	final figure of S in three-part imitation

Appendix B: Proportions

PRESENCE AND ABSENCE OF SUBJECT IN PERCENTAGES IN DESCENDING ORDER

Fugue	bars	length of subject	no. of entries		bars with subject	% of total	episode	bars w/o subject	% of total
I.4	115	3	S^i	28	107	93%	1	8	7%
			S^{ii}	16					
			S^{iii}	37					
I.1	27	1 ½		25	24	89%	0	3	11%
I.20	87	3		30	71	82%	2	16	18%
I.Pr.7	45	2	S^i	19	36	80%	3	9	20%
			S^{ii}	11					
II.7	70	6		11	51	73%	1	19	27%
II.9	43	1 ½		27	31	72%	1	12	28%
I.8	87	2 ½		36	63	72%	1	24	28%
I.21	48	4		9	34	71%	2	4	29%
II.2	28	1		25	20	71%	1	8	29%
I.23	34	2		12	24	71%	3	10	29%
II.Pr.3	26	4		6	18	69%	1	8	31%
II.3	35	1 ½ (½)		39	24	69%	2	11	31%
I.16	34	1 ½		17	23	68%	2	11	32%
I.14	40	3		9	27	68%	3	13	32%
II.8	46	2		15	30	65%	3	16	35%
I.6	44	2		18	28	64%	4	16	36%

cont.

Fugue	bars	length of subject	no. of entries		bars with subject	% of total	episode	bars w/o subject	% of total
I.Pr.19	24	2 ½		6	15	63%	2	9	37%
I.11	72	4		14	44	61%	3	28	39%
II.10	86	6		9	54	63%	5	32	37%
II.22	101	4		24	63	62%	7	38	38%
II.16	84	4		13	50	60%	6	34	40%
II.17	50	2		15	30	60%	2	20	40%
I.18	41	2		12	24	59%	5	17	41%
I.Pr.14	24	1		14	14	58%	5	10	42%
II.20	28	2		8	16	57%	6	12	43%
I.15	86	4		16	47	55%	6	39	45%
I.24	76	3		14	42	55%	9	34	45%
II.24	100	6		9	54	54%	7	46	46%
II.1	83	4		11	44	53%	4	39	47%
II.14	70	3	S^i	10	37	53%	5	33	47%
			S^{ii}	9					
			S^{iii}	6					
I.19	54	2		15	28	52%	2	26	48%
I.12	58	3		10	30	52%	7	28	48%
II.13	84	4		11	44	52%	4	40	48%
II.6	27	2		13	14	52%	3	13	48%
II.19	29	1 ½		10	15	52%	7	14	48%
II.4	71	2	S^i	16	36	51%	6	35	49%
			S^{ii}	8					
II.23	104	3	S^i	15	51	49%	7	53	51%
			S^{ii}	11					
II.5	50	1 ½		23	24	48%	5	26	52%
I.22	75			24	36	48%	4	39	52%
I.13	35	2		8	16	46%	5	19	54%
II.18	143	4	S^i	12	64	45%	9	79	55%
			S^{ii}	8					
I.2	31	2		7	14	45%	5	17	55%
I.3	55	2		12	24	44%	6	31	56%
I.17	35	1		15	15	43%	6	20	57%
II.21	93	4		10	40	43%	8	53	57%
I.10	42	2		10	18	43%	4	24	57%
II.15	72	5		6	30	42%	2	42	58%
I.5	27	1		11	11	41%	2	16	59%
II.12	85	4		8	32	38%	5	18	62%
I.9	29	1		11	11	38%	4	18	62%
I.7	37	1 ½		9	13	35%	7	24	65%
II.11	99	4		8	32	32%	5	67	68%

Notes

CHAPTER 1: FUGAL STYLE

1. *A New Dictionary of Music* (New York: Penguin, 1958), 139.

2. *Grove's Dictionary of Music and Musicians*, 5th ed., edited by Eric Blom (London: Macmillan, 1954), iii: 513.

3. Sometimes it is called "link" or "bridge" as well. See also note 5.

4. In German (including its English translation, e.g., Riemann and Keller), the equivalent term "Durchführung" is used in a slightly different context in their style of fugal analysis where every fugue is seen to be made of multiple "expositions" (in effect, meaning "sections").

5. Distinguishing between codetta and episode is not always easy and clear-cut, and many scholars have their own definition of them. While both refer to subject-free passages (and for this reason Bruhn does not bother to distinguish them), there are some important differences between them. The length or duration is one of these. Schulenberg: 394, n. 18, for instance, regards episodes to be "longer, more distinctly articulated passages." German scholars such as Czaczkes and Dürr use the term "Zwischentakt" for a short episode (*Zwischenspiel*). This sometimes causes problems, however, as their length depends on such matters as the way that thematic materials are developed and how modulations are handled. To remedy this inherent analytical problem, some scholars, such as Prout 1891: 92–93, take into account at which point in a fugue they appear; they regard those appearing during the course of the exposition as codettas (German scholars use the term "Expositionszwischenspiel" for this). The author, while basically acknowledging those principles, takes the view that episodes must contain elements of development, either pursuing thematic material or facilitating the modulation or both. Thus, a codetta lacks those elements, for its principal role is to refocus the tonal center professed by the subject or answer to prepare for the next event. He also uses another term, "extension," in a similar context. Its role is to maintain and

extend the tonal focus, often leading to a strong cadence that marks an important structural juncture in the fugue.

6. While this is the meaning used in this book, students should note that the same term also assumes several different meanings in different contexts.

CHAPTER 2: ANSWERING A FUGUE SUBJECT

1. Prout 1891: 18–71.

2. Oldroyd: 52–98. For a more comprehensive study on this topic, readers are encouraged to consult Nalden.

3. It may be worth quoting a similar claim by Nalden: 38: "It is when we come across a subject with a distinctive melodic pattern receiving, more often than not, a real rather than an expected tonal answer, that we may be fairly certain that considerations of character and shape are involved."

4. The whole discussion will be clearer if approached from the theory that this is a modulating subject from dominant to tonic, and likewise its answer modulates from tonic to dominant, which the author discusses on pp. 7–9. Scholars have been debating this point for many years, which readers may learn most conveniently from Nalden: 32, 155–156.

5. Cf. Higgs: 23 and Prout 1891: 56.

6. Again this discussion can be simplified if we view the subject being a modulating one. See also Nalden: 139–140, 154, who highlights the analytical pitfalls by which many earlier scholars (e.g., Prout, Bairstow, Gédalge, and Macpherson) are trapped.

7. According to Nalden: 140, Macpherson (*Studies in the Art of Counterpoint* [London, 1927], 103) claims that the first half of the answer is in the dominant; on this point, we agree with Nalden that Macpherson is incorrect.

8. See Riemann i: 116 for further discussion on this point.

9. That Nalden: 134–136 relates this to a binary form is interesting from both structural and harmonic standpoints.

CHAPTER 3: COUNTERSUBJECTS

1. See the main discussion of **I.17** on pp. 104–5.

CHAPTER 4: THE EXPOSITION

1. The following are small, but necessary, points to be mentioned: **II.18** (Type 1b) lacks C in the third entry; and **II.24** (Type 2b) has C in the alto in the third entry.

2. **I.18** (Type 2c) lacks C^{ii} from the fourth entry; **I.20** (Type 3b) has C in the alto (and not in the bass) in the fourth entry; **II.22** has C in the alto (and not in the soprano) in the third entry; and finally, in **I.12** the position of C^{ii} and C^{iii} in the fourth entry is revised by the editor.

CHAPTER 6: GROUP 1: FUGUES FOR TWO VOICES

1. Riemann i: 66–67 and Prout 1910: 31 claim the subject to end at the first note of bar 3.

2. It is possible to have a tonal answer by lowering the seventeenth note onward by a tone. Bach did not do that, presumably because this would lose the characteristic chromatic descent of the line as well as the diminished fifth interval at this junction. Furthermore, it is unnecessary to restore the tonality to the original key since this is a two-part fugue where there is no imminent subject entry in the tonic.

3. The second half of the subject appears in the soprano from the second beat of bar 41.

4. Note that Bach stresses its significance by resorting to homophonic texture in bars 19–20 and 39.

5. While this interpretation is shared by Perrachio: 96 and Dürr: 154, other scholars suggest different structures: 4+34+4 (Morgan and Iliffe), 10+28+4 (Prout 1910: 31–2); 19+23 (Sampson 1905–7: 107, Czaczkes 1982 i: 145, Hans T. David, "Bach Analyses: J. S. Bach's Fugue in E minor from The Well-Tempered Clavier, Book I," *Bach*, vol. 2, no. 3 (1971): 15–16, and Schulenberg: 181).

CHAPTER 7: GROUP 2: FUGUES FOR THREE VOICES, WITHOUT STRETTO

1. Czaczkes 1982 i: 63 and Dürr: 114 consider this entry as subject, while Iliffe: 9, Sampson 1905–7: 36, and Dickinson: 61 agree with the author.

2. Some authors (e.g., Iliffe and Bruhn) recognize three countersubjects, the third being the variant of the second countersubject found in bars 10–11 and 52–53. On the contrary, Knorr ignores the second countersubject at bars 10–12, 19–20 and 51–53 in his analysis.

3. Prout 1910: 16–17, Oldroyd: 47, and Horsley: 69–70 consider the first run of six semiquavers as codetta. For the argument in support of the author, see Kitson 1929: 36–37.

4. While Dürr: 139–140 agrees with the author, many earlier scholars perceive the episodes differently. Iliffe and Morgan, for instance, recognize five episodes only, since he regards episodes 1 and 4 as codettas; Czaczkes 1982 i: 121f. and Bruhn ii: 73 regard all subject-free passages as episodes, listing nine in total.

5. The precise ending point of the subject has remained controversial for over a century. While the author's suggestion wins the support of Prout 1891: 20, Iliffe: 33, Morgan, and Dürr: 148, other scholars put forward different interpretations, for example, ending at the first note of bar 2 (Brandts Buys: 185, Bruhn ii: 131, and Czaczkes 1982 i: 135), on the second beat of bar 2 (Stade i: 33 and Knorr), and at the first note of bar 3 (Keller: 81). For further discussion from an analytical perspective, see Renwick: 21–22.

6. All the answers are real in this fugue; for this reason, the distinction of the subject form can be difficult; while Czaczkes specifies the form in the exposition only, Bruhn and Dürr make no attempt to distinguish between subject and answer.

7. Bach rounds off the piece with an incomplete off-beat entry in the bass.

8. While Bruhn ii: 134 considers all the seven subject-free passages as episodes, Iliffe: 33 and Sampson 1905–7: 52 regard episode 1 as codetta.

9. Iliffe and Sampson consider this portion of episode as codetta.

10. Iliffe and Sampson recognize a subject entry in the soprano starting at the second beat of bar 12 (the head of the subject being distorted); in their view the first episode thus starts at the third beat of bar 13. Keller: 81, who also ratifies this view, proposes a rather untenable theory that bars 13–16 form a middle section of this fugue.

11. The point at which to end the first period of the fugue is a matter of debate. While the author's view (i.e., to end at bar 17) is shared with Iliffe: 72, there are several other possibilities put forward by other scholars: bar 19 (Carl Schachter, "Bach's Fugue in B♭ major, *Well-Tempered Clavier*, book I, No. XXI," *Music Forum* 3 (1973): 239–267); bar 22 (Czaczkes and Dürr).

12. Schachter: 243 and 259f. considers from a Schenkerian perspective that the final section begins at bar 37.

13. For a further detailed discussion, see Schachter: 251.

14. Schachter describes this section as "extension" and not a part of the episode. Likewise, Schulenberg: 192 excludes this section from episode.

15. It may be worth noting that there was an earlier reading of bars 45–47 with a different interchange between the upper voices. See Macpherson i: 94 or Dürr: 217 for details.

16. Iliffe: 141 considers the counterexposition to start from after episode 2 (i.e., bars 32–40).

17. It may be worth mentioning that in his treatise *Traité du Contre-point & de La Fugue,* Paris, 1824, ii: 53, Fétis "corrects" the shape of Bach's answer to tonal—*a♯′–g♯′–a♯′–c♯′* (his example is transposed to F)—to conform with his own theories.

18. The reason is simply that it results in parallel fifths against the subject entry placed above. Note that Stade ii: 52f., Morgan, Czaczkes 1982 ii: 138, Keller 169, Schulenberg: 217, Bruhn iii: 86 and Dürr: 343 regard this idea as the second countersubject. In addition to the two segments mentioned by the author, the melodic segment found in bars 33–35 (first in the soprano in bar 33–34, which continues in the alto in the following bar) can be considered as the variation of it. Czaczkes suggests further variations (i.e., bars 40–44 and 76–80 in the bass), but they are melodically too remote to be considered as such; this Stade calls the third countersubject.

19. A fascinating case study of this device by Daniel Harrison ("Some Group Properties of Triple Counterpoint and Their Influence on Compositions by J. S. Bach," *Journal of Music Theory* 32, no. 1 (1998): 23–49) demonstrates how Bach achieved a highly unified and economical composition.

20. Following this pattern of two-bar phrase, the episode constantly modulates in a circle of fifths starting from I, through vi, ii, V and back in I, viz., F♯→d♯→g♯→c♯→F♯.

21. The harmonic contents are similar to the previous episode; but instead of returning to I, it modulates to V through vi, ii, vii, and iii, viz., F♯→d♯→g♯→e♯→a♯→C♯.

22. The harmony also shifts in a similar manner: vi, ii, V, I, and IV, viz., d♯→g♯→C♯→F♯→B.

23. The harmony shifts from IV, through ii, V, iii, vi to I, viz., B→g♯→C♯→a♯→d♯→F♯.

24. The overall design of this fugue is a matter for dispute. Julius Herford ("J. S. Bach's Fugue II in C Minor (*The Well-Tempered Clavier*, Book I)," *Bach*, vol. 4, no. 3 (1973): 36–40 at 37) claims that while one can see a ternary division from the tonal design of this fugue (in which he recognizes the final section to start at bar 20, the view endorsed by Prout 1910: 15 and Morgan), he argues that the binary design is more audible (i.e., bars 1–17 and 17–31). Dürr: 110, who is also in favor of the binary design, claims episode 3 as the pivot of the symmetry, viz., bars 1–12 and 15–31.

25. Iliffe: 6 and Prout 1910: 14–15 do not recognize Bach's use of the second countersubject in this fugue.

26. While the author's view is supported by Tovey, Macpherson: 11 and Dickinson (*The Art of J. S. Bach* [London: Hinrichsen, 1950], 48), a majority of scholars (e.g., Higgs: 49, Iliffe: 6, Prout 1891: 92–93, Kitson 1929: 57, Oldroyd: 99, Bullivant: 99, Schulenberg: 170) consider this section as codetta. Ulrich Siegele's fascinating study on the conceptual studies of this fugue ("The Four Conceptual Stages of the Fugue in C Minor, WTC I," *Bach Studies*, edited by Don Franklin [Cambridge: Cambridge University Press, 1989], 197–224) is worth mentioning; he is of the opinion that this episode was absent from the initial stage of its conception, which was added when Bach felt the necessity to improve the balance between thematic and nonthematic sections.

27. This episode modulates from the tonic to relative major through iv and ♭VII, viz., c→f→B♭→E♭.

28. The harmonic contents differ from episode 2, however; this time there is no modulation.

29. This section was an extension worked out subsequently. The shorter version (seventy-one bars long, without this extension) is found in the so-called London autograph (Add. MS. 35021, the British Library, London).

30. The author is presumably referring to the staccati that were supplied by Bach on all non-tied crotchets in bars 1–4.

31. German scholars (e.g., Knorr, Czaczkes, and Dürr) tend to disregard the use of codetta at this point, placing the beginning of the countersubject at the eighth note of bar 3. Stade ii: 36 interprets slightly differently; he considers the countersubject as starting at the same time as the answer (on the eleventh note of bar 3).

32. Czaczkes 1982 ii: 125 claims that there is also the second countersubject in free variant form, which first appears at bar 14 in the soprano. In the editor's view it is insignificant.

33. This rhythm alteration at this point, from ♩♪♫ *d'* to ♩♪♪, is certainly considered with the performance on the keyboard in mind, since the note *d'* needs to be struck by the answer in the alto.

34. Keller: 187 considers it to last until the fifth note of bar 3.

35. Stade ii: 90 and Czaczkes 1984 interpret the countersubject to follow the subject immediately (i.e., without having the codetta in between).

36. Prout 1891: 110 claims that this is the subject taking the form of the answer. See also Macpherson ii: 64.

37. The alternative reading—*e'*—given in Bach's earlier version entitled "Fugetta" (transmitted in the hand of J. C. Altnickol).

38. Iliffe: 173 considers that the countersubject is absent here.

39. Prout 1892: 107–111, Iliffe: 173, Gray: 136–137, and Fuller-Maitland ii: 32–33 make no mention of this device.

40. Earlier scholars (e.g., Prout, Iliffe, Sampson, and Morgan) describe this section as codetta. It is worth noting that the syncopation ♪♩♪ *e'–a'–g♯'* in the alto, bar 6, was a revised figure modified from ♪♪♩ *e'–c'–b–g♯'* (attested to in Altnickol's copy), a figure that has a clear thematic reference.

41. In the early version, the distance was two octaves only.

42. This section was added when Bach was working on the fugue in the last stage of compiling the "Well-Tempered Clavier," Book II (WTC II) in c. 1742.

43. Renwick: 192 attempts to explain its significance from Schenkerian analysis. He observes that this design is structurally significant as it marks a deeper level of a back-relating dominant.

44. Stade ii: 4, Knorr, Schulenberg: 203, Bruhn i: 87, and Dürr: 255–256 call this section the coda, while Keller: 137 regards it as "the fourth exposition."

45. It should be noted that, as Riemann ii: 7 points out, the original running passage is a decorated version of the head motive. See also Renwick: 30, 193.

46. Czaczkes 1984 ignores it in his analysis, and so does Knorr, who recognized that in bar 39 in the soprano only.

47. Iliffe: 87 appears to be the only commentator who explicitly denies Bach's use of countersubject in this fugue.

48. Of all commentators consulted, Czaczkes 1982 ii: 128–129 and Dürr: 330 are in the minority in claiming that this entry is answer. A particularly notable commentary given by Renwick: 155–156 explains from an analytical perspective how the subject evolved to this shape during the course of fugal discourse and how subject and episode are united as a conclusion to the fugue.

49. This fugue was extensively reworked from an early composition entitled "fughetta" (BWV 902/2: see the *Neue Bach Ausgabe*, vol. 5, no. 6.2 [Kassel: Bärenreiter, 1995], 332) at the time when Bach was compiling the WTC II in c. 1738/39. It is sixty bars in length, and Bach not only added this final section as an extension to the existing work but also revitalized the contrapuntal texture of this piece. For further details, see Dürr: 358–359.

50. There are several possible interpretations; the author's suggestion is the shortest and most convincing, which is shared by Bruyck: 155, Iliffe: 150, Knorr, Prout 1910: 74, Morgan, Gray: 120, Macpherson ii: 48, and Czaczkes 1982 ii: 164; Riemann ii: 130 and Souchay: 65 claim that the subject ends at the third note of bar 6, whereas Dürr: 360 goes up to the first note of bar 7; Keller: 175 goes so far as the first note of bar 8.

51. For this reason, Stade ii: 62, Sampson 1905–7: 151, Knorr, Czaczkes 1982 ii: 165, Bruhn iii: 144 and Dürr: 360 consider this idea as countersubject.

52. Iliffe takes the same view, though he gives no reasons.

53. The case of bar 16 requires some explanation from a study of sources: the leap (♫♫ *AA–E–A–B*) is found in the version of the "London autograph," whereas the plain version (♪♫ *A–B*) is given in the other tradition of sources (i.e.,

Altnickol's copies). This issue is not just a matter of Bach's revision from the latter to the former since it also involves the keyboard compass beyond the bottom C.

54. The idea can, in fact, be traced as early as in bar 4 in the alto. It may be worth noting that those accidentals in bars 21 and 28 were subsequent additions in Bach's autograph, a proof that the idea was gradually developed when copying the score. See Yo Tomita, *J. S. Bach's "Das Wohltemperierte Clavier II": A Critical Commentary* (Leeds: Household World, 1993), i: 118 for further details.

55. As Czaczkes 1982 ii: 219–220 demonstrates, it makes good sense if we accept that there are two countersubjects used in this fugue whereby the jerky melody placed below the answer (bars 2–4) is a condensed form of both in a single line, which develops into two separate countersubjects in bars 5–6.

56. There are some differences among scholars in the way that episodes are defined and recognized. Iliffe: 169, Prout 1910: 80–81, and Morgan consider those of bars 13, 17, 21, and 25 as episodes and the rest as codetta.

57. Although the author does not discuss how long the subject lasts, it is clear from the diagram that he considers it to last until the first note of bar 4. This view is shared by Iliffe, Prout 1891: 84, Knorr: 33, and Brandts Buys: 264. The majority of scholars (e.g., Bruyck, Boekelman, Souchay: 58, Macpherson ii: 36, Czaczkes 1982 ii: 132, Bruhn ii: 238, and Dürr: 335) believe, however, that it lasts until the fifth note of the bar. The fact that more than half of all the entries reach to the fifth note is one reason; more importantly, they consider the rhythmic character of the subject ($\flat|\sqcup\sqcup$) to be paramount, which becomes the basis for the semiquaver figurations that follow.

58. Here the author is referring to the mordent (✳) placed on the first strong beat on the subject at bars 1 and 25, where the ornaments are playable.

59. The effect is so minimal that it is not perceived as a stretto.

60. Kennan: 213 claims that bar 8 is a "link" (codetta) and that the "bridge" (episode) starts at bar 9.

CHAPTER 9: GROUP 3: FUGUES FOR THREE VOICES, WITH STRETTO

1. Riemann i: 72 and Busoni T.1, H.2: 17 consider the subject to last until the third note of bar 4, followed immediately by the countersubject.

2. Several alternative interpretations have been offered in the past. Stade i: 38 and Sampson 1905–7: 110 suggest that the countersubject starts on the fifth note of bar 4, vertically coinciding with the answer; Czaczkes, Bruhn, and Dürr consider that it starts on the second note of bar 4 (i.e., immediately after the subject entry), thus disregarding the use of codetta. (See also note 1.) The author seems to think that the codetta lasts until the end of bar 4 (or possibly to the first note of bar 5) and that the countersubject starts from the first note of bar 5 (possibly by allowing the overlap of a note between the codetta and the countersubject). This interpretation makes good sense when one notices that two particular figures in the countersubject—the head ($\sqcup\sqcup\sqcup$) and the tail ($\epsilon\epsilon\epsilon\epsilon|\sqcup$)—actually emerged from the codetta.

3. As Iliffe: 39, Sampson 1905–7: 60, and Dürr: 159 point out, there is another possible entry not mentioned by the author: an incomplete entry at bar 65 in the

middle voice (shown in the diagram in square brackets). This creates a stretto with the highly decorated entry in the soprano (bars 64–68).

4. See note 2.

5. It appears that the author is in the minority on this occasion. While Iliffe considers the final section (which he calls "recapitulation") to start at bar 79, a great majority of scholars recognize it as starting at bar 69 (e.g. Prout 1910: 39, Morgan, Macpherson i: 62, Czaczkes 1982 i: 165, Bruhn iii: 138, and Dürr: 182).

6. Sampson 1905–7: 111 considers the countersubject to begin at bar 6 for the reason that "the first bar in each entry (of countersubject) being different." Iliffe: 52 suggests even later that he regards the first half of this passage (from the second note of bar 5 to the fourth note of bar 6) as codetta.

7. It may be worth adding here that there is also a subject entry in the middle voice in bar 79, a third below the more prominent entry in the soprano. However incomplete and distorted in form, it conforms to the correct pitch level of the entry in the tonic key.

8. See p. 16.

9. Dehn: 1 thinks that it lasts until the first note of bar 3.

10. Both the clarity and stability of tonal structure given in the exposition are exemplary, preparing for an almost chaotic range of fugal permutations being explored in the following sections. For further discussion, see Schenker, *Free Composition* (New York: Longman, 1984), 143 f.; John J. Daverio, "The 'Unravelling' of Schoenberg's Bach," in *Johann Sebastian: A Tercentenary Celebration*, edited by Seymour L. Benstock (Westport, CT: Greenwood Press, 1992), 33–44, and Renwick: 109.

11. Iliffe: 20 regards the inverted entries in bars 14, 22, 27, and 29 as answers.

12. To illustrate the point, Iliffe includes the bass entry in bar 26 as subject in G minor. From the editor's point of view, this is clearly a false entry. Note that false entries of subjects are not indicated in the diagram.

13. It is usually the case that the subject entry manifests the key in the way that it is first introduced. Due to the ways that the treatment of subject is explored, some entries do not manifest the tonal center in the same way. The author interprets the entries of bars 13–14, 21–22, and 34–35 as starting in the dominant instead of tonic.

14. See note 13.

15. See note 13.

16. As Tovey: 144 correctly suggests, Bach needed to work out this variation in order to avoid octaves with the soprano (g'–a'/g–a).

17. Boekelman ignores this incomplete entry in his analysis.

18. Knorr does not recognize Bach's use of countersubject in this fugue.

19. Those of bars 13 and 30 are supplemented by the editor.

20. Boekelman ignores those partial forms of countersubject at bars 17, 24, and 39 in his analysis.

21. See note 20.

22. See note 20.

23. The manner in which the cadence is reached in the dominant key at this midpoint of the fugue gives a strong impression that it has a binary design, hinting at early sonata form.

24. Keller: 70 suggests even further that the semiquaver passage of the previous bar is the first half, thus forming "the veiled subject entry."

25. Souchay: 58 claims that it lasts until the third note of bar 3.

26. Iliffe: 110 and Sampson 1905–7: 55 do not consider it as subject entry.

27. Iliffe considers it as answer.

28. Iliffe and Sampson 1905–7: 54–55 take this view, regarding this section as stretto.

29. Stade ii: 20 claims that it begins at the first note of bar 3. Knorr failed to recognize it in his analysis.

30. Iliffe and Sampson do not regard it as stretto, as they do not consider an entry in this bar. See note 26.

31. Czaczkes 1982 ii: 69 considers the episode to last until bar 25½.

32. The comparison with an early version of this fugue (transmitted in a copy by Agricola [Mus. ms. Bach. P 595 in the Staatsbibliothek zu Berlin Preußischer Kulturbesitz], c. 1738) reveals an interesting process of composition at this point; the succession of three fragmentary motives in the soprano were originally given as a sequence of plain triads, viz., i, ii, III, in rising arpeggio (♩ ♫). This new idea was later replaced with that of thematic reference, thus tightening the contrapuntal integrity.

33. Equally, the use of the leaping quavers in the middle voice appears to have been an afterthought; the original figure was a simple descending melody $d''-c''-b\natural'$ (bar 19) and $c''-b\flat'-a'$ (bar 20), respectively.

34. Stade ii: 22, Knorr, and Czaczkes 1982 ii: 71 do not consider the first two entries as such; hence, they do interpret this section as stretto.

35. Iliffe: 93 considers that the subject lasts until the first note of bar 28, ♪ $d\sharp'$.

36. The chromaticism was the idea that Bach subsequently introduced here when revising an early version of the piece (written in C major, transmitted in Mus. ms. Bach P 226 in the Staatsbibliothek zu Berlin Preußischer Kulturbesitz, copied by Anna Magdalena in c. 1738). The original passage descended diatonically from g' to d'.

37. Although Iliffe: 94 agrees with the author, the editor tends to share with the later scholars (e.g., Czaczkes 1982 ii: 36 and Dürr: 270) the view that this entry is answer.

38. Note that the author qualifies his statement to the subject at the beginning of the fugue; for the author's reasoning, see p. 9. For this fugue, he unusually allows shorter versions of the subject (the four-note motive as well as the six-note phrase) to appear in the diagram, for, as he observes, they are not treated as "motives" but the subjects themselves in the fugal development. The author's view that the subject consists of twelve notes is shared by Tovey, David: 21, Kennan: 214, and Schulenberg: 205; other scholars suggest various interpretations, however: four notes only (Iliffe: 94 and Brandts Buys: 235); six notes (Riemann ii: 20, Stade ii: 8 [who calls the 7–12th notes as "Nachsatz" (afterthought) distinguishing from the "Thema" of first six notes], Sampson 1905–7: 64, Macpherson ii: 10, Knorr, Czaczkes 1982 ii: 34 [who distinguishes the 7–12th notes as countersubject], Bruhn i: 144, Dürr: 268); eight notes (Keller: 142); eleven notes (Busoni, ii, H.1, 22), and possibly thirteen (Dickinson: 86 simply says "two bars").

39. Busoni suggests that this "new theme" is derived from the initial four-note motive, for example ♪♩♪♪ *c♯–e♯–c♯–f♯* in the bass at bar 8. See also Czaczkes 1982 ii: 38, who suggests the second half of the subject in the bass (bar 2) as an intermediate stage of this motivic metamophosis. It is worth adding here that Bach added the demisemiquavers subsequently. See Yo Tomita, "Analysing Bach's Ink through a Glass Darkly," *Musical Times* 139, no. 1865 (1998): 37–42.

40. Iliffe: 94 considers the middle voice as answer and the bass as subject.

41. Iliffe considers the bass as subject.

42. These demisemiquaver flourishes (with slurs) were originally conceived in the shape of the inverted subject in diminution (in an early version transmitted in Bach's surviving autograph). The use of the same figures in the middle voice and the bass from the end of bar 18 is therefore seen as a logical step.

43. The identification of countersubject depends on how the subject is to be interpreted (see note 38). Those who consider the subject to last for six notes would probably interpret the semiquaver figure in bar 2 as countersubject; those who believe that the subject has four notes (e.g., Iliffe) would declare that no countersubject was used in the fugue.

44. The augmentations were introduced in the new extension that Bach added to the semifinal version of this fugue (in the "London autograph") when he was working on the compilation of WTC II. The idea of augmentation occurred to him "accidentally." For further discussion on Bach's compositional process of this passage, see Tomita, "Analysing Bach's Ink."

45. Scholars disagree with each other as to where the final section should start, for example, bar 57 (Prout 1910: 29), bar 61 (Dürr: 145–146). Morgan states that "theoretically, this [final section] begins at bar 57: musically, it begins at bar 61 ... the author takes the latter view."

46. Renwick: 42 makes a fascinating observation from a Schenkerian analysis on the harmonic basis of a tonal answer and the inversion of the subject.

47. Keller: 77 believes that a countersubject was not used in this fugue so that "the subject may be counterpointed continually with itself." Stade i: 29f. points out, however, that even although the same melody does not appear, its concluding figure appears frequently: bars 10, 22, 29, 69, 74, 80, and 82.

48. In their respective studies Bullivant: 96–97 and Bruhn i: 103–104 discuss them as episodes. Macpherson i: 36, however, considers two episodes in this fugue, viz., bars 15–19 and 33–36.

49. Dickinson: 67 regards this entry as the beginning of the counterexposition (bars 12–30).

50. Readers may be interested to read Paul Badura-Skoda's theory regarding why Bach "evaded" the expected modulation to F♯ in this episode. See Badura-Skoda: 227.

51. Iliffe: 29 considers that this is answer. Schulenberg: 179 rightly observes that the quasi-augmented entries of bars 24 and 48 anticipate the true augmentation of the subject in the last section, hence achieving its culmination when the prime, augmented, and quasi-augmented forms are all combined in stretto at bar 77.

52. For a more technical harmonic analysis of this stretto section, see Renwick: 168–169.

CHAPTER 11: GROUP 4: FUGUES FOR FOUR VOICES, WITHOUT STRETTO

1. Many commentators (e.g., Knorr, Prout 1910, Morgan, Gray, Kennan, and Bruhn) actually fail to notice the second countersubject.

2. Czaczkes 1984 claims that there is a fragment of C^{ii} in the bass.

3. Czaczkes 1982 i: 216 and Dürr: 219 consider that this is subject. Also, Czaczkes 1984 recognizes a variant form of C^{ii} in the bass.

4. Czaczkes 1982 i: 217 and Dürr: 219 consider this as answer.

5. Czaczkes 1984 claims that there are C^{i} (placed in advance in the soprano) and C^{ii} (in the alto).

6. Czaczkes 1982 i: 218 claims that there is also C^{ii} in the bass in the second half of bar 30.

7. Prout 1910: 50 and Morgan call it a codetta.

8. BWV 901/2, composed c. 1720. For music, see *Neue Bach Ausgabe*, vol. 5, no. 6.2, 326–327.

9. Dürr: 380 considers this as subject.

10. The extent to which its shape is modified during the course of the fugal development is such that Iliffe: 160 and Sampson 1905–7: 124–125 and Knorr do not consider it as countersubject. Bruhn iii: 201 also dismisses it from bar 18 onward, noting that "it seems no longer meaningful to use the same name."

11. Readers using the Henle edition (edited by Otto von Irmer, 1970) should note that its text is based on the version known as the so-called "Berlin autograph" (Mus. ms. Bach P 274 in the Staatsbibliothek zu Berlin Preußischer Kulturbesitz), in which the upper two voices receive different treatment; here the soprano takes over the second countersubject, while the alto reads ♪♪♩ ab′. Another voice exchange occurs at bar 10 between the tenor and alto. The majority of editions follow the other tradition of text, that is, the "London autograph" and Altnickol's copy, which is the revised version of the former. Our diagram follows the version of Altnickol (e.g., *The Associated Board*, 1994; *Neue Bach Ausgabe*, 1995).

12. Stade ii: 74, Czaczkes 1982 ii: 189, and Bruhn iii: 210 claim that this is a flowing variant form of the first countersubject in the bass.

13. See note 10.

14. Dürr: 375 considers that the alto line is a resolution of the first countersubject in semiquavers.

15. Scholars are in disagreement on this point. While Iliffe: 160, Sampson 1905–7: 83 and Riemann ii: 149–150 agree with the author, Stade ii: 77, Macpherson ii: 53, Czaczkes 1982 i: 198, and Dürr: 380 consider that it is an answer.

16. Some editions, such as Henle, fail to give the first note of the first countersubject, that is, ♩ ab.

17. Prout 1910: 34 and Morgan consider the final section to start at bar 47.

18. Knorr, Iliffe: 42, Prout 1910: 34, Morgan, and Macpherson i: 51–52 do not consider the use of the third countersubject in this fugue.

19. The interpretation of the voice-crossing between two inner voices is revised by the editor. Although the voice range at the end of bar 13 is too low for the alto, this is how Bach set the score in two-stave system. The shortened note ab on the third beat in the tenor (♪♪), which was merely to facilitate the performer (to play E♮ on the next semiquaver beat), is followed by ♩f′ (and not ♪♪♫ c–d–e♭). The

erroneous rendering of the texture is given by Stade i: 41, Iliffe: 42 , Sampson 1905–7: 145, Czaczkes 1982 i: 149, and Renwick: 99.

20. Prout 1910: 34 suggests that these entries constitute a partial and irregular counterexposition.

21. This is a controversial point. While Riemann i: 81 and Sampson 1905–7: 89 agree with the author, Iliffe: 42 and Dürr: 163 consider that this is subject.

22. Iliffe: 42 considers this entry as real answer.

23. Sampson 1905–7: 89, Riemann i: 81, and Prout 1910: 34 consider that this is a real answer.

24. Prout 1910: 34 and Morgan regard this episode as codetta.

25. Note that the treatment of imitation is less obvious than episode 1. See Bullivant: 104 for his discussion of "four-part developmental episodes."

26. Prout 1910: 37 and Morgan consider the final section to begin with the tenor entry of bar 29.

27. Scholars in recent decades (e.g., Czaczkes 1982 i: 158, Bruhn iii: 100, and Dürr: 174) seem to agree on the point that this tenor part is the second countersubject, which reappears in bars 15–18 (tenor) and 29–32 (alto) in a much altered form.

28. Many earlier scholars, including Iliffe: 49, Prout 1891: 95, and Sampson 1905–7: 90, consider this episode as codetta.

29. The use of subject form at this point is facilitated by the preceding episode.

30. Iliffe: 49 and Sampson 1905–7: 90 consider that the opening section ends before this episode; Dürr: 176 agrees with the author, though he recognizes the piece in binary structure (bars 1–20 and 20–40)

31. Iliffe considers this entry as answer.

32. Iliffe, Prout 1891: 95, and Macpherson i: 58 do not consider this as extension but as episode.

33. Iliffe considers that countersubject is absent here.

34. This is a rare example of a quadruple canon used in episodes in which all voices participate.

35. Prout 1910: 48 and Morgan suggest that the entries in bars 11, 15, 17, and 19 may be regarded as an irregular counterexposition; in their view, the middle section starts at bar 21.

36. This was first discussed in Marpurg 1753 i: 30 and Plate 14, Figure 4. For a fuller discussion on this topic, see Riemann i: 116 and Nalden: 139–140.

37. Iliffe does not recognize the use of the second subject.

38. Czaczkes 1982 i: 183 recognizes a variant form of C^{ii} in the alto.

39. Earlier scholars (e.g., Iliffe: 62 and Sampson 1905–7: 77–78, 147) tend to view this as real answer.

40. Czaczkes 1982 i: 184 claims that they are present in a very free form, C^i in the bass and C^{ii} in the soprano.

41. Czaczkes 1982 i: 185 claims that the countersubjects are present in a very free form, C^i in the alto and C^{ii} in the tenor.

42. Czaczkes 1982 i: 186 claims that the countersubjects are present in a very varied form, C^i in the soprano and C^{ii} in the alto.

43. This was presumably to avoid the false relation with the alto two semiquaver beats earlier, although there is another problem awaiting Bach a quaver beat later in the soprano (*b*).

44. This "real" entry has been a controversial point whether it is to be understood as subject or answer; while Stade i: 66, Macpherson i: 76, Czaczkes 1982 i: 186, and Dürr: 199 agree with the author, Riemann i: 119, Iliffe: 62, and Sampson 1905–7: 78 consider this entry as answer.

45. Prout 1910: 52 and Morgan consider the middle section to start at bar 24.

46. Prout 1910: 52 and Morgan consider the middle section to begin at bar 60.

47. Due to the way that Bach uses this portion separately from the rest of the countersubject, some commentators do not consider it as a part of the countersubject (e.g., Prout 1891: 76, Sampson 1905–7: 114, Czaczkes 1982 i: 224).

48. Iliffe: 82, Sampson 1905–7: 80–81 and Oldroyd: 50 consider this short episode as codetta.

49. The remaining segment in the alto is its variant form in sequence, which Czaczkes 1982 i: 224 calls the second countersubject.

50. Iliffe and Sampson also consider this episode as codetta.

51. The source study serves to show that Bach was testing the possibility of a real answer at this point, in an intermediate version of this fugue. The former is the intermediate reading, and the latter is the final (*post correcturam*) reading attested in the autograph of Book I (D-B, Mus. ms. Bach P 415). For further details, see *Neue Bach Ausgabe, Kritischer Bericht*, vol. 5, no. 6.1 (1989): 141–142 or Jones: 163.

52. While Keller: 127 argues the significance of this "false entry" of the subject as the anticipation of the entry, Schulenberg: 195 suggests that it originated from an error made during the composition. All the "false entries" are added to the diagram by the editor, so that a reader may be able to follow the following discussion.

53. Scholars offer various interpretations of episodes 5 and 6. Among scholars who do not regard these as episodes, Iliffe and Riemann i: 167 believe that they are stretto sections, the view also supported by Prout 1891: 119 when he discusses bars 33–41 of this fugue, saying that "one voice in a stretto may discontinue the subject as soon as another voice enters with it, but that the last voice that enters should complete the subject." Sampson 1905–7: 81 argues from a different angle, saying that "these imitations can hardly be called 'stretti' because they are not *canonic*." The author's view is endorsed by Tovey, Czaczkes 1982 i: 226–227, and Dürr: 239.

54. As discussed in note 53, some scholars believe that bars 41–46 form a second stretto.

55. Iliffe: 82 fails to mention this short episode in his analysis, while Sampson 1905–7: 81 considers it as codetta.

56. Iliffe considers this entry as the third stretto (cf. episodes 5 and 6; see note 53). Dürr: 239 considers this as "false entry," which is more logical in the editor's view.

57. Stade i: 27 and Knorr disregard the initial falling steps as part of the countersubject.

58. Iliffe: 118, Sampson 1905–7: 79, and Macpherson ii: 22 regard this section as codetta.

59. Iliffe considers this entry as answer.

60. Czaczkes 1982 i: 85 interprets the bass to be a variant form of countersubject.

61. Knorr does not think that there is a countersubject here. Czaczkes 1982 i: 86 considers the alto to be "a branch" (*Nebenarm*) of countersubject. In the editor's view, its role is far less certain when compared with the corresponding part of the next entry in the bass (bars 21–23).

62. Czaczkes 1984 offers a radically different interpretation; on the one hand, he continues to recognize the presence of countersubject in a varied form in the subsequent entries (i.e. bass: 27–29; alto: 43–45), on the other hand, he recognizes the first appearance of the second countersubject (descending scale) in the bass. In the editor's view, this is simply the last segment of the subject that has been used as a free part.

63. Prout 1910: 76 and Morgan consider the "middle section" to begin with episode 2 (bars 24–28), when free modulation takes place.

64. This fugue is often used to explain how one can use invertible counterpoint since the day of Bach's pupils: Kirnberger, who wrote in "10" and "12" in his personal copy of the "48" (Am.B.57/2 in the Staatsbibliothek zu Berlin Preußischer Kulturbesitz), apparently analyzed the piece in this light. Readers who need further explanation on this device may refer to the following: Bullivant: 117–119; Kennan: 116–117. For a more advanced harmonic analysis on this device, see Renwick: 103–105. Note that Bullivant does not consider the doubled subject entries (bar 45 onward) in the same way as the author.

65. In the "48" another instance of this device is found toward the end of **II.22** (bar 96f.). See p. 121 f.

66. Czaczkes 1982 ii: 173–174 considers this as the second countersubject, as he identifies the following as its variants: bars 28–32, tenor; bars 32–36, tenor; and bars 36–40, alto.

67. It may be added that a rapid modulation to the relative major coincides with an early climax at the midpoint of the episode. The second half of the episode is clearly articulated in $\frac{3}{2}$ (i.e., hemiola, which is most clearly manifested in bars 73–74).

68. Although the author does not discuss the alto, he presumably believes it is a free voice. Czaczkes 1982 ii: 173–174 suggests that this is the third countersubject, which reappears in the tenor at bar 36 in a modified form.

69. Czaczkes 1982 ii: 176–177 claims, on the contrary, that the alto is the chief voice. All the other scholars (e.g., Stade, Knorr, Bruhn, and Dürr) do not attempt to distinguish them.

70. The editor has added this entry to the diagram, for, having considered an interesting variant reading in the bass at bar 79 on the third beat: ♪ *d* (autograph)/ ♫ *B♭–c–d* (Altnickol's first copy [Mus. ms. P 430 in the Staatsbibliothek zu Berlin Preußischer Kulturbesitz], revised from the autograph reading), the transformation appears to be Bach's afterthought. It seems logical to infer that the initial conceptual reading must have been ♪ *B♭*, which was presumably abandoned at an early stage; it is not certain why Bach adopted the autograph reading in the first place; one possible explanation is playability, so that one can play the two lower voices with the left hand alone. The elaboration introduced subsequently to the subject in bars 81–82 forced Bach to rethink the passage in bar 79. If this reconstruction is correct, then this process of Bach's revision was first triggered by the ease of performance but then overridden

subsequently by his desire to increase the powerful drive at this closing phrase of the piece.

71. For a more serious Schenkerian approach to analysis, see Felix Salzer, *Structural Hearing* (New York: Dover, 1962), ii: 240–241.

72. This needs an explanation, as some scholars claim that Bach makes use of up to three countersubjects in this fugue (e.g., Stade i: 20f., Bruhn i: 201–202, and Dürr: 126). In fact, this particular passage reappears eight times during the course of the fugue, of which seven are in the bass (i.e., bars 4, 5, 8, 11, 12, 13, and 14; the only exception is bar 7 in the tenor). Clearly, this melodic device has such a strong character of functional bass that Czaczkes 1982 i: 107 is quite right when he describes it as the "fixed bass" (*festgehalten Baß*) for the subject. Riemann i: 35 agrees, saying that it "merely imitates the concluding motive of the theme, and then forms a cadence in bass fashion."

73. Riemann i: 36–37 shares the view here, saying that "it has the importance of a real countersubject."

74. Iliffe: 17 considers this entry as answer.

75. Iliffe and Keller: 67 erroneously interpret the bass (beat 1) as answer/subject, instead of the soprano (from beat 2). The bass is, in fact, derived from the figures of episode 1 and ultimately from the free voice in bar 2.

76. Iliffe also considers this entry as answer.

77. Except for Prout 1910: 41 and the author, all the other commentators consider that this entry is in V. Kitson 1929: 18 claims that this answer "should have been real."

78. Stade i: 59, Tovey, Czaczkes 1982 i: 177, and Dürr: 192 cautiously accept the view that it can be regarded as a countersubject. Iliffe: 59 calls it "free countersubject."

79. Iliffe recognizes, for instance, that these are fragments of subject in the alto and of answer in the treble.

80. Iliffe considers that the entry in the alto is an answer.

81. Iliffe considers all the mixed-shape entries (bars 28, 29, and 30) as answers.

82. Prout 1910: 42 and Morgan consider that this section is a part of coda (bars 31–35).

CHAPTER 12: GROUP 5: FUGUES FOR FOUR VOICES, WITH STRETTO

1. It is more common to regard the subject as lasting until the first note of bar 7 than what the author suggests. The former is claimed by the following: Dehn: 7, Higgs: 5, Boekelman, Iliffe: 114, Sampson 1905–7: 67, Knorr, Macpherson ii: 21, Bruhn ii: 85f., Dürr: 298. The latter is supported by Jadassohn: 18, Riemann ii: 48–9, Stade ii: 23, and Czaczkes 1982 ii: 72. Stade calls this bar the "connecting bar" (*Überleitungstakt*).

2. Boekelman, Iliffe: 114, Knorr, and Gray: 100, on the contrary, do not recognize a countersubject in this fugue.

3. Dürr: 299 also makes the same distinction between the two segments as variable and fixed (*variabel und fest*), whereas Stade ii: 23 and Czaczkes 1984 simply state that the countersubject begins at bar 7, which is misleading.

4. Jadassohn: 19, Iliffe: 114, Sampson 1905–7: 68, and Dürr: 301 call this extension an episode, while Macpherson ii: 21 calls it codetta.

5. Iliffe: 114 claims that the episode starts on the second note of bar 44.

6. Other scholars recognize more than one episode in this fugue, as already discussed in note 4.

7. In fact, the early version manifested in the copy in the hand of Johann Friedrich Agricola (Mus. ms. Bach P 595 in the Staatsbibliothek zu Berlin Preußischer Kulturbesitz, written in D major) shows that the quaver runs in the bass in bars 47, 49, and 51 were originally conceived in the codetta figure, which Bach presumably revised when he transposed the fugue into E♭ major for WTC II.

8. As Knorr: 29 and Dürr: 301 point out, the alto part can be seen as the incomplete entry of the subject where the beginning of the subject is missing. In this light, one may see that all the subject entries after the counterexposition take the stretto form throughout.

9. The structural role of this section is interpreted differently by other scholars; while Sampson 1905–7: 69 views it as codetta, Jadassohn: 21, Iliffe: 122, and Dürr: 316 consider it as episode.

10. Sampson 1905–7: 69 regards this section as codetta.

11. Dürr: 316 regards it as episode, while Sampson 1905–7: 69 regards it as codetta.

12. Sampson 1905–7: 69 regards this section as codetta.

13. Iliffe: 122, Sampson 1905–7: 69, and Dürr: 317 consider this section as episode.

14. It is difficult to determine the precise point at which the countersubject starts. While many scholars suggest that the countersubject begins at the last crotchet of bar 2, Knorr does not recognize it at all. As far as the author is concerned, he believes it to start at the third note of bar 2 (overlapping with the end of the subject). For a greatly expanded discussion of this point, see Kitson 1929: 33. It may be worth adding that Higgs: 41, Prout 1891: 117, Iliffe: 122, Czaczkes 1984, and Bruhn ii: 155 claim that the tenor in bars 11–12 is countersubject. In addition, Prout 1891: 117 considers the tenor in bar 8 as countersubject as well. In our view they are not countersubjects but a free voice based on the figure derived from it. See also p. 15.

15. In fact, a closer analysis reveals that in bars 35–38 this free segment of the countersubject is transformed into the inverted subject in diminution, which first developed independently in bars 30–33. As it does not seem productive to distinguish all the variants for this study, they are not distinguished from the countersubject proper in our diagram.

16. Sampson 1905–7: 155 and Bruhn ii: 150f. refer to these two themes (*sogetti*) as the second and third countersubjects, respectively. Note that, as Dehn: 25 illustrates, this stretto section demonstrates the interchange of a quadruple counterpoint.

17. Iliffe: 122, in stating that this section (from bar 22 to the third beat of bar 26) should be considered as episode, reflects the fact that the subjects do not enter in their original form and that the tonal shift is obvious, modulating from F♯ minor to C♯ minor. Note that Knorr does not recognize two entries of bars 25–26 in his analysis.

18. Kirkpatrick: 103 interprets that the harmony is vi of V, however.

19. Iliffe: 122, Riemann ii: 74f., Stade ii: 35 and Czaczkes 1982 ii: 110–112 regard the figure in the soprano in the second half of bar 35 as the inverted subject in diminution. If so, the motivically related figures starting in the tenor, bars 30–32 (which are added by the editor in the diagram), should also be recognized as such.

20. As Tovey points out, the first two notes ♩♩ e–d♯ are transposed down by an octave for the sake of playability.

21. Boekelman and Czaczkes consider it differently; in their view, the countersubject starts immediately after the subject, from ♩g on the fourth beat of bar 2, the portion often absent in the subsequent entries.

22. As Kennan: 226 points out, there is a false entry in the alto at bar 7, forming a "mock stretto."

23. Riemann i: 105, Czaczkes 1982 i: 172–173, and Dürr: 186 regard this entry as subject.

24. Czaczkes 1982 i: 172–173 and Dürr: 186 consider this entry as subject.

25. Sampson 1905–7: 84 calls it episode.

26. Scholars are generally in agreement in that there is no firm countersubject employed here. As Dürr: 221 demonstrates, it consists of three elements, all derived from the subject itself—bar 4: ♪♩♪ in sequence (from bar 3, second half); bar 5: ♫♫ ♪ in sequence (from bar 2, first half); bar 6: ♫ ♪ in sequence (from bar 1, head motive).

27. Iliffe: 68 continues to distinguish the answers throughout the piece, and indeed it is possible to do so.

28. Note the use of the inflected note *f♯″* (instead of *f″*) here, which contributes significantly to the modulation.

29. Here the author expands Tovey's theory of analytical classification by contrapuntal devices. Sampson 1905–7: 85 and Fuller-Maitland: 32, on the contrary, recognize fourteen individual stretti.

30. It may be worth noting that Bach retains the key relationship of the exposition, viz., i–v–i, up to this point.

31. Its fluid character assists the establishment of the modulation to the relative major.

32. In this extension there are noteworthy stretto entries of the second half of the subject in the inner voices. This is the only instance in this fugue where Bach uses only the second half of the subject in stretto.

33. In the editor's view, this imitation is significant, as it can be seen to be paving its way to employing the truncated subject entries, which become predominant from bars 76 onward. Musically, too, the dominant pedal suggests the appearance of something substantial for the piece.

34. Readers may have noticed Bach's powerful harmonic language at this dramatic halt, where, on the subdominant pedal, Bach unfolds the Neapolitan six and the third inversion of the dominant seventh chord in six voices; it prepares for the dominant pedal (bars 81), which in turn anticipates the convincing perfect cadence in the tonic (with a *tierce de Picardie*) in bar 83. For the further discussion of Bach's "colourful harmony," see Bullivant: 153–154.

35. Presumably the author is referring to Tovey's (p. 27) critical remark on Kroll, which, incidentally, is a false accusation. Among the analytical studies, Jadassohn,

Iliffe, and Stade take this approach. Such distinction is purely academic and unnecessary, as it is characteristic of the fugues of Bach's predecessors.

36. This refers to the copy in the hand of his second wife, Anna Magdalena (the "London autograph," f. 2^v), presumably copied from Bach's autograph (now lost); it is thought to reflect Bach's notational details closely.

37. The countersubject disappears after the exposition. Czaczkes 1982 ii: 26, however, claims that it is still present in modified form as the new running theme (first appearing in episode 1) until bar 16.

38. Jadassohn: 9 thinks that the entry of bar 10 is subject and that of bar 11 is answer.

39. The editorial supplement is also suggested by a number of other scholars, including Sampson 1905–7: 53, 183, Czaczkes 1982 ii: 28, and Dürr: 261.

40. The author follows Tovey's analytical description of its structure and stretti. Iliffe: 90 groups stretti differently: stretto I (= stretto 1 + 2); stretto II (= stretto 3 + 4).

41. Sampson 1905–7: 53 divides this stretto into two stretti (grouping the first three entries as one and the remaining two as the other).

42. The editor believes that there is an inverted subject in the soprano in bar 19 (as suggested by Iliffe and Czaczkes 1982 ii: 29), although many scholars, including Bruhn, Dürr, and the author, do not recognize it.

43. Macpherson ii: 7 and Keller: 140 call this section coda.

44. Czaczkes 1982 ii: 32 claims that the soprano at the last note of bar 26 is also a variant form of subject entry.

45. More precisely, it is iii♯ to i of the dominant key. It may also be added that the countersubject disappears after bar 60 almost completely (with the exception of a brief reappearance in bar 82).

46. Iliffe: 183, Sampson 1905–7: 87, Prout 1910: 85, and Morgan regard this episode as codetta.

47. Many commentators, including Riemann: 183–184, Keller: 193, Czaczkes 1982 ii: 259, Bruhn iv: 176, and Dürr: 418, regard this idea (particularly the rhythm ♩♪♩♪♩♪) as the second countersubject, which reappears in bars 19, 29–30, 35–36, 44, 48, 54, 60, 75, and 91.

48. Iliffe, Sampson 1905–7, Prout 1910: 85, and Morgan regard this episode as codetta.

49. For a more detailed harmonic analysis, see Renwick: 146–147.

50. Iliffe divides this section into two stretti. For the discussion of stretti on harmonic grounds, see Renwick: 177–178, 199–202, who carefully examines both the contrapuntal relationship among the stretto parts and their implications within the tonal structure.

51. Iliffe considers all the second entries of the stretti in this fugue as answers.

52. For a detailed harmonic analysis, see Renwick: 148.

53. For a detailed harmonic analysis, see Renwick: 158.

54. For a detailed harmonic analysis, see Renwick: 177–179.

55. Several scholars (including Iliffe, Riemann: 186, and Dickinson: 92) consider that the second entries of the stretti are "answers."

56. For a detailed harmonic analysis, see Renwick: 159.

57. For a detailed harmonic analysis, see Renwick: 177–179.

58. For a detailed harmonic analysis, see Renwick: 178–180.

59. However unusual it may be, it is a misconception that this idea—as believed by many scholars in the past—is "exceptional" and that Bach is "defying the fusty old rules and showing at the very outset of his collection that he was going to do just what he liked" (as Bullivant: 32 puts it). It is now considered to be one of many possible procedures available in Bach's time, as we now know more about the fugues composed by Bach's predecessors, particularly Froberger, Fischer, and Fux. See Bullivant: 32, 86.

60. It may be added that the semiquaver figure evolved from the tail section of the subject (♫♫♩ ♩), in itself an inverted diminution of the first four notes of the subject (♩ ♫♩ ♩.).

61. It may be worth noting an interesting theory put forward by Boekelman that "the subject is metamorphosed into what may be termed a countersubject at the 7th measure, which peculiarly explains the origin of the large number of strettos in this composition."

62. Some scholars (e.g., Iliffe: 3, Prout, 1910: 11–12, Morgan, Macpherson i: 8, and Dickinson: 71) consider bars 7–10 as a sort of counterexposition, despite the fact that only three of the four voices participate, whereas Fuller-Maitland i: 13 explicitly states that there is no counterexposition.

63. Iliffe and Gedalge continue to specify subject–answer types throughout the piece, with a few differences in interpretation.

64. Dürr: 103 puts D as the tonality at this point, which is correct if we examine the inherent harmony of the melody in the subject entry alone, with no contextualization; if we examine the actual harmony in which the subject entry is placed, Dürr's harmonic analysis is invalid.

65. Dürr: 103 claims the tonality as E minor. See also note 64.

66. Dürr: 103 suggests the tonality as G major at this point, with which we disagree.

67. Riemann ii: 35, Stade ii: 16, Fuller-Maitland ii: 12, and Gedalge: 223 call this figure countersubject.

68. Macpherson ii: 15 regards it as codetta.

69. This observation by the author is both unique and compelling: other commentators (including Iliffe: 106 and Bruhn i: 219) commonly claim that the episode starts after the subject entry.

70. Prout 1891: 150 calls it episode.

71. Dürr: 285 describes the tonality as A major. See also note 64.

72. Iliffe: 106 and Dürr: 285 describe the tonality of this tenor entry in bar 21 as B minor. See also note 64.

73. Iliffe: 106, Prout 1891: 150, and Gedalge: 221 claim that this entry is answer, not subject.

74. The author originally wrote "subject" for these entries, but the editor amended them to "answer."

75. Several commentators, including Prout 1891: 151, Macpherson ii: 16, and Dürr: 283, consider that this entry marks the beginning of the final section.

76. Iliffe: 106, Prout 1891: 152, and Gedalge: 223 consider this entry as answer, with which the editor tends to agree.

77. The soprano entry at bar 44 looks more likely to be answer, a view that is supported by Iliffe and Sampson.

CHAPTER 13: GROUP 6: FUGUES WITH COUNTERSUBJECTS INTRODUCED AFTER THE EXPOSITION

1. The author does not specify the origin of this opinion; the editor has so far been unsuccessful to identify him or her.

2. The author's view is shared by the majority of scholars, including Riemann i: 125, Macpherson i: 79, Gray: 65, Perrachio: 147, David: 74, Czaczkes 1982 i: 189, Bruhn iv: 63, and Dürr: 205. The next common view is to end at the fifth note of the second bar (Iliffe: 65, Sampson 1905–7: 41, Prout 1910: 44, and Morgan). Stade i: 67 considers it to last until the second note of bar 2 and calls the remaining portion "Nachsatz." Keller: 109 and Souchay: 58 claim that the subject lasts until the first note of the third bar.

3. Iliffe and Sampson consider this section a codetta.

4. Iliffe and Sampson consider this section an episode.

5. Iliffe and Sampson think differently; they consider bars 17(18)–23 an episode.

6. Iliffe does not consider this a countersubject but a "new and more rapid passage."

7. Iliffe regards this voice as alto. Bach's autograph (Mus. ms. Bach P 415 in the Staatsbibliothek zu Berlin Preußischer Kulturbesitz) shows that, at least notationally, Bach did not bother distinguishing the voice-crossing; the soprano was consistently written as down-stemmed notation below the alto in bars 25–26.

8. Iliffe considers that the episode starts from bar 34 (instead of bar 36, which the author suggests).

9. Bruhn iv: 67–69 supports this alternative theory.

10. Iliffe and Sampson consider the coda to start as early as bar 46.

11. Bruhn iv: 142–143 cautiously argues that it can be considered as the first countersubject along with another free part (which she calls the second countersubject) appearing in bars 14–17 in the soprano (and again in bars 22–25 in the middle voice). The editor supports, however, a different view proposed by Riemann: 176 and Gray: 139 in that the crotchet motive (♩♩♩|♩♩♩—which is later revised by Bach into a quaver figure to mirror the subject in tenths and sixths below the answer) develops into the first countersubject proper (♪ ♫♩♩♫♩♩ etc.), which appears in the soprano at bar 33 for the first time.

12. Several scholars, including Iliffe: 178, Sampson 1905–7: 59, Prout 1910: 83, Morgan, and Macpherson ii: 68, consider that this is a codetta.

13. Readers interested in a Schenkerian analysis of the exposition of the fugue (bars 1–17) will find Renwick: 127 useful.

14. German scholars (viz., Riemann ii: 177, Czaczkes 1982 ii: 242, and Dürr: 411) consider this entry as subject.

15. As with the previous entry at bar 21, Riemann, Czaczkes, and Dürr consider this entry as subject also.

16. Iliffe and Sampson play down the significance of this section, as they believe that a new section (which modulates into related keys) starts at bar 44. They thus claim the presence of counterexposition in this fugue, although they disagree with

regard to the place where it starts and how it interacts within the piece; Iliffe considers it to start at bar 32, whereas Sampson (and Fuller-Maitland ii: 79) choose at 21.

17. See note 11.

18. Renwick: 158–160 discusses this topic from harmonic analysis using Schenkerian methods.

19. Iliffe: 178 and Riemann ii: 178 consider that this is an answer. The distinction between subject and answer is difficult due to a complex reading of the last quaver note of bar 78, the note that determines the real or tonal shape of the answer; while the sources deriving from Bach's lost autograph (the so-called Altnickol tradition) unanimously give c'' (real), Bach's surviving autograph in the British Library, London, gives ambiguous reading—either bb' or c''—as a result of subsequently amending the position (and size) of the note-head. Jones: 192 considers that Bach altered it to bb' (tonal) to "underline the return to the tonic key," which is basically supported by Dürr: 408.

20. The two-bar section that leads to the last four bars of the fugue was revisited by Bach, where the voice-texture received different, more convincing treatment. The earlier version is preserved in Bach's autograph in London.

21. Prout 1910: 89 considers the final section to start at bar 69.

22. It is necessary to supplement a little, for this countersubject not only plays an important role in this fugue but also is in itself controversial, as Gray: 147 points out. While Iliffe: 193 does not consider it as countersubject, the majority of commentators consider that it is, although there is a disagreement whether it should start at the second semiquaver of bar 7 (author, Czaczkes 1982 ii: 301, Bruhn iv: 248) or the fifth semiquaver of the bar (Macpherson ii: 77, Dürr: 434). In any case, it resembles the subject closely; furthermore, they are arranged in quasi stretto (which recurs at bars 15–17, 26–28), evolving into a clearer stretto later on (viz., bars 69–71 and 97–100).

23. Iliffe, Prout 1910: 89, and Morgan consider that this is codetta, not episode.

24. The author is referring to the text transmitted in the so-called Altnickol tradition. *Neue Bach Ausgabe* gives this text as "Fassung B." The version transmitted in the London autograph gives a different text (S: ♩♩♩♩ $d'-e'-f\!\!\sharp'-g'-f\!\!\sharp'$; A: ♪♩♩♪ $b-e'$), which retains the original shape of the first countersubject announced at bar 7.

25. Stade ii: 113 thinks it is a variant form of the head motive of the subject, while Czaczkes and Knorr ignore it completely in their analysis.

26. Iliffe: 193 and Sampson 1905–7: 48 consider that this entry is a real answer.

27. Bruhn considers this the first countersubject. See also note 21.

28. This subject first appears as if it is the first countersubject but it soon establishes (from bar 72) that it is a proper subject entry.

29. Bruhn iv: 255 interprets the bass (bars 97–99) as the first countersubject.

30. For a detailed harmonic analysis of the exposition, see Renwick: 118, 195–196.

31. Note that a part of countersubject (from the third beat of bar 15) is inverted in double counterpoint in the twelfth instead of octave. The free part in the soprano thus assumes a new contrapuntal role, as it recurs in bars 32–35. Czaczkes 1982 i: 156 labels this idea as "countersubject 2b" (*Gegensatz IIb*).

CHAPTER 14: GROUP 7: FUGUES WITH SUBSIDIARY SUBJECTS

1. The ending point of the subject is usually interpreted in one of the following ways: (1) the last note of bar 2—the view of the author, shared by Taylor: 57, Riemann ii: 29, Gray: 91, Keller: 144, and Dürr: 278; (2) the seventh note of bar 2—Higgs: 8, Iliffe: 100, Stade ii: 11, Sampson 1905–7: 61, Brandts Buys: 237, Knorr, Macpherson ii: 12, Czaczkes 1982 ii: 47, and Bruhn i: 183.

2. In the editor's view, this is a crucial point for the better understanding of the construction of this fugue, especially how the introduction of the second subject (bar 35) can be justified. It is a mistake to think that the lack of a stable shape is an unimportant topic. Iliffe, who denies the presence of any subsidiary subjects in this fugue and ignores them in his discussion, thus made a serious error in judgment, as he completely misunderstood their roles and contributions in the fugue. As our analysis reveals, the second subject is a product of the gradual metamorphosis of the countersubject. This view is endorsed by the following scholars: Macpherson ii: 13, Bruhn i: 185, and Dürr: 277.

3. Bruhn does not consider this device as countersubject.

4. The countersubject, now modified further, is in the soprano.

5. Iliffe: 100 regards the counterexposition to be incomplete, as he excludes the bass entry (bars 20–21) from this section.

6. Iliffe and Sampson 1905–7: 61 do not recognize this section as such; they include it in a large episodic section, engulfing both episodes 2 and 3. Note that Knorr does not recognize the second subject in his analysis but calls it countersubject (from bar 48, in the same way as that of bar 38).

7. Czaczkes 1982 ii: 50 and Dürr: 278 give the tonality "fis–gis" here.

8. Bruhn iv: 191 does not consider that S^{ii} appears here.

9. Knorr does not consider countersubjects to be present in this fugue.

10. Iliffe: 165 and Sampson 1905–7: 45 consider this episode a codetta (cf. episodes 5 and 7).

11. As was the case with **II.4**, the second subject can be traced back to the countersubject announced at bar 5. See Riemann ii: 154, Gray: 130–131, and Dürr: 384–385.

12. The episode temporarily modulates to III (bar 41) before settling in v.

13. It briefly modulates to III again (bar 51), before heading back to i.

14. Iliffe and Sampson call this extension "codetta."

15. Iliffe calls this a countersubject (cf. **II.4**); he ignores the second countersubject in his analysis.

16. Iliffe and Sampson also consider this episode a codetta (cf. episodes 1 and 7).

17. Iliffe interprets this entry as answer.

18. Iliffe and Sampson also consider this episode a codetta (cf. episodes 1 and 5).

19. Iliffe: 187 and Knorr do not recognize this device. See also p. 15.

20. Riemann ii: 196, Iliffe: 187, and Sampson 1905–7: 70–71 consider this entry as answer.

21. Scholars are divided whether this should be interpreted as the second subject, as the author claims (with Riemann ii: 197, Tovey, Fuller-Maitland ii: 36, and Macpherson ii: 73), or a "new" countersubject, the view that has a wider support (e.g., Dickinson: 95, Prout 1891: 79, Iliffe: 187, Sampson 1905–7: 159, Morgan, Czaczkes 1982 ii: 283, Bullivant: 134, Bruhn iv: 208, and Dürr: 426). Whichever

view one may take, it is important to notice that unlike the double fugues that we examined earlier (viz., **II.4** and **II.18**), there is no comparable exposition of the second subject (though one may argue that bars 28–35 can be considered as such). This "subject" is much more widely and freely used during the course of the piece (as indicated in the diagram).

22. Iliffe: 187 and Sampson 1905–7: 71 regard this as an episode that lasts until bar 35, as they do not consider the second subject as such in their analysis. See also note 19.

23. Riemann ii: 197 considers this soprano entry as answer.

24. It may be necessary to mention the role of the tenor, which initially accompanies the subject entry in the alto but then gives its role away to the bass in the following bar (as shown in the diagram in square brackets). The same textural treatment is found again in bars 48 and 75.

25. Riemann ii: 199, Iliffe: 187, and Sampson 1905–7: 71 consider this soprano entry as answer.

26. For an in-depth harmonic analysis of this episode, see Renwick: 151, 161.

27. Riemann ii: 202, Iliffe: 187, and Sampson 1905–7: 71 consider this tenor entry as answer.

28. Czaczkes 1982 ii: 149 takes a different view, claiming that this is a countersubject that recurs in a variant form at bars 9 (soprano) and 17 (bass).

29. Iliffe: 145 and Sampson 1905–7: 49 consider that the phrase starting on the third note ($g\sharp$) of bar 14 in the bass is the real answer. Prout 1910: 72 goes one step further to claim that this is followed by the subject in stretto in the soprano in bar 16, forming a partial counterexposition (bars 14–16).

30. It is worth adding that the "walking-bass" that accompanies the soprano entry starts as a sequence of the first four notes of the subject in inversion, the idea first employed in bar 11 (though only three notes were used then); as the sequence continues freely, it gradually loses its identity, paving the way for introducing a new subject at bar 20.

31. Iliffe: 145, who does not recognize the second and third subject, interprets this section as episode (bars 19–28).

32. Some scholars have different views as to the length of this subject. Fuller-Maitland ii: 25 thinks, for instance, that it consists of four notes only, whereas Prout 1910: 73 and Macpherson ii: 45, claim six notes; Dürr: 352 suggests that it lasts until the second note of bar 22 (i.e., nine notes).

33. Iliffe: 145 regards this section as part of episode (bars 36–51). See note 31. Czaczkes 1982 ii: 153–158 and Dürr: 553–554 also consider this section to be an integral part of a much wider section (which they call the fourth exposition), consisting of three rounds: bars 36–40 (middle, soprano, bass, middle [redundant]), 40–43 (bass, middle), and 43–51 (soprano, bass, soprano [redundant], soprano [inversion, redundant], episode, and cadence). They are added to the diagram by the editor.

34. Czaczkes 1982 ii: 159 and Dürr: 353 think that this entry is answer.

35. For the further analytical discussion of how each subject retains its essential melodic structure while being governed by the underlying harmonic motion, see Renwick: 94–95.

36. Iliffe: 23 and Bruhn ii: 64 reverse the way that they refer to respective subjects, while the majority of commentators agree with the author. It may be worth mentioning that Riemann i: 48 refers to them as "theme" and "countersubject."

37. Note that even at this early stage of fugal development, it is abundantly clear that this toccata theme, which became the head figure of the second subject, is also employed freely outside this thematic device as a motive.

38. Iliffe: 24 and Bruhn ii: 69 do not recognize this as subject entry.

39. As in the previous episode, it begins with a similar tonal deflection to ii.

40. Dürr: 136 considers that the final section begins at the next entry in the bass in bar 61, while Bruhn ii: 69 suggests much earlier at bar 58.

41. Iliffe: 25 and Bruhn ii: 69 do not recognize this as a variant form of subject.

42. Iliffe: 63 divides the sections differently in two: bars 1–14½, and 14½–24.

CHAPTER 15: GROUP 8: FUGUES FOR FIVE VOICES

1. Prout 1910: 21 and Morgan consider the final section to begin at bar 73.

2. See Bruhn i: 165 for her argument for the presence of countersubject in bars 4–9. It is important to recognize that this melody provides not only the descending-scale figure but also the suspension motive. See also Stade i: 14 and Dürr: 119.

3. Riemann, Jadassohn, and Iliffe: 134 continue to distinguish them in their analysis.

4. Czaczkes 1984 claims that "consistently retained preparatory motives of the second countersubject" [i.e., S^{ii}] first appears in bar 6 in the bass.

5. In his analysis Boekelman: 5 considers that the four notes starting on the second quaver of bar 38 (plus second-eighth quavers of bars 62 and 84) do not belong to the second subject.

6. As Gray: 26 suggests, the emergence of S^{iii} is already hinted at in bars 39–41 in the tenor. Czaczkes 1984 suggests even earlier, claiming that its "adorned variant of its opening" is already suggested in bar 4 in the bass and then in bar 7 in the tenor.

7. This is, in fact, a stretto between the highest two voices.

8. All the commentators whom I have examined failed to recognize this alto entry of S^i except Knorr, who claims that it stays in the alto.

9. Boekelman does not recognize the second subject here. Prout 1910: 21 considers bars 57–58 as the second episode.

10. Prout 1910: 21 and Morgan consider bars 62–65 as the third episode.

11. Prout 1910: 21 and Morgan consider bars 69–72 as the fourth episode.

12. Iliffe considers that bars 62–65 constitute the second episode, modulating from i to V.

13. Iliffe considers that bars 84–86 constitute the third episode, modulating from i to iv; in Morgan's analysis this is the fifth episode.

14. Prout 1910: 22 considers this section as the fifth and the last episode in this fugue; in Morgan's analysis, this is the sixth.

15. The point at which the final section begins is a subject of debate; while Iliffe: 14 places it at bar 97, Czaczkes 1982 i: 98, Bruhn i: 173, and Dürr: 122 consider that it starts at bar 94. According to Macpherson i: 19, Prout regards the final period as starting at bar 73.

16. Prout 1910: 22 considers that the coda begins at bar 100.

17. Riemann i: 146–147 explains how this chain of syncopated figures assumes the role of a countersubject, and although it does not appear consistently, it can be traced "pretty well throughout the whole fugue."

18. Iliffe: 75, Sampson 1905–7: 92, Prout 1910: 48, and Morgan call it "codetta" rather than "episode." Schulenberg: 193 goes a step further to claim that there are only two "sequential bridges" in this fugue (bars 6[f.] and 42[f.]), as "the severe style adopted here permits no real episodes."

19. Iliffe: 75 regards this bass entry as answer.

20. Dürr: 225 gives the tonality of this entry as ♭VII (A♭), which is imprecise and misleading; although the entry is formulated in the shape of A♭, the underlying harmony, and the resultant tonality of this phrase, is D♭.

21. These irregular entries are not always recognized by the commentators; while Stade i: 86, Czaczkes 1982 i: 211, and Dürr: 225 ignore the alto in their analysis, Boekelman, Knorr, and Bruhn iv: 158–159, 165 ignore both.

CHATPER 16: EPISODES (2)

1. See note 5 to Chapter 1.

2. See note 19 to Chapter 7.

CHAPTER 17: TONALITY IN THE "48"

1. In the editor's opinion **II.12** should be classified outside this category, as it uses a tonal answer whose first note is harmonized in the tonic.

2. **II.7, 9**, and **22** may be better classified under a different category, as they all feature a much larger structural plan where the entries in question not only start a new section but also appear in stretto.

3. **II.16** may be better placed under a different category (e.g., with **I.10**), as it does not fit to this group of pieces in strict sense.

4. See note 23 to Chapter 13.

Annotated Bibliography

The following are the books and articles chosen for the notes of this book. In the editor's view, they broadly represent the analytical writings on the "48." Other sources discuss specific movements of the "48" and thus are cited less frequently; these are described in the notes themselves. For a more complete, searchable bibliography, consult the on-line Bach Bibliography:

http://www.music.qub.ac.uk/tomita/bachbib/

Altschuler, Eric Lewin. *Bachanalia: The Essential Listener's Guide to Bach's Well-Tempered Clavier.* Boston: Little, Brown, 1994. xv+254 pp. Written in an informal style, it introduces the ingenuity of Bach's contrapuntal art to those readers who have had no formal musical education. The scope of his analytical discussion is restricted to the listing of subject entries.

Badura-Skoda, Paul. *Interpreting Bach at the Keyboard.* Translated by Alfred Clayton. Oxford: Clarendon Press, 1993. xvi+573 pp. Originally published in German under the title of *Bach-Interpretation: Die Klavierwerke Johann Sebastian Bachs* from Laaber-Verlag in 1990. A monograph devoted to the performance aspect of Bach's keyboard works.

Boekelman, Bern. *Acht Fugen aus J. S. Bach's Wohltemperirtem Clavier durch farben analytisch dargestellt, mit beigefügter harmonischer Structur zum gebrauch in Musikschulen und zur Selbstbelehrung.* Serie I [and II]. Leipzig: F. M. Geidel, 1895. 18 ff + 19 ff. Analysis of sixteen fugues (I.1, 2, 3, 4, 5, 6, 7, 10, 16, 21, 22; II.1, 2, 7, 11 and 12) on the piano score, using colors to distinguish between thematic and nonthematic parts. His analysis is not always thorough.

Brandts Buys, Hans. *Het Wohltemperirte Clavier van Johann Sebastian Bach.* Arnhem: van Loghum Slaterus, 1942. 308 pp. Reissued in 1955 and 1984. Analytical commentary of each movement of the "48" preceded by brief discussions on the technique of fugal writing and a wide range of historical issues.

Bruhn, Siglind. *J. S. Bach's Well-Tempered Clavier: In-Depth Analysis and Interpretation.* Hong Kong: Mainer International, 1993, 4 vols. 264+250+248+260 pp. With advanced performers in mind, the author discusses each movement of the "48" methodically and systematically. Within this rigid framework of discussion, she attempts to cover everything from the obvious to the trivial, which unfortunately deprives her of opportunities to effectively deal with the issues of real import. For readers with the agenda of analysis, her policy not to distinguish answers from subjects and codettas from episodes is unhelpful, for without this distinction one cannot fathom a sense of direction and structure in a fugue. Her color diagram provided after the analysis of each fugue is well conceived and user-friendly.

Bruyck, Carl van. *Technische und ästhetische Analysen des Wohltemperirten Claviers nebst einer allgemeinen, Sebastian Bach und die sogenannte kontrapunktische Kunst betreffenden Einleitung.* Leipzig: Breitkopf, 1867. [2/1889] iv+188p. One of the earliest monographs devoted to the analysis of the "48." His discussion of individual movements is often too brief to be useful; some of his analytical observations are approached aesthetically and are not always well conceived.

Bullivant, Roger. *Fugue.* London: Hutchinson University Library, 1971. 198 pp. Probably the most insightful monograph, examining fugues from both historical and analytical angles while attempting to clear up the confusions arising from the divergence between academic fugue and live composition. Numerous examples are drawn from the "48."

Busoni, Ferruccio. *Johann Sebastian Bach: Klavierwerke.* Unter Mitwirkung von Egon Petri und Bruno Mugellini hrsg. von Ferruccio Busoni. Leipzig: VEB Breitkopf & Härtel, [1894]. Practical edition full of dynamic marks. Analytical indications are also added to some fugues.

Czaczkes, Ludwig. *Analyse des Wohltemperierten Klaviers. Form und Aufbau der Fuge bei Bach.* Vienna: Österreichischer Bundesverlag, [i: 1956, ii: 1965] 2nd revised ed., 1982. 235+332 pp. Very detailed analysis on the form and structure of all the movements from the "48." It was considered by many in the past as the "classic" textbook. His indulged analysis is sometimes speculative.

————. *Die Fugen des Wohltemperierten Klaviers in bildlicher Darstellung.* Vienna: Österreichischer Bundesverlag, 1984. Very detailed analytical diagrams of all the fugues from the "48" based on his earlier publication.

David, Johann Nepomuk. *Das Wohltemperierte Klavier. Der Versuch einer Synopsis.* Göttingen: Vandenhoeck & Ruprecht, 1962. 92 pp. Brief, but speculative analysis of all the movements of the "48"; it attempts to demonstrate how a motive or subject is derived from others and how every piece in the same key is thematically related to each other.

Dehn, Siegfried Wilhelm. *Analysen dreier Fugen aus Joh. Seb. Bach's wohltemperiertem Klavier und einer Vocal Doppelfuge A. M. Bononcini's.* Leipzig: C. F. Peters, 1858, 37p., pl. 11. Detailed analysis of I.6, II.7 and II.9, scrutinizing both the motivic and (a rather limited) harmonic contents of almost every bar.

Dickinson, Alan Edgar Frederic. *Bach's Fugal Works. With an Account of Fugue before and after Bach.* London: Pitman, 1956. ix+280 pp. Brief commentary on numerous fugues, focusing on their main stylistic and structural traits, covering not only those from the "48" and his other fugues for organ but also those by other composers before and after Bach.

Dürr, Alfred. *Johann Sebastian Bach. Das Wohltemperierte Klavier.* Kassel: Bärenreiter, 1998. 459 pp. Considered by many as a groundbreaking monograph on the "48" written by the editor of the *Neue Bach Ausgabe* (Kassel: Bärenreiter, 1989, 1995). It not only addresses historical and analytical issues but also incorporates into the discussion notable variants found in the principal traditions of sources. While discussing the salient features of various aspects of fugal construction, the author evaluates other scholars' interpretations. Like many other German scholars, he concludes his study of fugues with the summary of their constructions in two levels of hierarchy (i.e., sections and expositions).

Fuller-Maitland, John Alexander. *The "48": Bach's Wohltemperirtes Clavier.* London: Humphrey Milford and Oxford University Press, 1925. 2 vols. 38+38p. Very brief commentary of each movement of the "48."

Gedalge, André. *Treatise on the Fugue.* Translated and edited by Ferdinand Davis. Norman: University of Oklahoma Press, 1965. 435 pp. First published in French in 1900 under the title of *Traité de la fugue*, this is a well-laid-out textbook for students. Some examples are taken from the "48" for a specific discussion: I.18 (answer), II.22 (episodes), I.I, 4, II.5, 9, 22, 23 (stretto).

Gray, Cecil William Turpie. *The Forty-eight Preludes and Fugues of J. S. Bach.* London: Oxford University Press, 1/1938 [2/1948, R/1952]. viii+148 pp. Written as a concise analytical commentary, it focuses on musical style and its effect of each movement of the "48."

Higgs, James. *Fugue.* London and New York: Novello, [preface dated 1878]. iv+115p. A concise textbook on fugue written for students learning to write fugues.

Horsley, Imogene. *Fugue: History and Practice.* New York: Free Press; London: Collier-Macmillan, 1966. 399 pp. This is a textbook designed for students learning the historical background of, and how to write, fugues; some examples are drawn from the "48," but the discussion is rather basic.

Iliffe, Frederick. *The Forty-eight Preludes and Fugues of John Sebastian Bach Analysed for the Use of Students.* London: Novello, 1896, 1897. v+194 pp. Very brief outline analysis (or description) of each movement of the "48." Interesting details of Bach's compositional techniques are mostly untouched, however.

Jadassohn, Salomon. *Erläuterungen zu ausgewählten Fugen aus Johann Sebastian Bach's wohltemperirtem Clavier.* Supplement zu des Verfassers Lehrbuch des Kanons und der Fuge. Leipzig: F.E.C. Leuckart, [Vorwort dated 1887], 58 pp. A fairly detailed structural analysis of nineteen selected fugues of the "48" (I.1, 4, 6, 12, 14, 16, 17, 18, 20, 22, 23, 24; II.2, 5, 7, 9, 10, 22, 23).

Jones, Richard. *J. S. Bach: The Well-Tempered Clavier, Part I* [and *II*]. Edited and annotated by Richard Jones. Commentary by Donald Francis Tovey. London: Associated Board of the Royal Schools of Music, 1994. A well-researched critical edition with excellent commentaries on the genesis, sources, and editorial issues. Tovey's famous commentary (1924), albeit slightly revised and updated by the editor, is reproduced here.

Keller, Hermann. *The Well-Tempered Clavier by Johann Sebastian Bach.* Translated from German by Leigh Gerdine. London: Allen & Unwin, 1976. 207 pp. Original title: *Das Wohltemperierte Klavier von Johann Sebastian Bach* (Kassel, 1965). It captures well the emotional content of the individual movements of the "48." While his interpretation is often unique and controversial, his analysis is mostly limited to the fugue subject and salient features of the form, style, and techniques, thus lacking the details needed for a serious analytical study.

Kennan, Kent Wheeler. *Counterpoint based on Eighteenth-Century Practice.* 2nd edition. Englewood Cliffs, NJ: Prentice-Hall, 1972. xiii+289 pp. Basic textbook for studying counterpoint, gradually introducing to students how to write fugues. Many examples are taking from the "48" to illustrate fugal techniques and style.

Kirkpatrick, Ralph. *Interpreting Bach's Well-Tempered Clavier. A Performer's Discourse of Method.* New Haven, CT, and London: Yale University Press, 1984. xvii+132 pp. Written by an author who maintains that the conventional analytical studies are of little use for an interpreter, ridiculing them as "the autopsy of the Bach fugue" (p. 30). By resorting to a range of issues drawn from historical, theoretical, and aesthetic approaches, the author attempts to show how one can interpret the "48" with conviction.

Kirnberger, Johann Philipp. *Die Kunst des reinen Satzes in der Musik.* Berlin, 1771–79. 2 vols. Kirnberger's magnum opus, covering a diverse range of topics in music theory. Six examples are cited from the "48" (I.1, 4; II.4, 10, 11, 22) to demonstrate some aspects of time-signatures, rhythm, harmony, and counterpoint.

————. *Die wahren Grundsätze zum Gebrauch der Harmonie.* Berlin, 1773. Includes harmonic analysis of I.24 and II.Pr.20 (by his pupil, Johann Abraham Peter Schulz) with figured bass. Repr. in *Bach Dokumente*, vol. 3, no. 781; Engl. trans. by David W. Beach and Jurgen Thym, in *Journal of Music Theory* 23 (1979), pp. 163–225. Fascinating details of controversy between Marpurg and Kirnberger are discussed in Howard Serwer, "Marpurg versus Kirnberger: Theories of Fugal Composition", *Journal of Music Theory* 104 (1970), pp. 209–236.

Kitson, Charles Herbert. *Studies in Fugue.* Oxford: Clarendon Press, 1909. 104 pp. Textbook on writing fugues with particular emphasis on writing good countersubjects and episodes. Some examples are drawn from the "48," but with little value for analytical purposes.

————. *Elements of Fugal Construction.* London: Oxford University Press, 1929. 76pp. Concise textbook for students learning to write fugues. Through many examples taken from the "48" the author occasionally discusses pitfalls associated with certain fugal devices.

Knorr, Iwan Otto Armand. *Die Fugen des "Wohltemperierten Klaviers" von Joh. Seb. Bach in bildlicher Darstellung.* Leipzig: Breitkopf & Härtel, 1912. 48 pp. Very brief and rough outline analysis of all the fugues of the "48" shown in diagram, merely indicating the entries of subjects.

Macpherson, Stewart. *A Commentary on Book I* [and *Book II*] *of the Forty-Eight Preludes and Fugues of Johann Sebastian Bach.* London: Novello & Co., [1934–37]. 107+79 pp. Analytical commentary of each movement of the "48," focusing on several important structural features. Among similar books published in this period, it is probably the most useful one for students.

Marpurg, Friedrich Wilhelm. *Abhandlung von der Fuge, nach dem Grundsätzen der besten deutschen und ausländischen Meister.* Berlin, 1753–54. 2 vols. The first substantial discussion of Bach's fugal art from a conservative point of view at the time when the genre of fugue was mostly regarded as old-fashioned. Sixteen examples are taken from the "48" (I.1, 8, 10, 18, 20, 24; II.1, 2, 5, 6, 8, 11, 13, 16, 21, 22). The English translation of a selected portion is available in Alfred Mann, *The Study of Fugue* (London: Faber and Faber, 1958), x+341 pp. at pp. 142–212.

Morgan, Orlando. *J. S. Bach: Forty-eight Preludes and Fugues. Analysis of the Fugues.* London: Edwin Ashdown, 1931. [16 pp.] Very concise discussion on the constructional aspect of all the fugues of the "48." While largely based on Prout's *Forty-Eight Fugues*, the author stresses and expands his views where he disagrees with his mentor.

Nalden, Charles. *Fugal Answer.* London: Auckland University Press and Oxford University Press, 1970. xiii+192 pp. Comprehensive discussion of fugal answer from a theoretical standpoint. While examining the answering technique from a wider historical perspective, the author critically examines the theories and interpretations put forward by other scholars.

Oldroyd, George. *The Technique and Spirit of Fugue: An Historical Study.* London: Oxford University Press, 1948. viii+220 pp. Systematic study of technique and style of writing fugues by an author who regards the "48" as "an embodiment of truth" (p. 1). Numerous examples are taken from the "48," but his analysis is rather limited as well as too fragmented to be useful for analytical purposes.

Perrachio, Luigi. *G. S. Bach: Il Clavicembalo ben temperato.* Milano: Bottega di Poesia, 1926. 309 pp. Analytical commentary of each movement of the "48". There is also an expanded edition published by Ed. Palatine of Parma, Torino in 1947 (but not consulted).

Potgieter, Zelda. "Analyses of Selected Works from the Well-Tempered Clavier of J. S. Bach: A Synthesis of Existing Approaches." D.Phil. dissertation, University of Port Elizabeth, South Africa, 1999. 2 vols. 449+58 pp. Through the examination of a range of analytical approaches, the author puts into perspective their strengths and weaknesses, merits and defects, and suggests a model of the single, multifaceted musical experience using II.16 as an example.

Prout, Ebenezer. *Fugue.* London: Augener & Co., [1891]. xi+258p. Classic textbook on fugue, making ample reference to "48" examples (taking twenty-one fugues from Book 1 and twelve from Book 2).

———. *Fugal Analysis. A Companion to "Fugue."* London: Augener, 1892. viii+257 pp. "A collection of fugues of various styles put into score and analyzed." Bach is the main author; others include Handel, Haydn, Mendelssohn, Mozart, and Schumann. II.20 is the only one discussed from the "48."

———. *Analysis of J. S. Bach's Forty-Eight Fugues (Das Wohltemperirte Clavier).* Edited by Louis B. Prout. London: Edwin Ashdown, [1910] ix+90 pp. Posthumous publication by his son. Concise discussion of all the fugues of the "48" from the constructional perspective.

Renwick, William. *Analyzing Fugue: A Schenkerian Approach.* Stuyvesant: Pendragon, 1995. 229 pp. Thorough and systematic application of Schenkerian analysis to nearly 300 fugues by Bach and his contemporaries. Many fugues of the "48" are used as examples, which are often insightful.

Riemann, Hugo. *Analysis of J. S. Bach's Wohltemperiertes Clavier.* Translated from German by J. S. Shedlock. London: Augener & Co., 1890. 2 vols. 168+210 p. Original title: *Analyse von Bachs wohltemperirtem Klavier. Handbuch der Fugen-Komposition* (also 1890). Serious and original analytical approach to all the movements of the "48" and critical on earlier scholars' views (especially Bruyck). Due partially to the poor translation and partially to the author's pedantic approach with no explicit reference to a piece, his discussion can be difficult to follow.

Sampson, Brook. *A Digest of the Analysis of J. S. Bach's Forty-eight Celebrated Fugues from the Well-Tempered Clavier.* London: Vincent Music Company, 1905–7. 404 pp. Very systematic analysis of constructional aspects of the fugues of the "48." The format of presentation is rather poor, and there are numerous errors in the text and examples.

———. *Outline Analysis of Each of Bach's Forty-Eight Fugues.* London: Vincent Music Company [1907?]. 2 ll+36 pp. Shorter version of the preceding source, merely showing the construction of each fugue with keys of entries.

Schulenberg, David. *The Keyboard Music of J. S. Bach.* New York: Schirmer Books, 1992. 473 pp. Broad discussion of all the keyboard music written by Bach from diverse points of view. His discussion of the "48" is strongly colored from both sources and style analysis, a refreshing approach to inspire performers.

Souchay, Marc-André. "Das Thema in der Fuge Bachs," *Bach-Jahrbuch* 24 (1927): 1–102. The first of two parts of his discussion on Bach's fugues. In this article he discusses aspects of fugue subjects, types, and construction. Numerous examples are drawn from the "48."

Stade, Fritz. *J. S. Bach. Die Fugen des wohltemperierten Klaviers partiturmässig dargestellt und nach ihrem Bau erläutert von Dr. F. Stade.* Leipzig: Steingräber Verlag, [1900]. 2 vols. 100+115 pp. All the "48" fugues are set in open score with detailed analytical remarks, highlighting comprehensively the main themes, motives, and their variants employed in the piece.

Taylor, Franklin. *Treatise on Canon and Fugue.* Translated and adapted from the German of Ernst Friedrich Richter. London: J. B. Cramer and Co. 1878. viii+159 pp. Literal translation of *Lehrbuch der Fuge* (1859), a practical guide for writing fugues, in which the editor amply revised many aspects of the original treatise, especially the harmonic analysis. Many movements of the "48" are used as examples. The discussion is not very critical, however.

Tovey, Donald Francis. "Commentary" in: *J. S. Bach: Forty-Eight Preludes and Fugues. Pianoforte.* Edited by Donald Francis Tovey. Fingered by Harold Samuel. Book I and II. London: Associated Board of the Royal Academy of Music and the Royal College of Music, 1924. Classic reading for advanced performers, providing succinctly salient analytical issues of each of the "48" as well as helpful advice on stylish and effective performance. It is reproduced and corrected in the new edition by Richard Jones (1994).

Index

Compiled by Dorene Groocock

INDEX OF FUGUES BY NUMBER

Book I

No. 1 C major	124	2, 5, 6, 14, 21, 130, 167, 174
No. 2 C minor	43	6, 12, 13, 16, 20, 169, 170, 172, 174, 175
No. 3 C# major	32	6, 12, 13, 16, 19, 167, 174, 175
No. 4 C# minor	160	5, 21, 175
No. 5 D major	102	5, 6, 15, 84, 174
No. 6 D minor	68	5, 6, 13, 15, 19, 80
No. 7 E♭ major (Prelude)	154	7, 8, 9, 17, 19
No. 7 E♭ major (Fugue)	34	
No. 8 D# minor	77	6, 14, 20, 174, 180
No. 9 E major	37	5, 6, 13, 15, 20, 172, 174, 175
No. 10 E minor	25	5, 6, 7, 13, 19, 169, 170, 177
No. 11 F major	64	6, 13, 16, 20, 80, 171, 174
No. 12 F minor	89	6, 12, 13, 16, 21, 82, 84, 171, 174, 175
No. 13 F# major	140	6, 13, 16, 19, 169, 174, 175
No. 14 F# minor (Prelude)	28	5, 6, 13, 19, 21, 33
No. 14 F# minor (Fugue)	91	15, 82, 84, 174
No. 15 G major	66	5, 6, 15, 16, 19, 80, 173
No. 16 G minor	114	6, 16, 20, 84, 130, 174
No. 17 A♭ major	104	6, 15, 21, 84, 170, 174, 175, 176
No. 18 G# minor	93	8, 13, 17, 20, 84, 169, 171, 172, 178
No. 19 A major (Prelude)	156	7, 174
No. 19 A major (Fugue)	132	15, 176
No. 20 A minor	116	5, 6, 13, 16, 20, 84, 130, 169
No. 21 B♭ major	38	6, 16, 19, 170, 174, 175
No. 22 B♭ minor	164	6, 14, 21, 169
No. 23 B major	85	6, 13, 16, 20, 84, 174, 176
No. 24 B minor	95	8, 13, 17, 21, 84, 168, 169, 179

Book II

GENERAL INDEX

About the Author and Editor

JOSEPH GROOCOCK was a Lecturer at Trinity College Dublin and at the Dublin Institute of Technology. An accomplished pianist and organist, conductor, and composer, Dr. Groocock died in 1997.

YO TOMITA is a Reader in the School of Music at the Queen's University, Belfast.

**Recent Titles in
Contributions to the Study of Music and Dance**

Domenico Cimarosa: His Life and His Operas
Nick Rossi and Talmage Fauntleroy

The Writings and Letters of Konrad Wolff
Ruth Gillen, editor

Nomai Dance Drama: A Surviving Spirit of Medieval Japan
Susan M. Asai

The Wind and Wind-Chorus Music of Anton Bruckner
Keith William Kinder

Modern Myths and Wagnerian Deconstructions: Hermeneutic Approaches to Wagner's
Music-Dramas
Mary A. Cicora

Virtue or Virtuosity? Explorations in the Ethics of Musical Performance
Jane O'Dea

Beethoven in Person: His Deafness, Illnesses, and Death
Peter J. Davies

The Character of a Genius: Beethoven in Perspective
Peter J. Davies

Sing Sorrow: Classics, History, and Heroines in Opera
Marianne McDonald

Feminist Aesthetics in Music
Sally Macarthur

Electroacoustic Music: Analytical Perspectives
Thomas Licata, editor

Discordant Melody: Alexander Zemlinsky, His Songs, and the Second Viennese School
Lorraine Gorrell